Infusionsoft Cookbook

Over 88 recipes to effectively use Infusionsoft to meet
your CRM needs, marketing automation, and conduct
online business optimally

Paul Sokol

PUBLISHING

BIRMINGHAM - MUMBAI

Infusionsoft Cookbook

First published: October 2015

Production reference: 1261015

Published by Packt Publishing Ltd.
Livery Place
35 Livery Street
Birmingham B3 2PB, UK.

ISBN 978-1-78355-089-0

www.packtpub.com

Credits

Author
Paul Sokol

Reviewers
Dimitar Iliev
Julian Mills

Commissioning Editor
Kunal Parikh

Acquisition Editor
Kevin Colaco

Content Development Editor
Zeeyan Pinheiro

Technical Editor
Gaurav Suri

Copy Editor
Dipti Mankame

Project Coordinator
Nidhi Joshi

Proofreader
Safis Editing

Indexer
Priya Sane

Graphics
Abhinash Sahu

Production Coordinator
Komal Ramchandani

Cover Work
Komal Ramchandani

About the Author

Paul Sokol is an electrical engineer by trade and the Campaign Builder Mad Scientist at Infusionsoft—a moniker earned due to his breadth of knowledge. His first experience with Infusionsoft was when he cofounded jiveSYSTEMS—a business-class video e-mail platform—in 2008 while obtaining his master's degree in signal processing from the University of Central Florida. The company still exists today and is successfully running very efficiently thanks to the automation capabilities of Infusionsoft.

Since joining Infusionsoft formally as an employee in June 2011, he has provided over 1,000 hours of small business consulting and helped launch more than 200 clients with Infusionsoft. He has authored numerous blog posts, been a guest on many webinars, and taught from stage at live events, such as Infusionsoft's annual ICON. Currently, he is works in the product development department as one of the first data scientists of the company.

Besides being a universally recognized trailblazer in automated experience design, he is also a generous philanthropist, talented musician, and respected heavy metal advocate. His purpose is to believe in the dreams of others and empower their greatest possibilities. His mission is to have a positive impact on individuals, communities, and the world via love, sharing, and contribution to others.

Originally a Florida native, Paul currently lives in Chandler, Arizona with his two cats Beebo and Winston. When he isn't working or running his charity Keep Children Rockin, he can be found drumming in the local black metal band Elivagar and being part of the growing Arizona heavy metal scene.

To become part of Paul's Inner Circle, join his "Under the Hair" newsletter at http://www.iscookbook.com/newsletter.

Acknowledgments

I want to first acknowledge the elder brother I never had, Will, for suggesting me to apply at Infusionsoft some years ago. His creation of that possibility started me on a journey for which I am eternally grateful.

A huge shout-out to Jordan Hatch for doing internal review of the chapter drafts and believing in my dream. Thank you. I'd also like to thank Marc Chesley, Greg Head, and the legal team at Infusionsoft for their blessings on this project.

Major thanks to Kevin, Manasi, and the team at Packt publishing. You've all been delightful to work with. Big thanks to the "beta tester" readers whom Packt recruited to ensure that this book is supremely valuable.

I want to acknowledge all my fellow Infusionites, former and current. We've all pushed ahead something with the potential to legitimately improve the lives and families of small businesses. High five!

To all the partners in the Infusionsoft ecosystem, thank you for everything you do every day. You're also helping Infusionsoft push ahead, and I'm excited that you've got this book. May it bring abundance to you and your clients.

To the lovely Infusionsoft customers, thanks for dreaming big and picking up this book. I hope it helps you get organized, grow sales, and save time faster.

I want to acknowledge my best friend on the West Coast, Rich Thurman, for always motivating me to think big and for being a great guy in general. His friendship has seen me at my worst and at my best, and there never has been any judgment in our friendship. Thanks buddy!

Finally, I want to acknowledge and thank my parents, Kathy and Kevin Sokol, for being amazing. I love you both very much.

To read a special foreword for this book written by Rich, go to `http://www.iscookbook.com/forward-2015`.

About the Reviewers

Dimitar Iliev has more than 10 years of experience in web development and LAMP stack. He is a PhD graduate in information security from Kyonggi University, Seoul, South Korea. He is currently living in Bulgaria. Besides working as a freelancer, Dimitar positions himself as a various API integration expert, problem solver, and web application architect. For the past three years, he has been deeply engaged in providing web development support for businesses using Infusionsoft CRM and sales system. Currently, Dimitar is a partner of a newborn company, `http://www.wickedreports.com/`, which provides deep tracking and analysis for Infusionsoft customers and beyond, to help businesses understand which marketing strategies work better than others. In case of any queries, Dimitar may be contacted via e-mail at `demetris@digitela.com`.

Julian Mills is a marketer at heart who realized back in 2009 that he needed a way to automate online marketing for his clients, and this led him to Infusionsoft. Unlike most marketers, Julian has a techie streak and is more than happy to get stuck in and figure out the techie stuff. Based in the UK, Julian is an Infusionsoft Certified Partner and enjoys helping a range of clients to transform and grow their businesses with Infusionsoft. Julian can be reached at `www.JulianMills.co.uk`.

www.PacktPub.com

Support files, eBooks, discount offers, and more

For support files and downloads related to your book, please visit www.PacktPub.com.

Did you know that Packt offers eBook versions of every book published, with PDF and ePub files available? You can upgrade to the eBook version at www.PacktPub.com and as a print book customer, you are entitled to a discount on the eBook copy. Get in touch with us at service@packtpub.com for more details.

At www.PacktPub.com, you can also read a collection of free technical articles, sign up for a range of free newsletters and receive exclusive discounts and offers on Packt books and eBooks.

https://www2.packtpub.com/books/subscription/packtlib

Do you need instant solutions to your IT questions? PacktLib is Packt's online digital book library. Here, you can search, access, and read Packt's entire library of books.

Why subscribe?

- ▶ Fully searchable across every book published by Packt
- ▶ Copy and paste, print, and bookmark content
- ▶ On demand and accessible via a web browser

Free access for Packt account holders

If you have an account with Packt at www.PacktPub.com, you can use this to access PacktLib today and view 9 entirely free books. Simply use your login credentials for immediate access.

Table of Contents

Preface

v

Chapter 1: Pre-Flight Checks

1

Introduction

1

Setting up your user signature

2

Configuring your calendar

4

Connecting your Facebook account

5

Connecting your Twitter account

6

Configuring your company's logo

6

Configuring the CAN-SPAM address block

8

Creating new users

10

Chapter 2: Critical Tools for Mastery

13

Introduction

13

Creating custom fields

14

Using merge fields

16

Using campaign merge fields

18

Using campaign links

20

Creating tags for database segmentation

23

Using internal forms for workflow

25

Using note templates for workflow

26

Creating great user experiences with tasks

28

Installing campaign templates from the Marketplace

31

Connecting web forms together

32

Chaining campaigns together

35

Working daily out of My Day

39

Chapter 3: Attracting Leads and Building Your List   **45**

Introduction   45
Creating a Contact Us form   46
Building a lead magnet delivery   50
Maximizing social sharing of your e-mails   55
Collecting leads from in-person events   60
Leveraging offline media for lead generation   64
Creating a simple referral request   68
Building an automated Twitter offer   73
Growing your social media following   83
Building an inbound phone call lead capture   88
Creating a PPC lead generation funnel   93
Setting up web analytics   102

Chapter 4: Selling Products Online and Getting Paid   **105**

Introduction   105
Setting up your merchant account   105
Creating products and subscriptions   111
Building order forms   118
Implementing an automated cart abandon follow-up   127
Collecting failed automated billing attempts   130
Creating a one-click upsell   136
Building a one-click upsell or downsell chain   146

Chapter 5: Selling with a Sales Team   **155**

Introduction   155
Setting up a sales pipeline   156
Working sales opportunities   162
Using round robins for sales teams   168
Saving time with FAQ workflows   174
Sending automated appointment reminders   179
Merging custom opportunity fields into e-mails   184
Setting up lead scoring   193
Automating based on lead score achievement   198
Building a long-term prospect nurture   202

Chapter 6: Wowing New Customers with Great Experiences   **215**

Introduction   215
Segmenting by last purchase date   216
Building a new customer welcome campaign   222

Creating a customer satisfaction survey 228

Asking for testimonials automatically 238

Setting up a birthday collection mechanism 247

Building automated Happy Birthday messages 258

Chapter 7: Wowing Existing Customers with Great Experiences 267

Introduction 267

Updating a soon-to-be-expired credit card automatically 268

Re-engaging inactive e-mails in your database 275

Building a Vaynerchuk opt-out 284

Setting up a basic referral partner program 290

Building a referral partner sign-up form 299

Chapter 8: Administrative - Conquer Internal Chaos 307

Introduction 307

Reconciling hard bounced e-mail addresses 308

Tracking e-mail engagement levels 315

Filtering out new hire applicants 323

Creating a true e-mail preferences center 334

Using lead sources to track ROI 340

Managing campaign model variations with versioning 347

Adding groups of contacts to a campaign sequence 351

Checking for duplicate contact records 353

Cleaning up duplicate contact records 357

Collecting W-9 forms from referral partners automatically 360

Chapter 9: Your Dashboard and Reporting - Make Better Decisions 367

Introduction 368

Creating a saved search or report 368

Adding custom statistics to your dashboard 382

Configuring your dashboard 388

Setting a user's default start page 392

Automating saved search or report delivery 394

Building the perfect sales rep dashboard 396

Reporting on who is in a campaign 405

Reporting on who is in (or was in) a specific campaign sequence 406

Reporting on who is queued to receive a specific campaign step 409

Reporting on who received a specific campaign step 411

Reporting on who completed a specific campaign goal 414

Chapter 10: Pushing the System with Hacks   417

Introduction   417
Creating a custom confirmation link inside campaign builder   418
Creating a custom unsubscribe link inside campaign builder   425
Triggering automation from an e-mail open   428
Sending form submissions to different thank you pages based
on custom fields   434
Adding a calendar dropdown to date type fields on forms   436
Hiding order forms until a link is clicked   438
Using images as form submit buttons   440
Making any text a social sharing link   442
Making any link an unsubscribe link   443
Creating an evergreen sales funnel with an expiring offer   445

Index   451

Preface

Infusionsoft is the premiere all-in-one sales and marketing software for small business. Inside this all-in-one tool, beats the heart of a customer database, surrounded by an e-commerce platform with automation capabilities flowing throughout. Needless to say there is a lot that can be done using Infusionsoft.

This cookbook is designed to help you learn more about the system and get you to the end results your business is looking for faster.

What this book covers

Chapter 1, Pre-Flight Checks, ensures that you have everything configured to ensure maximum functionality. So, even a skilled user should start with this chapter.

Chapter 2, Critical Tools for Mastery, has the tools that are used in many of the recipes. Even if you are a skilled user, it would be wise to give this chapter a quick skim to ensure that you are familiar with all these tools.

Chapter 3, Attracting Leads and Building Your List, Infusionsoft teaches a three-phase framework named Lifecycle Marketing. The first of three phases is *Attract,* and all the recipes in this chapter are designed to help your lead generation efforts.

Chapter 4, Selling Products Online and Getting Paid, explains the second phase of Lifecycle Marketing, *Sell.* This chapter deals primarily with e-commerce selling.

Chapter 5, Selling with a Sales Team, shows that Infusionsoft is a very powerful tool for managing a sales force, even if you are the lone salesperson. This chapter focuses on selling with a human-managed pipeline.

Chapter 6, Wowing New Customers with Great Experiences, explains the final phase of Lifecycle Marketing, *Wow.* All the recipes in this chapter focus on providing world-class experiences for your new customers.

Chapter 7, Wowing Existing Customers with Great Experiences, extends the final phase of Lifecycle Marketing, *Wow*. All recipes in this chapter are focused around providing world-class experiences for your existing customers.

Chapter 8, Administrative – Conquer Internal Chaos, provides some streamlined recipes to tame your internal processes. Infusionsoft is often overlooked for its powerful workflow and process automation.

Chapter 9, Your Dashboard and Reporting – Make Better Decisions, will empower you to search and report confidently because an important discipline in automated experience design is extracting performance data and using that to inform improvements.

Chapter 10, Pushing the System with Hacks, is a grab bag of unsupported Infusionsoft hacks. These little tactics, when properly executed, can empower some amazing automated experiences.

What you need for this book

You will need an Infusionsoft account and an active login. Preferably, a login with admin rights to ensure that you have proper permissions to configure all the recipes in this book. At the very least, if you are not an admin, you'll want permissions to use the campaign builder, as a lot of recipes are implemented from there.

Who this book is for

Intended for those who have at least a cursory understanding of Infusionsoft and already know how to use the visual drag and drop builders (campaign builder, e-mail builder, and so on). Perhaps you've set up a couple of things already and want to take it to the next level. Maybe you are very fluent in the software but lack the high-level strategic understanding of how to take your business and automate it for the better. If you are a certified partner that has been around for a long time, this book will empower you to provide better results for your clients, faster!

Conventions

In this book, you will find a number of text styles that distinguish between different kinds of information. Here are some examples of these styles and an explanation of their meaning.

Code words in text, database table names, folder names, filenames, file extensions, pathnames, dummy URLs, user input, and Twitter handles are shown as follows: "Click on the name of the merge field we want to insert; this will insert a variable that looks like ~xxx.xxx~."

New terms and **important words** are shown in bold for example, **Infusionsoft**. Words that you see on the screen, for example, in menus or dialog boxes, appear in the text like this: "Hover over the Infusionsoft symbol in the upper-left corner of the page, navigate to the **Admin** column, and click on **Settings** in the bottom row."

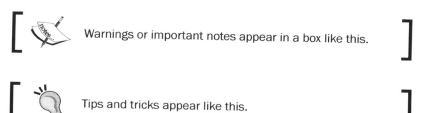

> Warnings or important notes appear in a box like this.

> Tips and tricks appear like this.

Reader feedback

Feedback from our readers is always welcome. Let us know what you think about this book—what you liked or disliked. Reader feedback is important for us as it helps us develop titles that you will really get the most out of.

To send us general feedback, simply e-mail feedback@packtpub.com, and mention the book's title in the subject of your message.

If there is a topic that you have expertise in and you are interested in either writing or contributing to a book, see our author guide at www.packtpub.com/authors.

Customer support

Now that you are the proud owner of a Packt book, we have a number of things to help you to get the most from your purchase.

Downloading the color images of this book

We also provide you with a PDF file that has color images of the screenshots/diagrams used in this book. The color images will help you better understand the changes in the output. You can download this file from https://www.packtpub.com/sites/default/files/downloads/0890OT_ColoredImages.pdf.

Errata

Although we have taken every care to ensure the accuracy of our content, mistakes do happen. If you find a mistake in one of our books—maybe a mistake in the text or the code—we would be grateful if you could report this to us. By doing so, you can save other readers from frustration and help us improve subsequent versions of this book. If you find any errata, please report them by visiting http://www.packtpub.com/submit-errata, selecting your book, clicking on the **Errata Submission Form** link, and entering the details of your errata. Once your errata are verified, your submission will be accepted and the errata will be uploaded to our website or added to any list of existing errata under the Errata section of that title.

To view the previously submitted errata, go to https://www.packtpub.com/books/content/support and enter the name of the book in the search field. The required information will appear under the **Errata** section.

Piracy

Piracy of copyrighted material on the Internet is an ongoing problem across all media. At Packt, we take the protection of our copyright and licenses very seriously. If you come across any illegal copies of our works in any form on the Internet, please provide us with the location address or website name immediately so that we can pursue a remedy.

Please contact us at copyright@packtpub.com with a link to the suspected pirated material.

We appreciate your help in protecting our authors and our ability to bring you valuable content.

Questions

If you have a problem with any aspect of this book, you can contact us at questions@packtpub.com, and we will do our best to address the problem.

1

Pre-Flight Checks

In this chapter, we will cover the following topics:

- ▶ Setting up your user signature
- ▶ Configuring your calendar
- ▶ Connecting your Facebook account
- ▶ Connecting your Twitter account
- ▶ Configuring your company's logo
- ▶ Configuring the CAN-SPAM address block
- ▶ Creating new users

Introduction

Before any professional caterer leaves for a job, they double-check to ensure that all food items and equipment, needed for the specific job, are present. This chapter is intended to operate as a *double-check* of your **Infusionsoft** before taking off into the recipes contained in this book.

The first four recipes are designed to be a good checklist to go through when adding a new user; the latter ones are mainly admin or *set it and forget it* functions.

By ensuring that the following things are set up, you'll be able to get things done faster while maximizing the functionality available to you.

For all recipes in this book, we are assuming that the user is logged in to a specific Infusionsoft account and has the necessary access permissions.

Setting up your user signature

Each user inside Infusionsoft has their own profile that contains a customizable signature, which can be merged into automated communications, such as letters and e-mails. Having a user's signature set will save time when configuring those communications.

Getting ready

We need to be logged in to Infusionsoft and inside a specific account.

How to do it...

1. Hover over the person symbol in the upper-right corner of the page and select **Edit My Profile** as shown in the following screenshot:

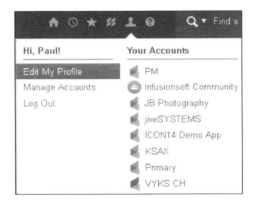

2. Click on the **Signatures** tab to display the plain text and HTML signatures.

3. Configure the user signatures.

4. Click on **Save** at the bottom of the page.

The following screenshot shows a preview of an HTML signature:

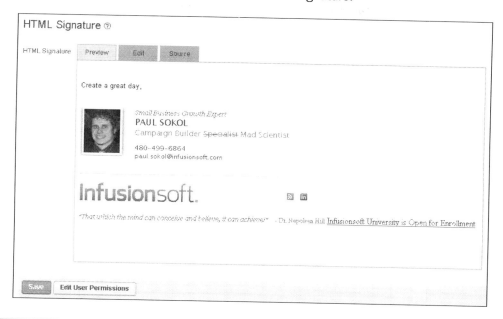

How it works...

Every communication sent affords us an opportunity to personalize it with one of the users' signatures (such as a sales representative signing off in an e-mail). When this occurs, the system will use whatever is set in this area of the user profile. In most cases, you can choose which signature type you want to merge—either the plain text or the full HTML signature, as shown in the following screenshot:

Hey ~Contact.FirstName~,

This is an email.

~Owner.HTMLSignature~

There's more...

There are many HTML e-mail signature generators and templates available online. To save time, use those as a starting point.

Configuring your calendar

Each user has a calendar that will show any scheduled tasks, appointments, or sales opportunities. The calendar settings can be configured to ensure smoother daily operations.

How to do it...

1. Hover over the person symbol in the upper-right corner of the page and select **Edit My Profile**.
2. Click on the **Preferences** tab to display the available user options.
3. In the **Calendar** section toward the middle of the page, we can configure the following:
   - **Default Calendar View**: This is what is displayed when you click on **Calendar** by navigating—the day when you log in (**Day**), the **Week**, or the **Month**
   - **Default Start Hour**: This indicates the time when the workday typically begins
   - **Default End Hour**: This indicates the time when the workday typically ends
   - **Time Zone**: This is the local time zone for the user; Infusionsoft assumes Eastern Time Zone by default
4. Click on **Save** at the bottom of the page.

How it works...

Depending on your job function, you may rely heavily on the calendar to plan and take action. By setting up the calendar to the user's specifications, it ensures that they will have the best user experience while performing their daily activities.

There's more...

While looking at a user's calendar, there are visual cues to inform what kind of item is in a time slot. A task will be symbolized by a checkmark. An appointment will be symbolized by a tiny calendar symbol. A sales opportunity will be symbolized by a **$** sign.

The following screenshot shows the three items in a time slot:

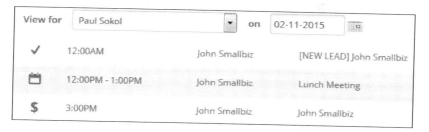

Connecting your Facebook account

Infusionsoft can leverage your Facebook account in the following two ways:

▶ First, you can post an e-mail broadcast, landing page, or web form out to your account

▶ Second, you can point a **Social** snippet inside an e-mail to your account and build your social network

Connecting your Facebook account to your user profile ensures you can maximize the social functions within the program.

How to do it...

1. Hover over the person symbol in the upper-right corner of the page and select **Edit My Profile**.
2. Scroll to the bottom of the page and click on the **Social Accounts** tab.
3. Using the **Add an Account** dropdown, select **Facebook**.
4. In the pop up message that appears, click on **Authorize Account**; this will open a new tab in the browser.
5. Follow the authorization instructions provided by Facebook.
6. Back in the browser tab with Infusionsoft, click on **Done**.

How it works...

Infusionsoft uses Facebook's secure authentication process to connect the user's Infusionsoft account with Facebook; technically the system is using **OAuth** to verify the user.

See also

For information about connecting a Twitter account, refer to the next recipe, *Connecting your Twitter account*.

Connecting your Twitter account

Infusionsoft can leverage your Twitter account in two ways:

► First, you can post an e-mail broadcast, landing page or web form out to your account

► Second, you can point a **Social** snippet inside an e-mail to your account and build your social network

Connecting your Twitter account to your user profile ensures that you can maximize the social functions within the program.

How to do it...

1. Hover over the person symbol in the upper-right corner of the page and select **Edit My Profile**.

2. Scroll to the bottom of the page and click on the **Social Accounts** tab.

3. Using the **Add an Account** dropdown, select **Twitter**.

4. In the pop-up message that appears, click on **Authorize Account**; this will open a new tab in the browser.

5. Follow the authorization instructions provided by Twitter.

6. Back in the browser tab with Infusionsoft, click on **Done**.

How it works...

Infusionsoft uses Twitter's secure authentication process to connect the user's Infusionsoft account with Twitter; it uses the same OAuth process as the Facebook connection.

See also

For information about connecting a Facebook account, refer to the previous recipe, *Connecting your Facebook account*.

Configuring your company's logo

One of the most common marketing assets used in your messaging is your company's logo. To save time while creating messages and stay consistent with your branding, there is a **Branding Center** where we can upload an image to be the company's logo. The system uses this logo where appropriate.

Getting ready

We need to be logged in to Infusionsoft, also inside a specific account, and have the appropriate access permissions.

How to do it...

1. Hover over the Infusionsoft symbol in the upper-left corner of the page, navigate to the **Admin** column, and click on **Branding Center** as shown in the following screenshot:

2. Click on the **Logos** tab.
3. In the **Default Logo** section, click on **Edit** in the lower-right corner of the logo preview.
4. From here, you can either:
   - Select an existing image from the file box using the dropdown
   - Upload your logo using the **Add New Image** button

5. Click on the **Save** button.

How it works...

Infusionsoft understands that a company's logo can be leveraged in many different ways. In other areas of the software where a logo is contextually relevant, it will pull from this area of the Branding Center.

The size of logo uploaded determines how it is displayed. Avoid using really large images to save time when configuring e-mails; having a 600 px width is a good size.

There's more...

There are three locations where a logo might show up:

- As a **Logo** snippet inside the **drag & drop** builder
- On hosted pages (such as the **opt-out** screen)
- On sign-in pages

When we upload a default logo using the mentioned recipe, the system automatically sets that for the three logo locations. If you want to further customize the logo for each of these locations, there is an **Edit** button that allows you to go through a similar process as the recipe mentioned earlier.

It is very important to use the formal **Logo** snippet while creating e-mails and other messages in the drag & drop builder. This ensures that updating your company's branding is easy. All we do is upload a new logo to the Branding Center, and the next time anything is sent containing a **Logo** snippet, Infusionsoft will use the new one. If we don't use the **Logo** snippet, but instead use a different method, such as an **Image** snippet, and our logo changes, we'll have to manually go into each individual e-mail, one by one, and update it to the new **Logo**. Using the **Logo** snippet is a huge time saver that also creates scalability.

There are other areas of the Branding Center that can help to save you a ton of time as well. It is here that we can create the default layouts for different objects in the system, such as e-mails, landing pages, and web forms. At the very least, create a branded **Campaign Email** template. This way, when we are cooking up the recipes in future chapters, every time we create a new e-mail, it will pull in our branding and we can begin writing immediately.

Configuring the CAN-SPAM address block

Legally, every e-mail that comes from an Infusionsoft e-mail server must contain the address of the company sending it and a link for the recipient to unsubscribe from future mailings. It is important to ensure that the address we set is real and can receive physical mails to protect the business legally should any disputes arise.

How to do it...

1. Hover over the Infusionsoft symbol in the upper-left corner of the page, navigate to the **Marketing** column and click on **Settings** in the bottom row as shown in the following screenshot:

2. Click on **Email Defaults** option in the **Template Settings** menu on the left-hand side of the page.

3. Fill in the contact information you would like to display at the bottom of every e-mail:

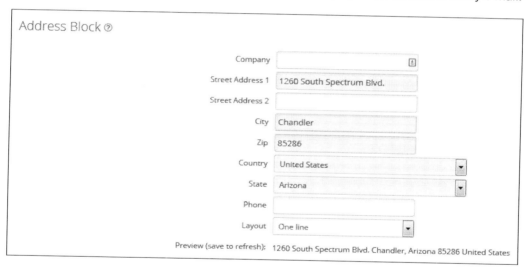

4. The **Layout** dropdown at the bottom of the **Address Block** fields lets you choose how the **CAN-SPAM** block displays; you can choose between a one-line and multiline layout. The preceding image is showing a preview of the one-line layout.

5. Scroll to the bottom of the page and click on **Save**.

How it works...

This is the specific area designed to set the CAN-SPAM address block for all e-mails sent by Infusionsoft. This ensures that all e-mails being sent are legally compliant with the CAN-SPAM laws. Otherwise, a user would be at legal risk if they experience excessive spam complaints.

There's more...

While the **Company** and **Phone** fields are available, they are not required. Only the address fields highlighted in orange are required.

In the **Email** section beneath the **Address Block** section of this page, there are some miscellaneous settings we might want to familiarize ourselves with. In particular, we can set the default **opt-in** (confirmation) and opt-out links to save time while creating e-mails. This is also where we would go to find the **action trigger** to cook the *Building a Vaynerchuk opt-out* recipe found in *Chapter 7, Wowing Existing Customers with Great Experiences*.

Creating new users

As a small business grows, there is a need to add more users to Infusionsoft.

How to do it...

1. Hover over the Infusionsoft symbol in the upper-left corner of the page, navigate to the **Admin** column, and click on **Users** as shown in the following screenshot:

My Nav	CRM	Marketing	E-Commerce	Admin
Contacts	Contacts	Campaign Builder	E-Commerce Setup	Branding Center
Campaign Builder	Companies	Email & Broadcasts	Orders	Infusionsoft Account
Email & Broadcasts	Opportunities	Lead Generation	Products	Users
Legacy	Referral Partners	Templates	Actions	Import Data
Templates	Visitors	Legacy	Promotions	Data Cleanup
Opportunities			Legacy	
Edit	Reports Settings	Reports Settings	Reports Settings	Reports Settings

2. Click on the green **Add Users** button:

3. Provide the new user's first name and e-mail address. You can also give them full system access by clicking on the switch to make them an admin.

4. Click on **Send Email Invitation**:

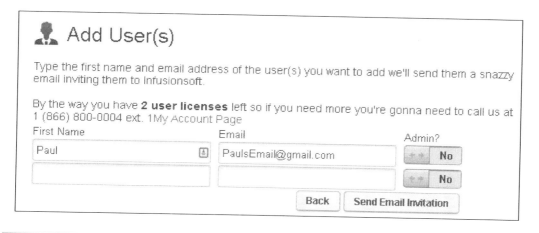

How it works...

After completing the preceding recipe, the new user will receive an e-mail invitation to log in to Infusionsoft. The new user will then need to follow the instructions to claim their invitation.

There's more...

From the list of users we see in the first step of this recipe, you can resend the user invite e-mail if someone is having difficulty locating the original invite e-mail.

Each Infusionsoft account has a certain number of available user licenses. However, next to the **Add Users** button, there is also a green **Add Partner** button. If we are working with an **Infusionsoft Certified Partner** and we want to give them access to our account without taking a user license, we can add their Infusionsoft ID there.

The number of user licenses is based on how many active users exist. Therefore, if we need to add a user but have no more licenses, we have the option to deactivate a user to free up space.

2
Critical Tools for Mastery

In this chapter, we will cover the following topics:

- ▸ Creating custom fields
- ▸ Using merge fields
- ▸ Using campaign merge fields
- ▸ Using campaign links
- ▸ Creating tags for database segmentation
- ▸ Using internal forms for workflow
- ▸ Using note templates for workflow
- ▸ Creating great user experiences with tasks
- ▸ Installing campaign templates from the Marketplace
- ▸ Connecting web forms together
- ▸ Chaining campaigns together
- ▸ Working daily out of My Day

Introduction

Now that we've ensured the user configuration is complete, we can begin to learn about the critical tools for mastery of automation experience design. The recipes in future chapters assume an understanding of the fundamental tactics introduced in this chapter.

There are two types of Infusionsoft users, and they use different tools for their needs.

The first type and target audience for this cookbook are the **builders**. These are the users who design and implement the automated experiences. These are the types of folks that would take a recipe out of this cookbook and use it for their business.

The second type of user is the end user. **End users** are the sales representatives and administrators who work daily with Infusionsoft. Often, they use things created by a builder are used by end users to stay organized, grow sales and save time.

Understanding both user types is critical in building a powerful automated experience. Therefore, mastery of both tool types is essential.

Creating custom fields

At its core, Infusionsoft is a **CRM** (short for **Customer Relationship Management**) system. In other words, it is a database of humans that contains information about their interactions with a business.

In this database, there are common pieces of information that all businesses would need to know about an individual: first/last name, addresses, phone numbers, e-mail addresses, and so on. There are even more interesting pieces of data as well, such as the person's birthday or their spouse's name.

However, there are pieces of data a business might need to collect that don't exist out of the box. Take a dog trainer for example. They might want to store a dog's name on the dog owner's **contact record**.

This recipe will show you how to create a custom data field on a contact record. A **custom field** can be merged into a communication or a **task**, submitted on a form, used as a search/report filter, and used to route automation logic.

How to do it...

1. Hover over the Infusionsoft symbol in the upper-left corner of the page, navigate to the **Admin** column, and click on **Settings** in the bottom row:

My Nav	CRM	Marketing	E-Commerce	Admin
Contacts	Contacts	Campaign Builder	E-Commerce Setup	Branding Center
Campaign Builder	Companies	Email & Broadcasts	Orders	Infusionsoft Account
Email & Broadcasts	Opportunities	Lead Generation	Products	Users
Legacy	Referral Partners	Templates	Actions	Import Data
Templates	Visitors	Legacy	Promotions	Data Cleanup
Opportunities			Legacy	
Edit	Reports Settings	Reports Settings	Reports Settings	Reports Settings

2. In the **Custom Fields** section at the top of the page, click on **Go**.

3. Click on **Add** next to the dropdown menu at the top of the page:

4. Give the custom field a name and select **Custom Fields** type from the dropdown menu.

5. Click on **Show Advanced Options...**; this will cause a submenu to be displayed.

6. Select a tab where we want the new custom field to be displayed on the contact record.

7. Select a header where we want the new custom field to be displayed on the contact record.

8. Click on **Save This Field**.

How it works...

This recipe is accessing the database table for a person's contact information. The tab/header chosen will control where the custom field shows up while viewing a contact record.

There's more...

A properly leveraged custom field can make both setup and the automated experience more powerful. Remember that a custom field can be merged into a communication or a task, submitted on a form, used as a search/report filter, and used to route automation logic. As we are creating and bumping into challenges, custom fields are a powerful tool in our back pocket.

There are many different types of custom fields besides a **Text** field. While creating a custom field, always choose the type closest to the type of data being stored. For example, if we wanted to store lifetime customer spend, we would want to create a **Currency** type custom field.

This is important for two reasons. First, when using a custom field to route automation logic, the field type helps with context. Infusionsoft understands what a date on the calendar is, and hence you can configure logic to say *if before a specific date*. Had we used a **Text** field to store the date instead, that kind of rule can't be created.

Similarly, when using a custom field to filter a search/report, the search parameters also understand the context of the field type. If we have a **Whole Number** type custom field that holds how many times someone has made a purchase, we could create a contact search saying *show me all those whose purchases are more than 5*.

When it comes to controlling automation logic based on human input, a **Yes/No** type, **Radio** type, or **Dropdown** can greatly reduce human error.

In step 3 of this recipe, we'll see a full list of all custom fields previously created. If we have more than one tab, there will be a blue arrow on the right-hand side that allows you to adjust the display order. Similarly, if there is more than one header within a tab, we will see the blue arrows as well. If you have more than one custom field in a header, we will also see the blue arrows. This is to organize how the custom fields display when looking at a contact record.

There are several places elsewhere in Infusionsoft where you can create a custom field on the fly. It is recommended to create a custom field first using this recipe as this ensures full control of the custom field generation.

It is important to realize that we can only have 100 custom fields per record type. This recipe describes how to create a custom **Contact** field. If we adjust the dropdown next to the **Go** button in step 2, we can create custom fields within other record types. For example, a sales representative might want a *Time Zone* dropdown inside an **opportunity record** to help them plan their calls for the day more efficiently.

Since there is a limit, conserve the custom fields only for situations where we have no other option. Also, we can often cut down on custom field bandwidth by spreading out the needed fields across different record types. For example, if we need four fields for a purchase, explore whether we can put two on the **order record** and two on the contact record.

While talking to the database directly through the API, often we'll need to find the names of the custom fields in the database, as these are different to their display names. To find these, in step 3 of this recipe, there is a **Show database names** link toward the top-right corner of the page. This will open a popup window with the database names of our custom fields.

See also

We can sometimes save our precious custom fields by leveraging campaign merge fields. See the *Using campaign merge fields* recipe later in this chapter.

Using merge fields

Merging contact information into an automated communication can be an extremely powerful tool to create a relevant, personal experience for the recipient. It can also ruin the customer experience if not properly implemented. As a tool itself, it thrives on context and so **merge fields** always need to be used strategically.

While this recipe specifically covers how to insert a merge field into an e-mail, the concept extends to any object with merging capabilities (tasks, letters, and so on).

Getting ready

We need to edit an e-mail inside a campaign.

How to do it...

1. Place the cursor where we want to merge some information.
2. Next to the **Subject** line, click on **Merge**; this will open a tool palette:

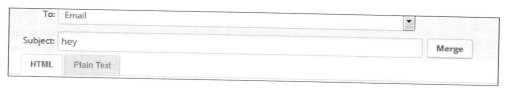

3. Click on the merge field category containing the field we want to insert.
4. Click on the name of the merge field we want to insert. This will insert a variable that looks like this: `~xxx.xxx~`.

How it works...

Before Infusionsoft sends the e-mail, it will replace any of these merge field code with the appropriate data. For example, `~Contact.FirstName~` becomes Bob, Joe, or Mary. This all depends on the contact record that caused the e-mail to be sent:

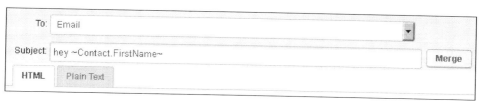

There's more...

There are more merge types available than just basic contact information. We can merge information from the user managing the relationship: the owner of the contact record. This can be handy when sending an automated e-mail from the user. We can also merge the custom field, referral partner, general company, and date information, such as the day of the week.

If any campaign merge fields have been created, they will show up at the bottom of the merge tool palette.

If the merge palette is getting in the way, we can move it by clicking and dragging the top of the palette.

See also

To learn how to merge opportunity record information, see the recipe *Merging custom opportunity fields into e-mails* in *Chapter 5, Selling with a Sales Team*. To learn how to merge credit card record information, see the recipe *Updating a soon-to-be-expired credit card automatically* in *Chapter 6, Wowing New Customers with Great Experiences*.

Using campaign merge fields

Sometimes, there is information that needs to be merged into a communication or process that is the same for all contacts that flow through a campaign. The date and location of an event is an example of this kind of information because that information is fixed for all contacts flowing through the campaign. A **campaign merge field** is the tool we can leverage for this kind of data.

Getting ready

We need to be inside a campaign.

How to do it...

1. Click on the **Campaign** dropdown in the upper-left corner of the page and select **Merge Fields...**:

2. Click on the green **Add Merge Field** button.

3. Give the new field a label. This is what will be displayed in the merge tool palette. For example, if this field were to hold the date of an event, the label could be *event date*.

4. Give the new field a value. This is what will be merged into a communication or process. For example, if the date of an event is January 1, the value can be January 1st.

5. Click on the *save* icon (floppy disk) in the right column to add the field to this campaign.

How it works...

Similar to how a regular merge field works, when Infusionsoft generates a communication or process, it will insert the value of the campaign merge wherever the merge code is present.

There's more...

Campaign merge fields can be found at the bottom of the standard merge menu; this menu will not be displayed if no campaign merge fields have been configured:

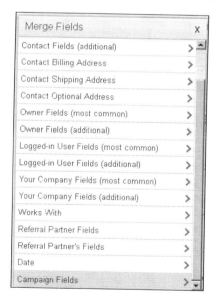

Campaign merge fields are very useful to build a reusable campaign. A great example of this is a **recurring event**. We can create an event date, an event time, and an event location merge field within the campaign. The next time we have the same event, we just have to update those fields and republish the campaign. There is no need to drill down into the individual campaign steps to display that information.

In general, any time there is an important piece of information that is the same across multiple campaign assets, we should consider using a campaign merge field.

See also

This recipe only shows how to create a campaign merge field. To learn how to insert it into a communication or process after creation, see the previous recipe *Using merge fields*.

Using campaign links

Quite often in a marketing, e-mail we will set the same URL multiple times, sometimes across multiple e-mails too. A **campaign link** is the tool we can leverage for these kinds of links to ensure easy maintenance and reusability.

This recipe has two parts: creating the campaign link and inserting it into an e-mail.

Getting ready

We need to be inside a campaign.

How to do it...

1. Click on the **Campaign** dropdown in the upper-left corner of the page and select **Links...**:

2. Click on the green **Add Link** button.

3. Give the new link a name. This is what will be displayed in the campaign link dropdown when setting a link in an e-mail.

4. Give the new link a destination URL. This is where contacts will go when they click on this campaign link.

5. Give the new link a description. Be sure to provide enough context behind why we are creating the link and how it is used.

6. Click on the **Save** button in the right column to add the link to this campaign.

7. Click on the **Close** button at the bottom of the **Campaign Link** menu to close it.

8. Go through an e-mail in this same campaign.

9. Highlight the text you want to connect to this **Campaign Link**.

10. Click on the **Link** button in the center of the **Format** toolbar; this will open the **Link Options** menu:

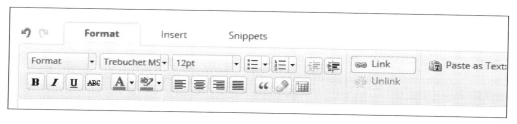

11. Change the **Link to:** dropdown to **Campaign link**:

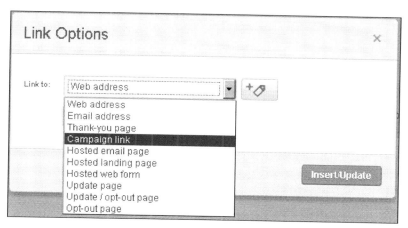

12. Select the campaign link you want from the second dropdown that appears:

13. Click on the green **Insert/Update** button.

    The following screenshot shows the name and URL of the **Event Registration Page** campaign link:

How it works...

Whenever someone clicks on a campaign link in an e-mail, Infusionsoft first checks the value of the campaign link and then redirects the recipient to that location.

There's more...

Campaign links are great for reusable campaigns or when a particular URL may change over time. For example, we could use a campaign link that points directly to a PDF on your server and use that to deliver the PDF in an e-mail. If we ever want to update the PDF, we simply have to update the campaign link URL and not update every link within each e-mail individually.

This could also be used to *close* a shopping cart. We can create a *Sales Page* campaign link, which takes people to a checkout URL. Then use the campaign link in every e-mail that is asking for the order. After the promotion is over, we can update the campaign link URL to a cart-closed page and republish the campaign. The next time someone clicks on a link in those old e-mails, they will be taken to the cart-closed page as the campaign link has changed since they originally received it.

Merge field variables will properly work in the URL of a campaign link. This can be a really handy trick in certain scenarios.

Creating tags for database segmentation

The more targeted and relevant our marketing is, the more effective it will be. In order to segment the database so we can be targeted and relevant, Infusionsoft uses tags. A **tag** can be thought of as a specific list or specific segment of people within your database.

We can apply or remove a tag manually from an individual or a group of individuals. A campaign can automatically apply or remove a tag as well.

Besides segmentation, a tag can route automation logic or filter a search/report. They can also be used as a goal within a campaign to start or stop it.

In short, understanding how to create a tag is a critical skill for automated experience design.

How to do it...

1. Hover over the Infusionsoft symbol in the upper-left corner of the page, navigate to the **CRM** column, and click on **Settings** in the bottom row:

My Nav	CRM	Marketing	E-Commerce	Admin
Contacts	Contacts	Campaign Builder	E-Commerce Setup	Branding Center
Campaign Builder	Companies	Email & Broadcasts	Orders	Infusionsoft Account
Email & Broadcasts	Opportunities	Lead Generation	Products	Users
Legacy	Referral Partners	Templates	Actions	Import Data
Templates	Visitors	Legacy	Promotions	Data Cleanup
Opportunities			Legacy	
Edit	Reports Settings	Reports Settings	Reports Settings	Reports Settings

2. Click on **Tags** in the left-hand side menu:

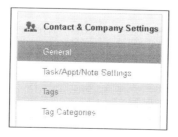

3. Click on the green **Add Tag** button:

4. Give the tag a meaningful name.
5. Add the tag to a tag category by selecting one from the **Category** dropdown or type a new tag category in the **Other** field.
6. Give the tag a proper full sentence description. If it helps, answer the question, *What do we know 100% about contacts with this tag?*
7. Click on the green **Add Tag(s)** button at the bottom of the page.

How it works...

This recipe directly modifies the database table for tags so that Infusionsoft and its users can use them.

There's more...

When adding new tags, we can create multiple tags by separating the names with commas. For example, if we created a new tag and named it `Widget 1, Widget 2`, the system would create a `Widget 1` and a `Widget 2` tag.

The name and category of tag are displayed when looking at a contact record. Keep this in mind when naming tags to ensure things make sense for the end user. If a tag means something very precise, we definitely want to denote this in the description. However, keep in mind that the name and category are the only context an end user receives from a tag and both will be truncated if they are too long. Infusionsoft will display the first 16 characters of each before adding an ellipsis to indicate that the name is too long to fully display. Err on the shorter side for tag names and categories and be long-winded in the description.

There are other areas in Infusionsoft where you can create a tag on the fly. It is recommended to follow this recipe always when creating a tag to ensure proper categorization and description; it is a good habit for easy-to-admin automation.

Using internal forms for workflow

An **internal form** is just like a normal web form, but it can only be submitted by a user inside Infusionsoft. While creating process workflows, especially task-based workflows, a well-placed internal form can create a time-saving experience for the Infusionsoft user, thus improving productivity.

Many of the recipes in this book leverage internal forms, so understanding the experience of submitting one is a key to building a great workflow.

Getting ready

We need to look at a full contact record, not in **My Day**.

How to do it...

1. Scroll down to the **Tasks** section of the contact record.

2. In the **Form Submissions** section, select the form we need to submit on the **Internal Forms...** dropdown and click on the **Fill Out** button:

3. Fill out the form with the information it requires.

4. Click on the green **Save** button at the bottom of the form.

How it works...

Submitting an internal form will update the contact fields provided by the user and trigger any associated automation.

There's more...

When adding a new contact, we can also fill out an internal form, which can also trigger automation.

If there is a date type field on the internal form, the user should place their cursor in the date field and press *i* on the keyboard; a popup of keyboard shortcuts will be displayed as follows:

Quick Date Keys

t: Set date to today
= : Add one day
+ : Subtract one day
w : Add one week
k : Subtract one week
y : Add one year
e : Subtract one year
m : Add one month
h : Subtract one month
q : Clear the date
f : Go to the first day of the month
l : Go to the last day of the month
z : Go to Monday of the week selected
x : Go to Tuesday of the week selected
c : Go to Wednesday of the week selected
v : Go to Thursday of the week selected
b : Go to Friday of the week selected

OK

These **Quick Date Keys** work anywhere in the system where a formal date field exists. End users who deal with lots of dates can greatly improve productivity by learning the shortcut keys they would most commonly need.

See also

An internal form can also be submitted from the **My Day** view. See the recipe *Working daily out of My Day* later in this chapter. To learn how a task can drive an Infusionsoft user to an internal form, see the recipe *Creating great user experiences with tasks* later in this chapter.

Using note templates for workflow

A **note template** is like a big red *AUTOMATION* button. Any time we need to automate or track something and we aren't sure how to do it, we can create a note template. Applying a note template can trigger an e-mail, a task, the application of a tag, and so on.

Many of the recipes in this book leverage note templates, so understanding the experience of applying one to a contact record is a key to building a great workflow.

Getting ready

We need to look at a full contact record, not in My Day.

How to do it...

1. Scroll down to the **Tasks** section of the contact record.

2. In the **Notes** section, select the note we need to apply using the **Note Template...** dropdown and click on the **Add Note** button:

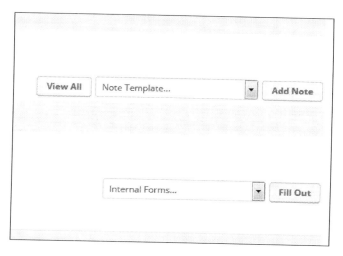

How it works...

Applying the note will add the predefined information to the contact's **note history** and trigger any associated automation.

There's more...

If we click on **Add Note** without selecting a note template from the dropdown, a pop-up window will open. The user can manually type a note, select a template, or do both from here. Selecting a template from here will trigger the automation tool upon **Save** even if the user makes edits to the information that gets populated.

See also

A note template can also be submitted from the **My Day** view. See the recipe *Working daily out of My Day* later in this chapter. To learn how a task can drive an Infusionsoft user to apply a note template, see the recipe *Creating great user experiences with tasks* later in this chapter.

Creating great user experiences with tasks

Not everything can be automated. There are certain activities that are too precise or too costly to automate. For example, making an outbound phone call to a new lead or adding a new customer to a third-party membership site. In these cases, an Infusionsoft user can be assigned a task.

A task is a key tactic in the human-machine interaction within Infusionsoft. When the automation cannot go any further and needs human intervention, empowering the end user to quickly take action and tell the automation machine to continue is a key skill towards designing productive automated experiences.

Since creating a great experience with tasks requires understanding the context in which the tasks will be performed, for this recipe, let's assume that we have a campaign model that looks like this:

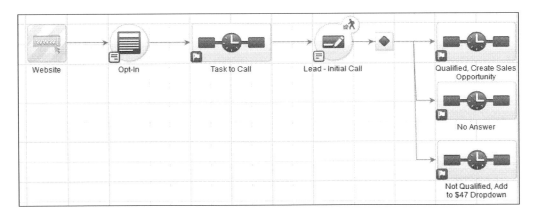

In plain English, when a lead comes in through the website, a human is tasked with calling them and filling out an internal form to push the lead ahead. Specifically, the user needs to submit the *Lead - Initial Call* form.

This recipe will build a task for this specific purpose.

For simplicity, we are assuming that the **Task to Call** sequence only contains a **Task** step and the same person will be performing these calls:

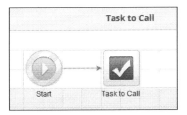

In a real-world application, there would most likely be more inside that sequence, such as tagging or e-mails.

Getting ready

The name of the internal form that needs to be filled out by the user should be finalized. We should be inside the **Task** step that is instructing the user to fill out an internal form.

How to do it...

1. Using the **Type** dropdown, select **Call**.

2. In the **Title** field, name it New Lead Call- -Contact.FirstName.

3. In the **Body** field, put Call - -Contact.FirstName - at -Contact.Phone1- to see if they qualify. Submit Internal Form "Lead - Initial Call" after you have made the call.

4. Using the dropdown for **Assign to (backup)**, select the user who will be assigned the task.

5. Using the dropdown for **Priority**, select **1. Critical**:

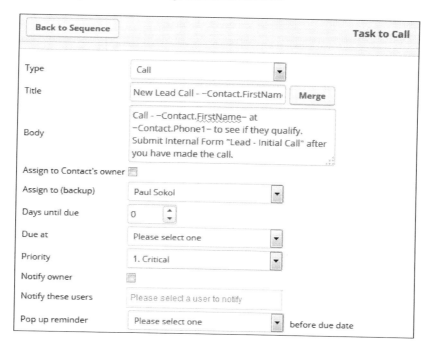

6. In the upper-right corner of the page, click on **Draft** to set this **Task** step as **Ready**.

7. Continue to build the campaign toward publishing.

How it works...

When a lead submits the opt-in form on the website, this task is created. Infusionsoft merges the information and assigns the task. All the information the end user needs to perform the task is in the task body, and the user is told explicitly what to do after the call has been made. This should allow the end user to focus and quickly call through new leads.

There's more...

While this recipe is telling the user to submit a specific internal form, we can also tell the user to apply a specific note template (or templates if there are multiple possible outcomes).

The name of the goal itself inside the campaign is what will be displayed for the end user while looking at the dropdown menus for internal forms or note templates. Using a naming convention, such as including Lead - in front of all internal forms associated with the lead development process, can further enhance productivity because the end user can find those items faster as they will be grouped.

This recipe assumes that the user making the calls has received the proper training to perform the phone call. We could have also included a script inside the task body. This would further systematize how those new lead calls are performed.

Selecting the most accurate task type ensures the best possible end user experience and tracking. Not only is it valuable for administrative reporting, the type is also leveraged in the **My Day** view and Infusionsoft's mobile app for contextual interactions around tasks.

We can create our own custom task types by navigating to **CRM | Settings | Task/Appt/Note Settings**:

The **task title** can be used as a search filter in the administrative **task note** reports, but not the **task body**. This can be leveraged for better administrative reporting by adding in naming conventions to the task title. For example, prefacing every new lead task's title with [LEAD] empowers an admin to easily find tasks with that in the title.

If you set a time for the task, that is when the task will show up on the user's calendar inside Infusionsoft. Selecting the most accurate priority ensures the best possible end user experience because they are used for visual cues in My Day. Priority can also be used to filter administrative task reports.

Installing campaign templates from the Marketplace

Some of the recipes in the following chapters can be implemented faster by using the prebuilt campaign templates as a starting point for the strategy's framework.

Getting ready

We need to be logged in to Infusionsoft, inside a specific account, and have the appropriate access permissions.

How to do it...

1. Hover over the main navigation, go to the **Marketing** column, and click on **Campaign Builder**, as follows:

2. In the upper-right corner of the page, click on the white **Get Campaign Templates** button; this will open up the campaign Marketplace.

3. Search for the campaign we need to install using the search box in the upper-right corner of the page.

4. Hover over the campaign listing we need to install and click on the white **Install** button in the lower-right corner as follows:

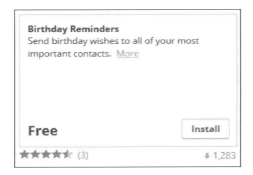

How it works...

Infusionsoft's platform has a campaign publishing tool, which gives the ability to export/import campaigns between applications. Infusionsoft also curates a library of publicly available campaigns on the Marketplace part of its platform. This recipe is leveraging the publishing tool to pull from this public repository of campaign templates and installing the chosen template into our specific Infusionsoft application.

There's more...

Most campaign templates come with launch instructions. Think of it as the recipe for that particular model. Even if we don't fully understand what is being done, by following the steps impeccably, we can confidently implement the campaign as it was intended.

Infusionsoft regularly releases new campaign models into the Marketplace. Each campaign solves for a specific problem, so keeping a finger on the pulse of new releases can potentially speed up implementation.

Quite often during implementation, we'll run into common structures, for example, a web form to purchase, which is used in most online launch models. These common structures are most likely in a campaign template somewhere, so becoming familiar with the library can give you a head start on different models.

Connecting web forms together

There are many reasons to create a multistep web form experience. As a conversion optimization tactic, progressively collecting information can help you identify the hottest leads while the automation handles those who drop off.

Getting ready

We need to be inside a campaign.

How to do it...

1. Drag out two web forms, as shown here:

2. Open the second web form.
3. Add a hidden e-mail field to the form, leave the **Field Value** completely empty, and click on **Save**. Be sure to delete a visible **Email** field as well if one is present:

4. Click on the **Settings** tab toward the top-left corner of the page and verify the **Auto-populate Form** setting is checked.
5. Click the **Code** tab and copy the web form URL from the **Use the Hosted Version** section.

6. Click **Back to Campaign** in the top-left corner of the page and open the first web form.

7. Click the **Thank-you Page** tab at the top-left corner of the page.

8. Change the **Thank-you Page to Display** dropdown to **Web address**:

9. Paste the web form URL into the second form we collected in step 5.

10. Check the box to pass the contact's information:

How it works...

Upon successful submission of the first form, the contact will be redirected to the second form and the contact's information is magically passed to the second form so they don't have to fill out the same details twice.

A form will check to see if someone is already in the database based on their e-mail address. By passing the contact's e-mail between the two forms in the background, Infusionsoft can track who is filling out each form without having the user input their e-mail every time.

There's more...

In order to autopopulate the hidden e-mail field on a form, the form must be presented using JavaScript or a hosted version of the form. Both of these versions contain JavaScript, which takes care of this for us. If you embed the form on your site using the HTML code, passing the contact information will not populate the hidden field unless we write custom code to do so.

Setting a form as a thank you page also works on **order forms**. This is how we can create one-click upsells and other post-purchase experiences.

Once we have a contact's e-mail address, we can chain as many forms and landing pages together as we want. We just have to make sure that each form in the process is sending the contact's info to the next in line, and that the receiving form has a hidden e-mail field autopopulating. This is a useful tactic in breaking up the online experience of a long intake form, such as one that an attorney or doctor would use.

Most of the time it makes sense to add a sequence between the different steps of a multistep form experience to recover those who don't make it through the first time. When setting a link in an e-mail, you can point directly to the hosted version of a web form or landing page (as long as the form's settings allow for autopopulation). This makes it easy to drive contacts back to a form if they fall out during a multistep process.

See also

If we search for **Two Step Web Form** in the Marketplace of campaign templates, we can find different variations of this recipe.

Chaining campaigns together

More often than not, when one campaign ends or reaches a certain point, another separate campaign has to respond accordingly.

A master builder not only has a clear strategy to chain campaigns together, they also leave plenty of breadcrumbs for others to follow and understand what is occurring.

For this recipe, let's assume that when **Campaign A** (*sales promo*) ends, we want to trigger **Campaign B** (*prospect nurture*) to start.

Getting ready

We need to create a tag in a **Functional** category that will be used to chain together the campaigns. Once that is created, we need to be inside Campaign A.

How to do it...

1. Open the sequence in Campaign A where we want to trigger Campaign B.

2. Add a new **Apply/Remove Tag** process to the sequence's flow at the appropriate point. In the example here, we are triggering Campaign B after the last e-mail in the Campaign A sequence:

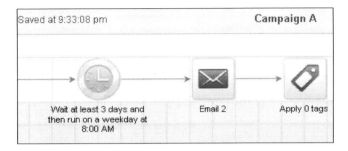

3. Apply the functional tag that is being used to chain the campaigns together:

4. Leave a canvas note explaining what campaign this tag application is impacting:

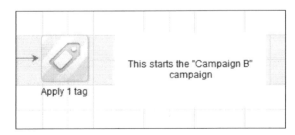

5. Exit out of **Campaign Builder** and go into Campaign B.

6. Drag out a new **Tag** goal and connect it to the sequence we need to start.

7. Name it to indicate that it is triggered by Campaign A. In the following image, we are assuming that the form for Campaign B already existed prior to the start of this recipe. The bottom chain is the result of this recipe:

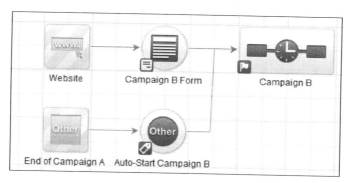

8. Double-click the **Tag** goal and configure it for the functional tag being applied in Campaign A:

9. Finish building the campaign and publish.

How it works...

When a contact reaches the step that applies the functional tag in Campaign A, the **Tag** goal in Campaign B will be triggered, effectively chaining Campaign B to Campaign A.

There's more...

We can have the same tag being listened for across multiple campaigns, such as, an **Escape Hatch** tag goal that we add to the end of every prospect marketing campaign. When a contact unsubscribes, the trigger can apply this **Escape Hatch** tag, effectively ending outbound marketing from any campaign with the hatch built-in:

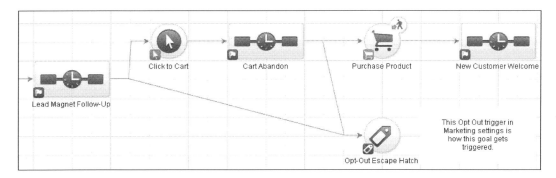

Since a **Tag** goal is used to chain campaigns together, they can also be used to stop sequences, as in the preceding **Escape Hatch** tactic.

This recipe can also be modified to control behavior within the same campaign. For example, for auto-tagging from a link, click on an e-mail to start another sequence without stopping the main sequence of e-mails:

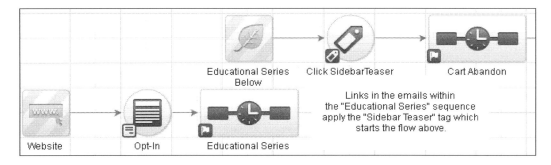

Remove any functional tags using a remove tag step within the resulting sequence to keep contact records clean. A functional tag should not be used for database segmentation.

Leaving notes isn't mandatory for functionality; however, it empowers others to perform maintenance without our presence.

Working daily out of My Day

To close out this chapter, we are going to explore the task completion workflow that an end user would experience in their daily responsibilities. Understanding this end user context helps us design automation that can truly streamline processes and boost productivity.

For this recipe, we are focusing on the workflow of someone who receives tasks to call new leads and must indicate the results via a note template or internal form. The recipe will take us through one call task.

Getting ready

We need to be logged in as the user assigned with the call tasks and in the *working* view of My Day. This can be accessed from the *Home* icon in the main navigation, as shown here:

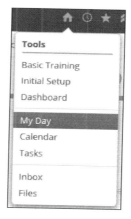

How to do it...

1. Click the task title from the list of tasks on the left-hand side of the screen, as shown here:

2. The task information and contact information will load in the right-hand side of the screen:

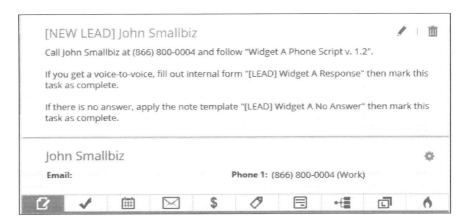

3. Perform the task as instructed and fill out any internal forms and/or apply any notes indicated.

4. In the left pane, check the box to the left of the task title to mark it as completed:

How it works...

My Day aggregates the tasks assigned to the logged in user. The *interactive* view on the right-hand side of the screen allows for most contact management functions without having to load separate web pages for each contact. This allows the user to quickly complete a list of tasks. The automated experience creator heavily influences how fast a user can be by providing the right amount of context and guidance for pushing along the automated experience.

There's more...

There is a setting in the user preferences where we can set My Day as the home page upon login.

If the logged in user has the appropriate permissions, they can edit the task by clicking on the *pencil* icon in the upper-right corner of the right-hand pane. This is great for pushing up due dates to follow up on task completion attempts. This ensures that a task can be addressed without being completed, and it will disappear from the list of tasks on the left. When the due date comes around again, it will show up on the list of tasks in the left pane.

Often, a user should push up the due date if they cannot complete a task. Include instructions in the task body to guide the user and maintain a pseudo-pipeline.

The left-hand panel will show (if any such tasks exist) **OVERDUE** tasks, tasks due today, and tasks with no due date, which are known as **SOMEDAY** tasks:

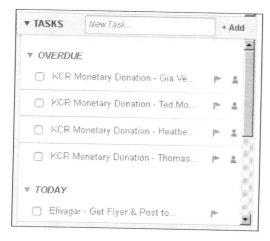

The user can adjust which contact fields are displayed in the right-hand pane using the *gear* icon, as shown in the following image:

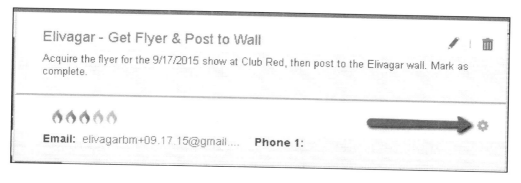

Depending on the nature of the task, displaying only the relevant fields can speed up productivity and enhance the focus:

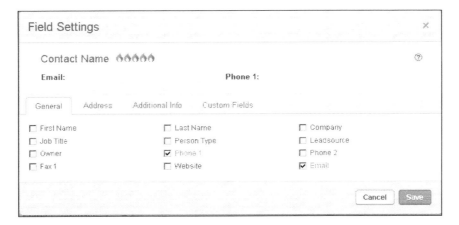

A task's priority is indicated with a visual queue on the right-hand side of the task's title. An *orange flag* indicates the task being critical, a *yellow flag* indicates that the task is essential, and *no flag* means that the task is non-essential.

For certain task types, a visual queue will be displayed to the left of the task title. For example, a **call type** displays as a *phone* icon, as shown in the following image:

If a task is connected to a **task completion goal** for more automation, we might want to include that context in the body of the task, so the user is careful to execute the task as it was designed. This is especially true when task completion will trigger an immediate e-mail.

When a user must fill out an internal form or apply a note template, it is recommended to instruct the user to finish those actions first, then mark the task as completed.

Any scheduled appointments assigned to the current user for today will be displayed on the top of the left-hand pane. Clicking on the appointment will load the right-hand panel. Instructions can also be included in an appointment's body, just like a task:

There is a quick-add task and an appointment button to the right of the **APPOINTMENTS/TASKS** headers, so the user can add new things without leaving My Day.

When adding a task or appointment using the quick-add, assigning it to a contact is not required. If this is the case, a *person* icon will not be displayed to the right of a task/appointment title in the left-hand pane.

Not all task fields are present in My Day, including custom task fields. If those are needed, they can be merged into the task itself upon creation or accessed by opening the full task view from the **Tasks** tab of the interactive view:

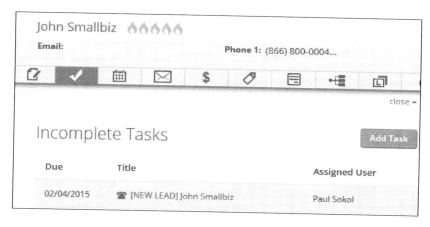

A plausible campaign model for the scenario presented in this recipe is as follows:

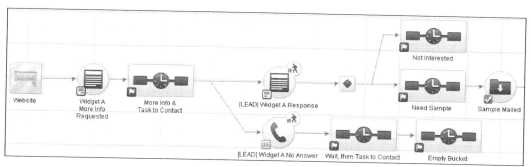

See also

Filling out an internal form or applying a note template can be performed following the same recipes as in *Using internal forms for workflow* or *Using note templates for workflow* directly from within My Day. The only difference is how you access the form or notes section.

For example, we can access internal forms using the *forms* symbol in the toolbar of My Day:

This is how we access the **Notes** section in the **My Day** toolbar:

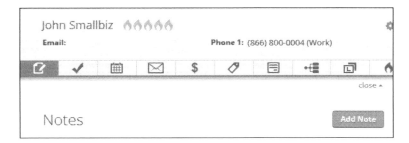

3

Attracting Leads and Building Your List

In this chapter, we will cover:

- ▸ Creating a *Contact Us* form
- ▸ Building a lead magnet delivery
- ▸ Maximizing social sharing of your e-mails
- ▸ Collecting leads from in-person events
- ▸ Leveraging offline media for lead generation
- ▸ Creating a simple referral request
- ▸ Building an automated Twitter offer
- ▸ Growing your social media following
- ▸ Building an inbound phone call lead capture
- ▸ Creating a PPC lead generation funnel
- ▸ Setting up web analytics

Introduction

Infusionsoft invented a holistic business strategy and customer experience journey framework called **Lifecycle Marketing**. There are three phases to Lifecycle Marketing: **Attract**, **Sell**, and **Wow**. This chapter concerns itself with different tactics to attract and capture leads.

Any business can use these recipes in one way or another. How you use them is up to you. Be creative!

Creating a Contact Us form

Every website needs to have some method for people to make general inquiries. This is particularly important for service-based businesses that operate locally. If a website is missing a simple *Contact Us* form, that means good leads from our hard-earned traffic are slipping away. Fixing this hole in our online presence creates another lead channel for the business.

Getting ready

We need to be editing a new campaign and have some manner of getting a form on our site (either ourselves or via the webmaster).

How to do it...

1. Drag out a new, **web form goal** and **sequence**.

2. Connect them as shown in the following image and rename all elements for visual clarity:

www.paulsokol.me   Contact Us Form   Task to Follow Up

3. Double-click on the web form goal to edit its content.

4. Add four fields to the form:
   - **First Name**
   - **Last Name**
   - **Email**
   - **Phone** (can be left as optional)

   The following screenshot shows these four fields:

5. Create a custom **Text Area** field for inquiry comments.

6. Add this custom field to the form using the **Other** snippet and leave as optional:

7. Click on the **Submit** button to change the call to action.

8. Change the **Button Label** button to `Please Contact Me!` and select **Center** alignment; click on **Save**.

9. Add a **Title** snippet above all the fields and provide some instruction for the visitor:

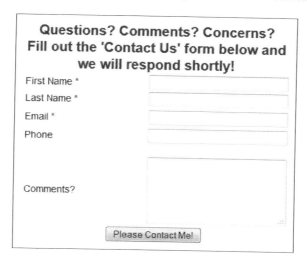

10. Click on the **Thank-you Page** tab at the top-left of the page.

11. Remove all elements and replace with a single **Title** snippet with a confirmation message for the visitor:

> **Thank you for reaching out ~Contact.FirstName~! We will contact you shortly.**

12. Click on the **Draft** button in the upper-right side of the page to change the form to **Ready**.

13. Click on **Back to Campaign** in the upper-left side of the page and open the connected sequence.

14. Drag out a new **Task** step, connect, and rename it appropriately:

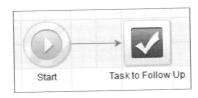

15. Double-click on the **Task** step and configure it accordingly. Don't forget to merge in any appropriate information or instructions for the end user:

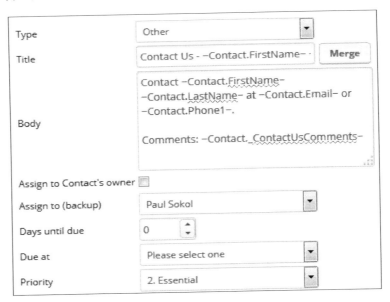

16. Click on the **Draft** button in the upper-right side of the page to change the task to **Ready**.

17. Click on **Back to Sequence** in the upper-left side of the page.
18. Click on the **Draft** button in the upper-right side of the page to change the sequence to **Ready**.
19. Click on **Back to Campaign** in the upper-left side of the page and publish the campaign.
20. Place the *Contact Us* form on our website.

How it works...

When a website visitor fills out the form, a task is created for someone to follow up with that visitor.

There's more...

For a better experience, add a *request received* e-mail in the post-form sequence to establish an inbox relationship. Be sure to respect their e-mail preferences as this kind of form submission isn't providing direct consent to be marketed to.

This out of the box recipe creates a *dead end* after the form submission. It is therefore recommended that you drive traffic from the thank you page somewhere else to capitalize on visitor momentum because they are very engaged after submitting a form. For example, we could point people to follow us on a particular social network, an FAQ page on our site, or our blog.

We can merge any captured information onto the thank you page. Use this to create a personalized experience for your brand voice:

> You got it ~Contact.FirstName~! We'll give you a call at ~Contact.Phone1~ as soon as we possibly can.
>
> In the meantime, why not check out the latest happenings on our Twitter feed.

We can add/remove form fields based on our needs. Just remember, a *Contact Us* form is for general inquiries and should be kept simple to reduce conversion friction; the fewer fields the better.

If we want to segment inquiries based on their type, we can use a radio button to segment inquiry types without sacrificing a custom field because the form's radio buttons can be used within a decision node directly coming out of the form.

See also

For a template similar to this recipe, download the **Automate Contact Requests** campaign from the **Marketplace**.

To learn how to download Marketplace campaign templates, see the recipe *Installing campaign templates from the Marketplace* in *Chapter 2, Critical Tools for Mastery*.

Building a lead magnet delivery

A **lead magnet** is exactly what it sounds like: it is something designed to attract new leads like a magnet. Offering some digital resource in exchange for contact information is a common example of a lead magnet.

A lead magnet can take many different forms, such as:

- ▶ PDF
- ▶ E-book
- ▶ Slideshow
- ▶ Audio file

This is by no means an exhaustive list. Automating the delivery and follow-up of a lead magnet is a simple and very powerful way to save time and get organized. This recipe shows how to build a mechanism for capturing interested leads, delivering an online lead magnet via e-mail, and following up with people who download it.

Getting ready

We need to have the lead magnet hosted somewhere publicly that is accessible via a URL and be editing a new campaign.

How to do it...

1. Drag out a new web form goal, **link click** goal, and two sequences.
2. Connect them as shown in the following image and rename all elements for visual clarity:

www.paulsokol.me   Lead Magnet Request   Lead Magnet Delivery   Download Lead Magnet   Download Follow Up

3. Create a **Campaign Link** and set it as the public download URL for the lead magnet.

4. Double-click on the web form goal to edit its content.

5. Design the form to include:

   ❑ A **Title** snippet with the lead magnet's name and a call to action

   ❑ A first name and e-mail field

   ❑ A call to action

The form should look as follows:

6. Set a confirmation message driving the visitor to their e-mail on the thank you page:

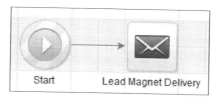

7. Mark the form as **Ready**, go **Back to Campaign**, and open the first sequence.

8. Drag out a new **Email** step, connect, and rename it appropriately:

9. Double-click on the **Email** step and write a simple delivery message. Make sure the download link(s) in the e-mail are using the campaign link. For best results, thank the person and tease some of the information contained in the lead magnet:

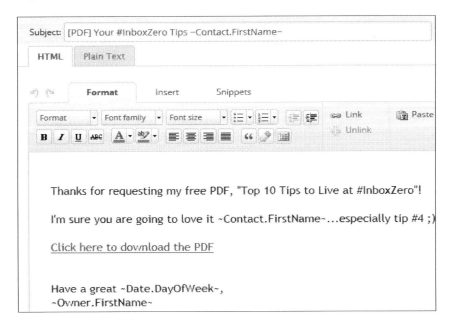

10. Mark the e-mail as **Ready** and go **Back to Sequence**.

11. Mark the Sequence as **Ready** to go **Back to Campaign**.

12. Double-click on the link click goal.

13. Check the download link within the e-mail and go **Back to Campaign**:

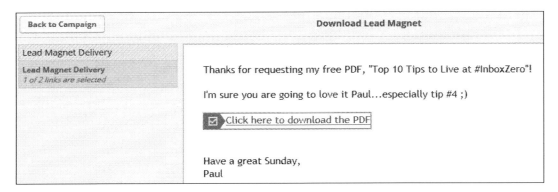

14. Open the post-link click goal sequence.

15. Drag out a **Delay Timer**, an **Email** step, and connect them accordingly.

16. Configure the **Delay Timer** to wait 1 day then run in the morning and rename the **Email** step:

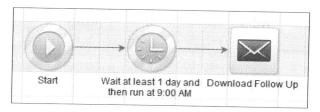

17. Double-click on the **Email** step and write a simple download follow-up. Make sure it furthers the sales conversation, feels personal, and gives a clear next step:

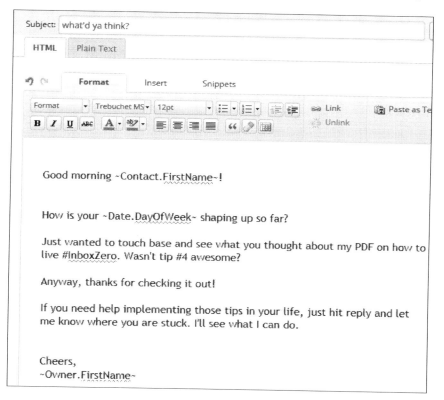

18. Mark the e-mail as **Ready** and go **Back to Sequence**.
19. Mark the sequence as **Ready** and go **Back to Campaign**; publish the campaign.
20. Place the lead magnet request form on our website.
21. Promote this new offering across social media to drive some initial traffic.

How it works...

When a visitor fills out the lead magnet request form, Infusionsoft immediately sends them an e-mail with a download link for the lead magnet. Then it waits until that person clicks the download link. When that happens, Infusionsoft waits one day then sends a follow-up e-mail addressing the download behavior.

There's more...

If the lead magnet is less than 10 MB, we can upload it to Infusionsoft's file box and grab a hosted URL from there. If the lead magnet is more than 10 MB, use a cloud-based file-sharing service that offers public URLs such as Dropbox, Google Drive, or Box.

Leveraging a campaign link ensures updating the resource is easy, especially if the link is used in multiple places. We can also use a campaign merge field for the lead magnet title to ensure scalability and easy duplication of this campaign.

It is important the word *Email* is present in the form's **Submit** button. This primes them for inbox engagement and creates clear expectations for what will occur after they request the lead magnet.

The download follow-up should get a conversation going and feel really personal. This tactic can bubble up hot clients; people appreciate it when others pay attention to them. For a more personal experience, the lead magnet delivery e-mail(s) can come from the company and the follow-up can come directly from an individual.

Not everyone is going to download the lead magnet right away. Add extra reminder e-mails into the mix, one at three days and then one at a week, to ensure those who are genuinely interested don't slip through the cracks.

Add a second form on the backend that collects addresses to ship a physical copy if appropriate. This would work well for a physical print of an e-book, a burned CD of an audio file, or a DVD of video content. This builds your direct mail database and helps further segment those who are most engaged and trusting. We can also leverage a second form to collect other information like a phone number or e-mail subscription preferences.

Adding an image of the lead magnet to the page containing the request web form can boost conversions. Even if there is never a physical version, there are lots of tools out there to create a digital image of an e-book, CD, report, and more.

This recipe is using a web form. We can also leverage a formal landing page at the beginning if desired.

Although we can tag those who request the lead magnet, we don't have to because a **Campaign Goal Completion** report can show us all the people who have submitted the form. We would only need to tag them in instances where the goal completion needs to be universally searchable (for instance, doing an order search via a goal completion tag).

See also

For a template that can be used as a starting point for this recipe, download the **Free Resource** campaign from the Marketplace.

Maximizing social sharing of your e-mails

Infusionsoft makes it easy for e-mail recipients to share an e-mail on their social networks via the **Social** snippet. Being able to capture leads from these social shares is an esoteric function of Infusionsoft that is extremely powerful when used properly.

This recipe has two parts:

- First, we are going to build the web form that will be used to collect social leads
- Second, we will connect this web form to an e-mail so the form displays when the e-mail is shared socially

Getting ready

We need to be editing a new campaign and have an e-mail prepared that we wish to use with social sharing.

How to do it...

Here we would be building a web form. to do so:

1. Drag out a web form goal, and a sequence.
2. Connect them as shown in the following image and rename all elements for visual clarity:

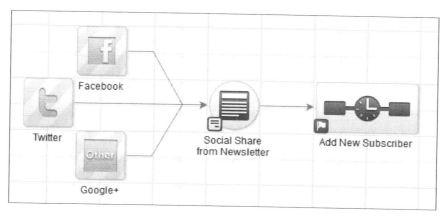

3. Double-click on the web form goal to edit its content.

4. Add two fields to the form:

   ❑ **First Name**

   ❑ **Email**

5. Click on the **Submit** button to change the call to action.

6. Change the **Button Label** to Add Me To Your Email List! and select **Center** alignment; click on **Save**:

7. Add a **Spotlight** snippet and provide some context for the form. Remember, whoever sees this will have arrived here from a social share of an e-mail:

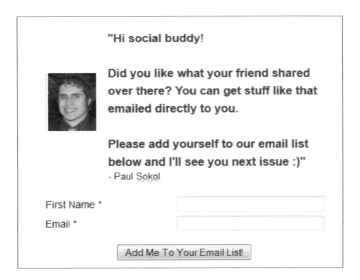

8. Click on the **Thank-you Page** tab at the top-left of the page.

9. Remove all elements and replace with a single **Title** snippet with a confirmation message for the visitor:

> You got it ~Contact.FirstName~! You're on the email list and will get the next issue.

10. Click on the **Draft** button in the upper-right side of the page to change the form to **Ready**.

11. Click on **Back to Campaign** in the upper-left side of the page and open the connected sequence.

12. Configure the necessary tag and/or field updates so the contact is on your broadcast list.

13. Click on the **Draft** button in the upper-right side of the page to change the the sequence to **Ready**.

14. Click on **Back to Sequence** in the upper-left side of the page.

15. Click on the **Draft** button in the upper-right side of the page to change the sequence to **Ready**.

16. Click on **Back to Campaign** in the upper-left side of the page and publish the campaign.

Here we would be connecting the web form to the e-mail. To do so:

1. Open the e-mail you wish to use with social sharing.

2. Add a **Social** snippet to the e-mail, and ensure the **Sharing Options** are not selected and **Labels** are **Off**; click on **Save**:

3. Add a **Title** snippet and provide a call to action to share:

4. Click on the **Layout & Style** button in the upper-right side of the **Format** toolbar to open the **Layout** and **Style** sub-menu:

5. In the **Layout** menu, turn on the **Social Sharing Layout**.

6. Type the name of the form we set up in the first part of this recipe and select it:

7. Click on the **Draft** button in the upper-right side of the page to change the e-mail to **Ready**.

8. Click on **Back to Sequence** in the upper-left side of the page.

9. Click on the **Draft** button in the upper-right side of the page to change the sequence to **Ready**.

10. Click on **Back to Campaign** in the upper-left side of the page and publish the campaign.

11. Send the e-mail we configured earlier.

How it works...

At the end of creating the web form section, we have a published web form. That enables the form to be selectable from within the **Layout** menu's **Social Sharing Layout** setting of an e-mail. Now, whenever someone shares the e-mail socially, their friends/followers will see the e-mail and the form:

Preview

Share this email with your friends
using the buttons below:
[f Like] [Tweet] [+1]

Here is the newsletter I want to use with the social sharing form.

When people share me, you'll see a form at my side.

Have a great Monday,
Paul

Update Your Information or Unsubscribe
1260 South Spectrum Blvd. Chandler, Arizona 85286 United States

"Hi social buddy!

Did you like what your friend shared over there? You can get stuff like that emailed directly to you.

Please add yourself to our email list below and I'll see you next issue :)"
- Paul Sokol

First Name *

Email *

[Add Me To Your Email List]

There's more...

We can preview the e-mail to see what the social share will look like.

This tactic should only be used where it makes sense. Newsletters and other content-rich e-mails bode well. It is also important to avoid using social sharing in general on e-mails that include sensitive information.

Treat a socially added opt-in like a normal new subscriber and add a welcome e-mail to the sequence. Encourage a social follow since they are on social media already.

This tactic can be used during a launch to boost virality. In that case, we should create a unique web form for every e-mail that could potentially be shared socially. This ensures a highly customized experience for each share and more transparent reporting on which e-mails convert the best socially.

 Fair warning: If we choose this tactic, we will want to lay out the campaign model(s) adeptly to avoid an unmanageable structure of web forms.

Consider tagging socially opted-in contacts with a special tag so we can isolate those who are socially active and we can leverage this subset of our list strategically. For example, send the first launch e-mail to these contacts and include a heavy call to action for social sharing. Then, send the first launch e-mail to the rest of your list a little while after the social shares have begun to permeate, in essence, amplifying the social proof.

We can also use social share links for link click goals within a campaign. This can be used to create a game layer powered by social sharing. Tell people they will get something for sharing the e-mail socially and automate the delivery using the post-link click sequences.

Alternately, we use link click goals on social sharing to deliver surprises and hidden rewards for social engagement. Don't tell people they will get something and really reward those who are truly engaged with our message.

We can have multiple **Social** snippets within a single e-mail. Embed multiple sharing opportunities throughout the e-mail's content to boost sharing rates; track which ones are performing best using link click goals.

See also

To boost our social media following, see the recipe later in this chapter, *Growing your social media following*. For a template that can be used as a starting point for this recipe, download the **Grow Your Newsletter With Social Sharing** campaign from the Marketplace.

Collecting leads from in-person events

In-person events are frequently chaotic. Having an easy-to-access lead capture form can provide confidence that each new connection we make will be properly added to our database.

Getting ready

We need to be editing a new campaign.

How to do it...

1. Drag out a web form goal and sequence.
2. Connect them as shown in the following image and rename all elements for visual clarity:

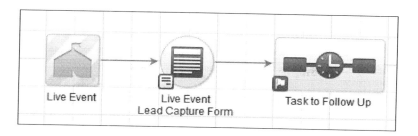

3. Double-click on the web form goal to edit its content.

4. Add the following fields to the form:

   ❑ **First Name**

   ❑ **Last Name**

   ❑ **Company**

   ❑ **Email**

   ❑ **Phone**

5. Click on the **Submit** button to change the call to action.

6. Change the **Button Label** to Add New Lead and select **Center** alignment; click on **Save**.

7. Add a **Title** snippet above all the fields and provide some instruction for the visitor. Remember, the only visitor will be internal employees/contractors:

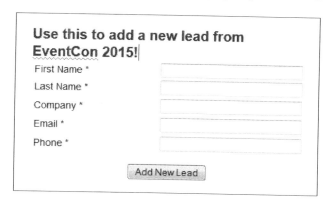

8. Click on the **Thank-you Page** tab at the top-left of the page.

9. Remove all elements and replace with a single **Title** snippet with a confirmation message:

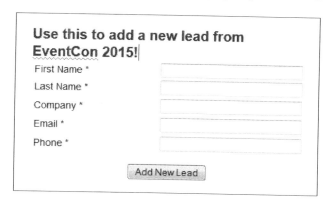

10. Click on the **Draft** button in the upper-right side of the page to change the form to **Ready**.

11. Click on **Back to Campaign** in the upper-left side of the page and open the connected sequence.

12. Drag out a new **Task** step, connect, and rename it appropriately:

13. Double-click on the **Task** step and configure it accordingly. Don't forget to merge in any appropriate information, context, or instructions for the end user:

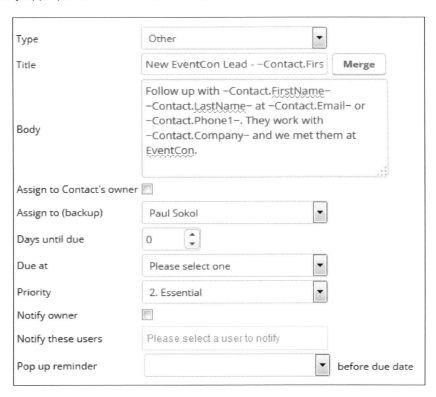

14. Click on the **Draft** button in the upper-right side of the page to change the task to **Ready**.

15. Click on **Back to Sequence** in the upper-left side of the page.

16. Click on the **Draft** button in the upper-right side of the page to change the sequence to **Ready**.

17. Click on **Back to Campaign** in the upper-left side of the page and publish the campaign.

18. Bookmark the form URL on our smartphone or laptop for easy access during the event.

How it works...

When we are at a live event and get a new lead, we can access the form on our phone quickly and enter their information. By building this habit we ensure there is a follow-up task for each new lead when we come home from the event and nobody slips through the cracks.

There's more...

Set the form width to 350 px for a better mobile experience.

Add other things besides a task into the sequence to streamline the follow-up. There are many other things that may need to happen with a new event lead such as tagging, sending a welcome e-mail, or starting another campaign.

To cut through the promotional haze of a live event, send a follow-up e-mail the day after the event is over or the following Monday.

Add more fields to the form per the business needs. Add radio buttons or checkboxes to be used in a decision node post-form. This can be used to assign owners, add to specific promotions, and tag for segmentation.

For easy distribution to company reps, shorten the form's URL using **Bit.ly** or another service. We can also e-mail the form URL and have them bookmark it.

Create a unique form for every event and use a hidden lead source field on the form. Populate the hidden field with a lead source for the event to enable easy **Return On Investment** (**ROI**) calculation in the future.

The smartphone app **Snap** by Infusionsoft can make data entry easy for new connections you make. In that case, we will want to start this campaign with a tag that is applied from within the app.

See also

For a template of this recipe, download the **Live Event Networking** campaign from the Marketplace.

Leveraging offline media for lead generation

Despite the proliferation of the Internet and smartphones, offline media can still be an extremely powerful lead generation channel. Strategically placing a URL somewhere within a letter, billboard, and so on gives us the ability to collect leads automatically.

Strategy is all based on context, so for this recipe, let's pretend we are going to be generating leads for a charity using a flyer that has already been designed.

Getting ready

We need to be editing a new campaign.

How to do it...

1. Drag out a new web form goal and sequence.

2. Connect them as shown in the following image and rename all elements for visual clarity:

3. Double-click on the web form goal to edit its content.

4. Add the following fields to the form:
   - **First Name**
   - **Last Name**
   - **Email**
   - **Phone**

5. Create a custom **Text Area** field for inquiry comments.

6. Add this custom field to the form using the **Other** snippet and leave as optional.

7. Click on the **Submit** button to change the call to action.

8. Change the **Button Label** to Call Me! and select **Center** alignment; click on **Save**.

9. Add a **Logo** and **Title** snippet above all the fields and provide some instruction for the visitor:

10. Click on the **Thank-you Page** tab at the top-left of the page.

11. Remove all elements and replace with a **Logo** and **Title** snippet with a confirmation message:

12. Click on the **Draft** button in the upper-right side of the page to change the form to **Ready**.

13. Click on **Back to Campaign** in the upper-left side of the page and open the connected sequence.

14. Drag out a new **Task** step, connect, and rename it appropriately:

15. Double-click on the **Task** step and configure it accordingly. Don't forget to merge in any appropriate information, context, or instructions for the end user:

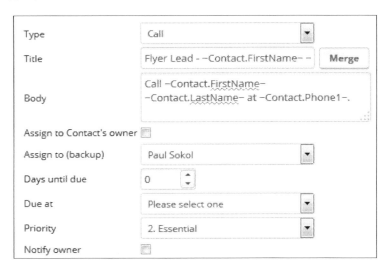

16. Click on the **Draft** button in the upper-right side of the page to change the task to **Ready**.

17. Click on **Back to Sequence** in the upper-left side of the page.

18. Click on the **Draft** button in the upper-right side of the page to change the sequence to **Ready**.

19. Click on **Back to Campaign** in the upper-left side of the page and publish the campaign.

20. Shorten the web form's hosted URL using a link-shortening service such as **Bit.ly** or **Goo.gl**.

21. Place this shortened URL somewhere on the flyer with a light call to action.

How it works...

When people see the flyer and are intrigued, having a short and simple URL makes it easy for them to take action. Driving them directly to an opt-in ensures hot leads can bubble up quickly.

There's more...

Set the form width to 350 px for a better mobile experience.

Add other things besides a task into the sequence to streamline the follow-up. There are many other things that may need to happen with a new lead such as tagging, sending a welcome e-mail, or starting another campaign.

Since we are switching messaging channels from offline to online, we need to make sure the branding on the form matches the branding of the offline media. Interested leads should never have any doubt they are on the right web page.

We can extend the form into a multi-step form for further segmentation and data collection. For example, if we are a home service business, we could ask for someone's address on the thank you page of the initial opt-in to help with scheduling appointments.

In general, the thank you page should never be a dead end. Drive new leads back to your website, to a social channel, or even to call you immediately. Make sure wherever we send them is mobile friendly!

The form's messaging should match the call to action on the offline media as much as possible. Even if there is a main call to action on the offline media, this recipe can work well as a secondary response mechanism for those not quite ready.

For added mobile friendliness, create a **QR code** for the form URL and place on the offline media in addition to the shortened URL.

To track the ROI of things like flyers and posters, pass through a lead source ID in a hidden field in the form's URL before shortening it. For example, if a flyer's lead source ID is 123, by appending `?inf_field_LeadSourceId=123` to the form's URL, Infusionsoft will assign that lead source to all people coming from that specific flyer. This enables us to drive different versions of offline media (each with their own lead sources) to the same form and track how each is performing.

Has the offline media already been printed? Still want to use this recipe? Get serious about lead generation and print out white label stickers with the shortened URL and place them on the media. It won't be pretty, but it will provide additional lead generation possibilities.

See also

For a similar model of this recipe that uses a physical letter, download the **Attract Traffic Using Direct Mail** campaign from the Marketplace.

Creating a simple referral request

Social proof is very persuasive. People tend to trust their friends and family more about a buying decision than anything else. Having a system to ask for referrals from your existing customers is a great way to lower customer acquisition costs because referrals are normally easier to close.

Getting ready

We need to be editing a new campaign.

How to do it...

1. Drag out a new **note goal**, web form goal, and two sequences.

2. Connect them as shown in the following image and rename all elements for visual clarity:

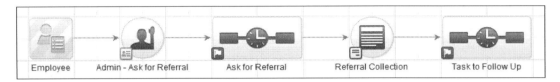

3. Double-click on the note goal, configure the information, and click on **Save**:

4. Double-click on the web form icon in the lower-left corner of the web form goal to open **Goal Settings**.

5. Change the goal so it can be achieved by any contact; click on **Save**:

6. Double-click on the web form goal to edit its content.

7. Add the following fields to the form and mark them as required:
    - ❑ **First Name**
    - ❑ **Phone**

8. Update those field labels to be My Friend's Name and My Friend's Phone Number.

9. Create a custom **Text** field for the referred friend's name.

10. Create a custom **Email** field for the referred friend's e-mail.

11. Add these custom fields to the form using the **Other** snippet and mark as required.

12. Update the field labels to be My Name Is and My Email Is.

13. Click on the **Submit** button to change the call to action.

14. Change the **Button Label** to Please Call Them and select **Center** alignment; click on **Save**.

15. Add a **Logo** and **Title** snippet above all the fields and provide some context for the visitor.

16. Click on the **Thank-you Page** tab at the top-left of the page.

17. Remove all elements and replace with a **Logo** and **Title** snippet with a confirmation message. Remember, the person filling out the form is actually the custom name field and not the normal contact fields:

18. Click on the **Settings** tab at the top-left of the page.

19. Uncheck the auto-population option:

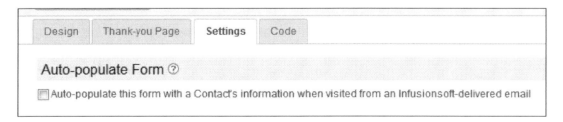

20. Click on the **Draft** button in the upper-right side of the page to change the form to **Ready**.

21. Click on **Back to Campaign** in the upper-left side of the page and open the post-form sequence.

22. Drag out a new **Task** step, connect, and rename it appropriately:

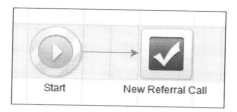

23. Double-click on the **Task** step and configure it accordingly. Don't forget to merge in any appropriate information, context, or instructions for the end user:

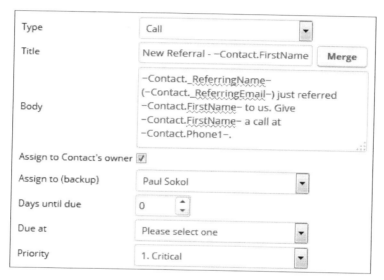

24. Click on the **Draft** button in the upper-right side of the page to change the task to **Ready**.

25. Click on **Back to Sequence** in the upper-left side of the page.

26. Click on the **Draft** button in the upper-right side of the page to change the sequence to **Ready**.

27. Click on **Back to Campaign** in the upper-left side of the page and publish the campaign.

28. Click on the **Edit** tab in the upper-left side of the page and open the first sequence.

29. Drag out a new **Email** step, connect, and rename it appropriately:

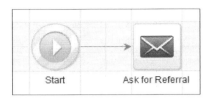

30. Double-click on the **Email** step and write a simple referral request:

Thanks for being a valued customer ~Contact.FirstName~!

I have a quick question: who do you know that could also benefit from what ~Company.Company~ offers?

If you have somebody in mind, would you please click here and share their phone number so we can give them a call?

Thanks,
~Owner.FirstName~

P.S. If you can't think of somebody thats ok, no hard feelings :)

31. Select the text we want to link to the referral collection form and create a link.

32. Select **Hosted web form** from the **Link to** dropdown and choose the form we just published; click on **Insert/Update**:

33. Mark the e-mail as **Ready** and go **Back to Sequence**.

34. Mark the sequence as **Ready** to go **Back to Campaign**.

35. Publish the campaign.

How it works...

When an employee wants to ask a customer for a referral, all they have to do is apply the *Admin - Ask for Referral* note to the contact record. This delivers an e-mail pointing to a referral collection form. When the form is submitted, it is creating a new contact record. This is why we uncheck the auto-population setting to ensure that the customer providing the referral doesn't get confused when they arrive at the form. If the setting was left on, they would see their own information in the `My Friend's` fields.

There's more...

In order to link to a hosted web form (or **landing page**), the form must be published at least once. This is why we published the campaign mid-recipe.

We can change this recipe to start with a **tag goal** and automate it from other campaigns. For example, triggering this campaign after a positive survey response.

We can use the admin task/note reporting to track which employees are asking for the most referrals. The note will be assigned to the user who applied it.

Collecting an e-mail address for a referral and e-mailing without permission would violate Infusionsoft's **Acceptable Usage Policy** (**AUP**). However, we can call the referral and get their permission to e-mail directly.

On the thank you page of the form, we can also link back to the form again so people can do multiple referrals.

See also

For a similar model to this recipe, download the **Refer a Friend** campaign from the Marketplace.

Building an automated Twitter offer

Twitter has an ad product called a **Lead Generation Card** where users can redeem offers directly from within their feed. This sends their name, username, and e-mail to whomever is running the offer. Infusionsoft has built-in integration that makes it easy to automatically follow up with new leads acquired in this way.

However, a Lead Generation Card is not an ad by itself. It has to be attached to a promoted tweet. Meaning you can use the same Lead Generation Card across many different ads.

Similar to a strategy, an offer is all about context. For this recipe we are going to pretend that the offer on the Lead Generation Card is for the user to redeem an e-book.

This recipe has two parts:

- ▸ First, we are going to build the Infusionsoft backend to deliver the e-book
- ▸ Then, we are going to create the Lead Generation Card

Getting ready

We need to have:

- ▸ A Twitter profile
- ▸ A Twitter ads account
- ▸ An image to use for the Lead Generation Card
- ▸ A URL for your company's privacy page
- ▸ A backup web form or landing page if the Twitter user views the card on a non-supported platform

We also need to have the e-book hosted somewhere publicly that is accessible via a URL and be editing a new campaign.

How to do it...

This recipe will be explained in two parts—*Part 1* and *Part 2*.

Part 1

1. Drag out a new **Twitter offer goal**, link click goal, and two sequences.
2. Connect them as shown in the following image and rename all elements for visual clarity:

3. Create a campaign link and set it as the public download URL for the e-book.
4. Double-click on the **Twitter** goal.
5. Mark the goal as **Ready**, go **Back to Campaign**, and open the first sequence.
6. Drag out a new **Email** step, connect, and rename it appropriately.

7. Double-click on the **Email** step and write an e-book delivery message. Make sure the download link(s) in the e-mail are using the campaign link. For best results, thank the person and tease some of the information contained in the e-book:

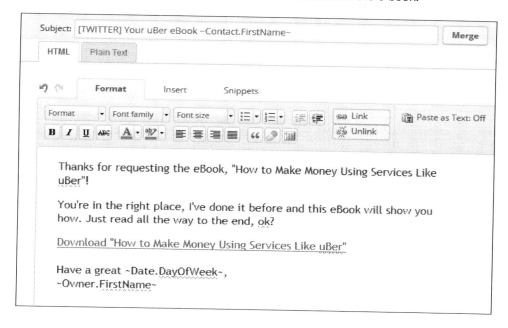

8. Mark the e-mail as **Ready** and go **Back to Sequence**.
9. Mark the sequence as **Ready** to go **Back to Campaign**.
10. Double-click on the link click goal.
11. Check the download link within the e-mail and go **Back to Campaign**:

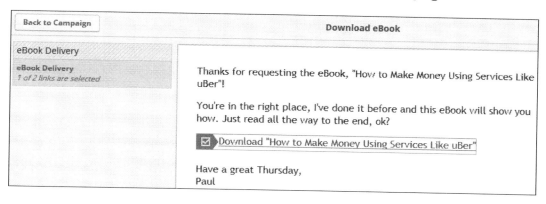

12. Open the post-link click goal sequence.
13. Drag out a **Delay Timer**, an **Email** step, and connect them accordingly.

14. Configure the **Delay Timer** to wait 1 day then run in the morning and rename the **Email** step:

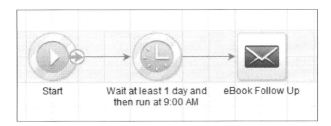

15. Double-click on the **Email** step and write a simple download follow-up. Make sure it furthers the sales conversation, feels personal, and gives a clear next step:

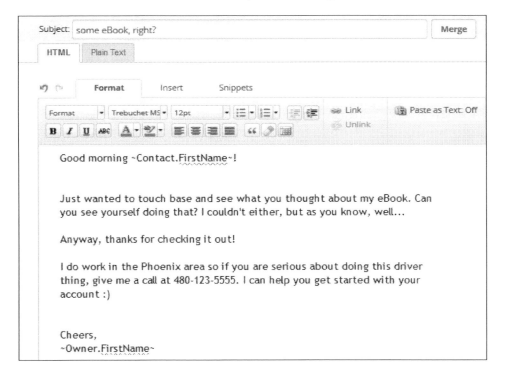

16. Mark the e-mail as **Ready** and go **Back to Sequence**.

17. Mark the sequence as **Ready** and go **Back to Campaign**; publish the campaign.

Part 2

1. Click on the **Edit** tab in the upper-left side of the page and open the Twitter goal.

2. Copy the URL provided by the Twitter goal:

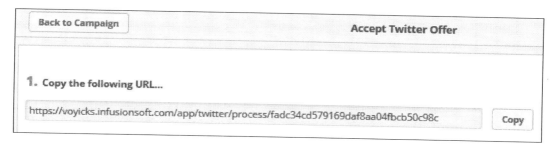

3. Log in to our Twitter ads account and find **Cards manager**. As of writing this book it resides in a URL that looks like: `https://ads.twitter.com/accounts/~Twitter.Hash~/cards`.

4. Click on the blue **Create Lead Generation card** button:

5. Provide a short description of the offer, the image to be used, and the call to action:

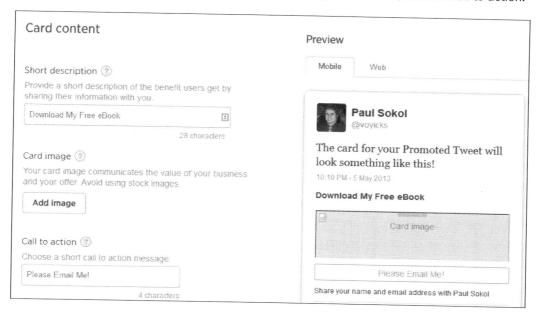

6. Add the privacy policy and fallback URL:

7. In the **Data settings (optional)** window, paste in the Twitter goal URL from Infusionsoft into the **Submit URL** field and change the **HTTP method** to **POST**:

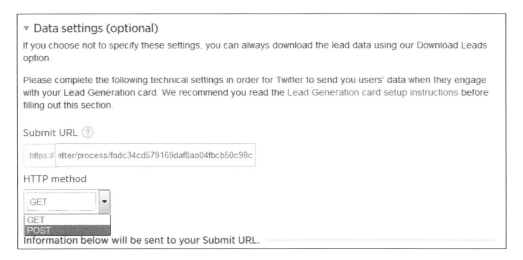

8. Give the card a name, agree to the terms, and click on **Create Card**:

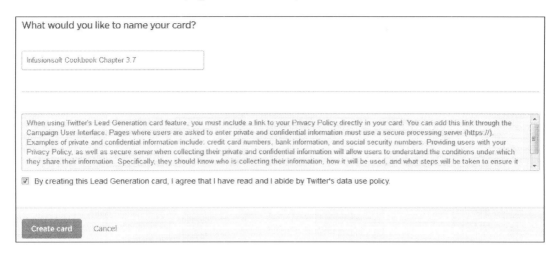

9. Verify the card was submitted successfully on the next page. We may also wish to check the **Historical Performance** view of the campaign to verify the goal was triggered.

10. Back at the main campaign dashboard, start a new **Leads on Twitter** campaign:

11. In the **Creative** section, there is an option to load this **Lead Generation Card**:

How it works...

When a Twitter user redeems the offer from the **Promoted tweet**, Twitter posts their user information directly to Infusionsoft, which triggers the offer delivery sequence.

There's more...

Remember that even though this recipe used the example of an e-book, the Twitter goal can be used to deliver any offer. The magic is in pushing the user's e-mail into Infusionsoft and starting some type of automation.

For maximum effectiveness, use a unique web form as the fallback URL for each Lead Generation Card. This way, we can customize the experience and address if their device doesn't work with the offer:

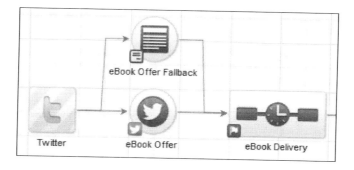

The following is an example fallback web form:

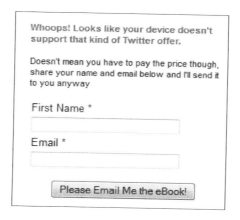

We can also add a destination URL where the user will be directed to when they redeem the offer:

▾ Destination URL settings (optional)

Adding a destination URL lets us redirect the user to your specified landing page after they submit the lead.

Destination URL

The user will be redirected to this URL after they submit the lead.

http://

Add a Facebook custom audience pixel to your destination URL page. If someone uses Twitter, they might also use Facebook. That would lay the groundwork for a multi-channel social campaign.

Point the destination URL to a hosted landing page to create a two or more step collection process. Since the user's e-mail will not be passed to the destination URL, remember to collect the e-mail address again on the landing page; label the e-mail field as `Confirm Your Email Address` for a smoother experience:

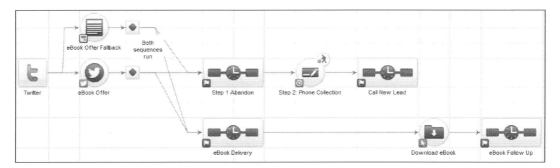

For faster implementation, connect a new **Twitter** goal to an existing offer sequence:

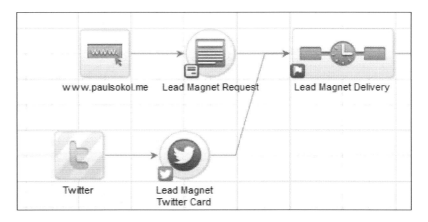

The download follow-up should get a conversation going and feel really personal. This tactic alone can bubble up hot clients just because someone is paying attention to them. For a more personal experience, the offer delivery e-mail(s) can come from the company and the follow-up can come directly from an individual.

Not everyone is going to download the offer right away. Add extra reminder e-mails into the mix, one at three days and then one at a week, to ensure those who are genuinely interested don't slip through the cracks.

Not every display platform shows all elements of the Lead Generation Card. Within Twitter there are ways to view how the ads will look on different devices. At a minimum, there will always be the image and the call to action button. Including the offer in a text overlay on the ad image ensures all users regardless of device will see your offer.

Adding the offer itself into the Lead Generation Card's image can boost conversions. Even if there is never a physical version, there are lots of tools out there to create a digital image of an e-book, coupon, report, and so on. If we *Google* stuff like "e-book cover generator", we can find those tools. These digital renderings can also be used in the offer delivery e-mails.

Although we can tag those who redeem the Lead Generation Card, we don't have to because a Campaign Goal Completion report can show us all people who have submitted the form.

See also

For a campaign template that uses the Twitter goal, download the **Automate Follow Up for Twitter Leads** campaign from the Marketplace. For a recipe that delivers an offer using a web form or landing page, see the *Building a lead magnet delivery* section earlier in this chapter.

Growing your social media following

In this age of technology, relationships are king. The more channels we can connect with someone, the greater the potential for a relationship. By intentionally asking people to follow us, we can systematically build more communication channels to the database.

For this recipe, let's pretend we want to invite people to follow us on Twitter.

Getting ready

We need to have a social profile URL and be editing a new campaign.

How to do it...

1. Drag out a new tag goal, link click goal, and one sequence.

2. Connect them as shown in the following image and rename all elements for visual clarity:

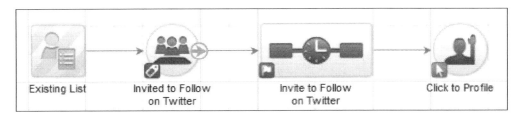

3. Create a campaign link and set it as the social profile URL.
4. Create a functional tag to trigger the campaign.
5. Double-click on the tag goal and configure it for this functional tag; click on **Save**:

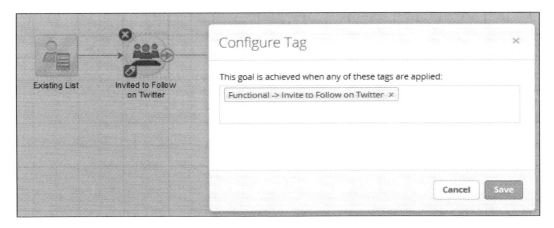

6. Open the connected sequence, drag out a new **Email** step, connect, and rename it appropriately:

7. Double-click on the **Email** step and write a simple follow request. Make sure the follow links in the e-mail are using the social URL campaign link. For best results, thank the person and provide a reason why they should follow us on that particular channel:

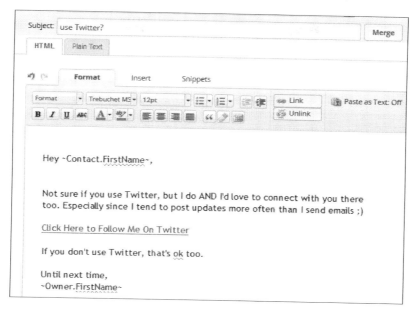

8. Mark the e-mail as **Ready** and go **Back to Sequence**.
9. Mark the sequence as **Ready** to go **Back to Campaign**.
10. Double-click on the link click goal.
11. Check the social link within the e-mail and go **Back to Campaign**:

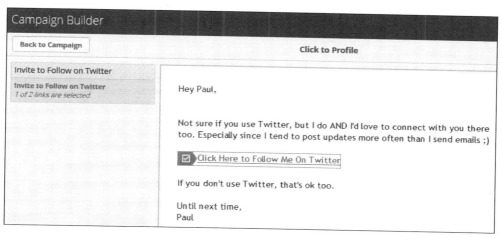

12. Publish the campaign.

13. Apply the functional tag from other campaigns where it is appropriate to invite someone to follow on social media.

How it works...

When the functional tag is applied to a contact record, an e-mail goes out driving them to our social profile. From there, the hope is they will add our profile. The link click goal allows us to track engagement.

There's more...

Not everyone is going to follow you right away. Add extra reminder e-mails into the mix but not too often to avoid list burnout. Doing another reminder in one month and then three months later is harmless. Make sure those reminders are configured in the link click goal as well so the series stops when they click to view our social profile.

By leveraging a campaign link this will ensure that updating the social URL is easy; especially if the link is used in multiple places. This also ensures you can copy the campaign easily for other social channels.

Set up two versions of this recipe: one for new leads and one for new customers. This will allow us to further target the follow request.

Add a delay timer to send during (or *NOT* during) normal business hours to create a more personal experience.

Use the proper lingo for the specific channel in the e-mail's call to action (for example, *Like us on Facebook* instead of *Follow us on Facebook*).

Build an *I don't use Twitter* link in the *P.S.* and tag those people. This creates an *anti-list* you can use strategically in other places:

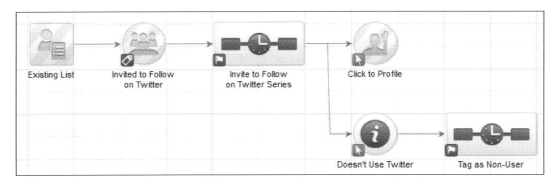

Keep these e-mails short because they are just driving them to your social profile quickly, not keeping them in their inbox.

Although we can tag those who click to the social profile, we don't have to because a Campaign Goal Completion report can show us all people who have clicked. There are only two times we would need to tag. First is, if the click will trigger some other sequence without stopping the current one, the tag can fire a tag goal. Tagging on click is also how we can segment a campaign based on engagement. We can configure a decision node to check for certain tags and respond accordingly.

Adjust this recipe by using a **note template** at the start instead. This can be particularly effective if using with a sales team and the e-mail comes directly from the sales representatives:

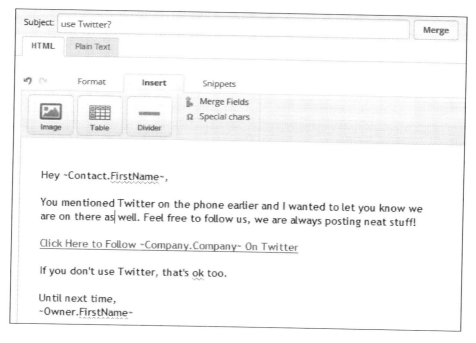

Create a task to check and verify a follow from the link click goal. Point that task to an internal form with a radio button to confirm whether or not that person followed. This allows us to segment based on their social activity:

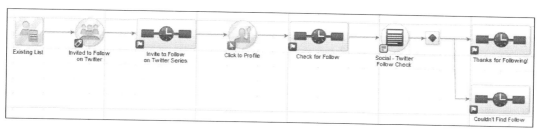

See also

For a template that can be used as a starting point for this recipe, download the **Grow Your Social Following** campaign from the Marketplace.

Building an inbound phone call lead capture

Having a system to reliably collect and distribute leads from inbound phone calls is critical for a well-oiled sales machine. This is also very important for any print media where the call to action is to call the company because it ensures easy ROI tracking.

The context behind why someone might call is important, so for this recipe let's pretend people are calling in to schedule a free consultation from an ad.

Getting ready

The ad needs to be finished and we need to be editing a new campaign.

How to do it...

1. Drag out a new web form goal, and two sequences.

2. Connect them as shown in the following image and rename all elements for visual clarity:

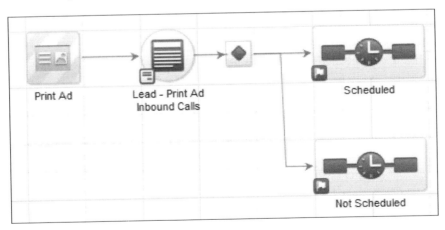

3. Double-click on the web form icon in the lower-left corner of the web form goal to open **Goal Settings**.

4. Change the goal so it is achieved when a user submits an internal form; click on **Save**:

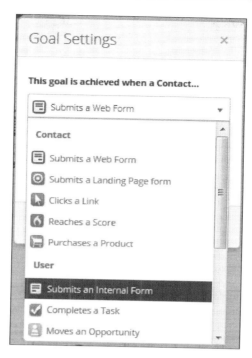

5. Double-click on the internal form goal to edit its content.
6. Add four fields to the form:
    - **First Name**
    - **Last Name**
    - **Email**
    - **Phone**

   The following screenshot shows these fields:

7. Add a radio button for the result of the call.

8. Add a **Title** snippet above all the fields and provide some instruction for the visitor:

9. Click on the **Draft** button in the upper-right side of the page to change the form to **Ready**.

10. Click on **Back to Campaign** in the upper-left side of the page and double-click on the **decision node** to open it.

11. Configure the rules for people to go into the **Scheduled** sequence if **Yes** is selected, and into the **Not Scheduled** sequence if **No** is selected; click on **Back to Campaign** in the upper-left side of the page:

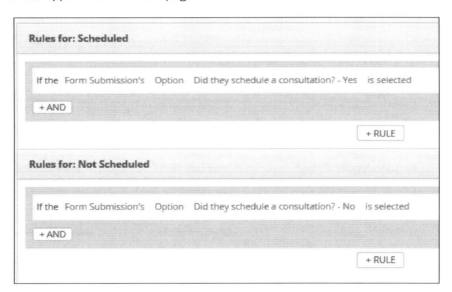

12. Open the **Scheduled** sequence, drag out a new **Email** step, connect, and rename it appropriately:

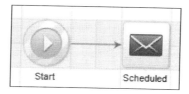

13. Double-click on the **Email** step and write a simple consultation follow-up:

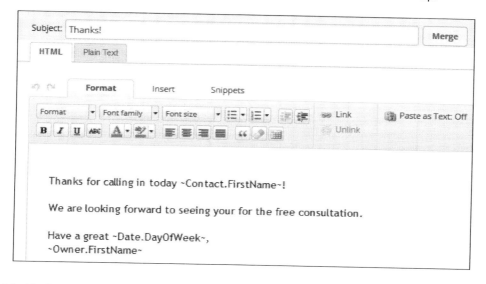

14. Mark the e-mail as **Ready** and go **Back to Sequence**.

15. Mark the sequence as **Ready** to go **Back to Campaign**.

16. Open the **Not Scheduled** sequence, drag out a new **Email** step, connect, and rename it appropriately:

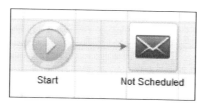

17. Double-click on the **Email** step and write a simple follow-up e-mail thanking them:

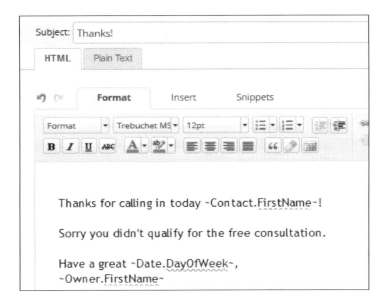

18. Mark the e-mail as **Ready** and go **Back to Sequence**.
19. Mark the sequence as **Ready** to go **Back to Campaign**.
20. Publish the campaign.
21. Run the ad.

How it works...

When someone calls in from the ad, the phone rep fills out the *Lead - Print Ad Inbound Calls*. Based on whether the caller scheduled or not, the proper automated follow-up is delivered.

There's more...

This recipe can easily be modified for a variety of inbound phone call outcomes.

We can add/remove form fields based on our needs. Just remember that this form is being used for inbound phone calls.

Use different phone numbers to track different ad versions. There are many different services out there that provide trackable phone numbers for this purpose. If we are using trackable phone numbers, add a lead source field to the form and create a unique lead source per phone number. Then make sure our phone reps are properly tracking which number was used using those lead sources. This will enable easier ROI reporting.

We can add a **Create Opportunity** step if the inbound call is for lead generation going to a sales representative:

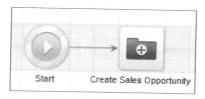

Sometimes we have a group of users to whom we want to distribute opportunities. In these situations, use a round robin step first to assign an owner. Check the user guide to learn how to set up a round robin.

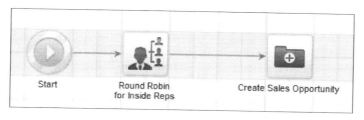

See also

For a template similar to this recipe, download the **Track Inbound Phone Calls for a Free Gift** campaign from the Marketplace.

Creating a PPC lead generation funnel

Having a progressive funnel allows the hottest leads to move at their own pace while normal leads can be nurtured and bubbled up over time. **Pay Per Click** (**PPC**) can be very expensive but those costs can be minimized over time using a progressive funnel.

For this recipe, let's pretend we are a service-based company (like a plumbing business) running PPC ads so people can request a service call.

Getting ready

We need to be editing a new campaign.

How to do it...

1. Drag out a new traffic source, three web form goals, and two sequences.

2. Connect them as shown in the following image and rename all elements for visual clarity:

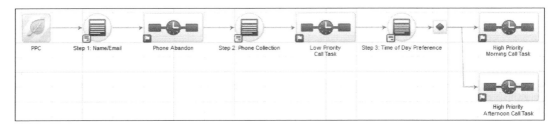

3. Double-click on the **Step 3: Time of Day Preference** web form goal to edit its content.

4. Add a hidden e-mail field to the form and a radio button for call time preferences.

5. Click on the **Submit** button to change the call to action.

6. Change the **Button Label** to Call Me Then! and select **Center** alignment; click on **Save**.

7. Add a **Title** snippet above all the fields and provide some instruction for the visitor:

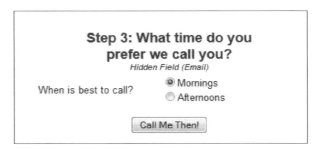

8. Click on the **Thank-you Page** tab at the top-left of the page.

9. Remove all elements and replace with a single **Title** snippet with a confirmation message for the visitor:

> **Success!**
>
> **We will give you a call at ~Contact.Phone1~ then, ~Contact.FirstName~!**

10. Click the **Code** tab and copy the web form URL from the **Use the Hosted Version** section.

11. Click on the **Draft** button in the upper-right side of the page to change the form to **Ready**.

12. Click on **Back to Campaign** in the upper-left side of the page and double-click on the decision node to open it.

13. Configure the rules for people to go into the **High Priority Morning Call Task** sequence if **Morning** is selected and into the **High Priority Afternoon Call Task** sequence if **Afternoon** is selected; click on **Back to Campaign** in the upper-left side of the page:

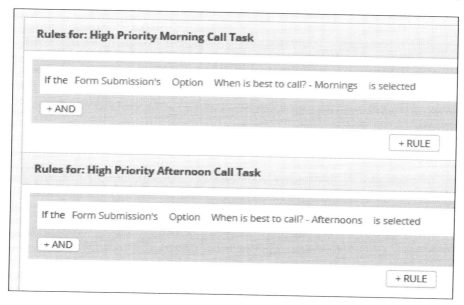

14. Open the **High Priority Morning Call Task** sequence, drag out a new **Task** step, connect, and rename it appropriately:

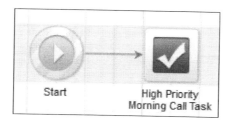

15. Double-click on the **Task** step and configure it accordingly. Make sure the **Priority** is set to **1.Critical** and the time is set for 08:00 AM. Don't forget to merge in any appropriate information or instructions for the end user:

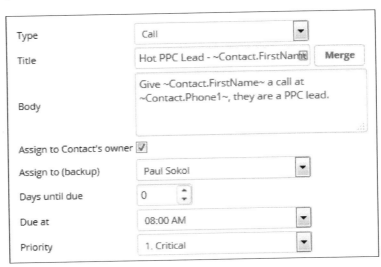

16. Click on the **Draft** button in the upper-right side of the page to change the task to **Ready**.

17. Click on **Back to Sequence** in the upper-left side of the page.

18. Click on the **Draft** button in the upper-right side of the page to change the sequence to **Ready**; click on **Back to Campaign** in the upper-left side of the page.

19. Open the **High Priority Afternoon Call Task** sequence, drag out a new **Task** step, connect, and rename it appropriately:

20. Double-click on the **Task** step and configure it accordingly. Make sure the **Priority** is set to **1. Critical** and the time is set for 01:00 PM. Don't forget to merge in any appropriate information or instructions for the end user:

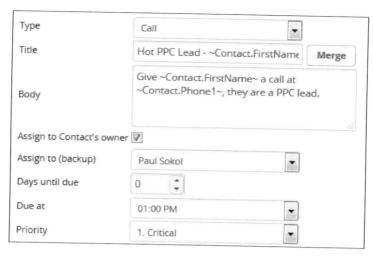

21. Click on the **Draft** button in the upper-right side of the page to change the task to **Ready**.

22. Click on **Back to Sequence** in the upper-left side of the page.

23. Click on the **Draft** button in the upper-right side of the page to change the sequence to **Ready**; click on **Back to Campaign** in the upper-left side of the page.

24. Double-click on the **Step 2: Phone Collection** web form goal to edit its content.

25. Add a hidden e-mail field to the form and a phone field.

26. Click on the **Submit** button to change the call to action.

27. Change the **Button Label** to Please Call Me! and select **Center** alignment; click on **Save**.

28. Add a **Title** snippet above all the fields and provide some instruction for the visitor:

29. Click on the **Thank-you Page** tab at the top-left of the page.

30. Change the **Thank-you Page to Display** dropdown to **Web address**, paste in the URL of the third web form we copied in Step 10, and make sure the **Pass contact's information to the thank-you page** box is checked:

31. Click on the **Code** tab and copy the web form URL from the **'Use the Hosted Version'** section.

32. Click on the **Draft** button in the upper-right side of the page to change the form to **Ready**.

33. Click on **Back to Campaign** in the upper-left side of the page.

34. Open the **Priority Call Task** sequence, drag out a **Delay Timer**, and set it to **Wait at least 15 minutes and then run between 12:00 AM - 11:45 PM**.

35. Drag out a new **Task** step, connect, and rename it appropriately:

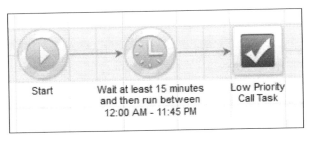

36. Double click the **Task** step and configure it accordingly. Make sure the **Priority** is set to **2. Essential**. Don't forget to merge in any appropriate information or instructions for the end user:

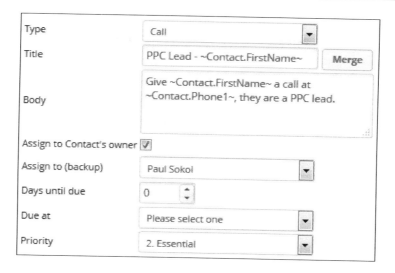

37. Click on the **Draft** button in the upper-right side of the page to change the task to **Ready**.

38. Click on **Back to Sequence** in the upper-left side of the page.

39. Click on the **Draft** button in the upper-right side of the page to change the sequence to **Ready**; click on **Back to Campaign** in the upper-left side of the page.

40. Double-click on the **Step 1: Name/Email** web form goal to edit its content.

41. Add a first name field to the form and an e-mail field.

42. Click on the **Submit** button to change the call to action.

43. Change the **Button Label** to `Proceed to Step 2: Scheduling` and select **Center** alignment; click on **Save**.

44. Add a **Title** snippet, a **Divider**, and another **Title** snippet above all the fields and provide the offer and redemption text:

45. Click on the **Thank-you Page** tab at the top-left of the page.

46. Change the **Thank-you Page to Display** dropdown to **Web address**, paste in the URL of the second web form we copied in Step 31, and make sure the **Pass contact's information to the thank-you page** box is checked:

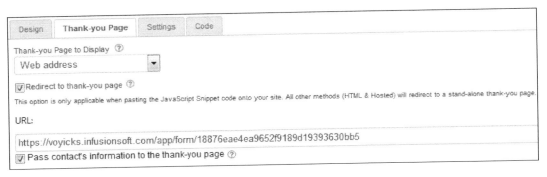

47. Click on the **Draft** button in the upper-right side of the page to change the form to **Ready**.

48. Click on **Back to Campaign** in the upper-left side of the page.

49. Publish the campaign.

50. After publishing, click on the **Edit** tab and double-click on into the **Phone Abandon** sequence.

51. Drag out a **Delay Timer** and set it to **Wait at least 15 minutes and then run between 12:00 AM - 11:45 PM**.

52. Drag out a new **Email** step, connect, and rename it appropriately:

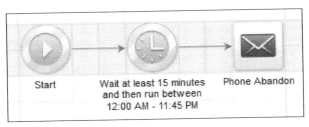

53. Double click the **Email** step and drive the reader back to the Step 2 form.

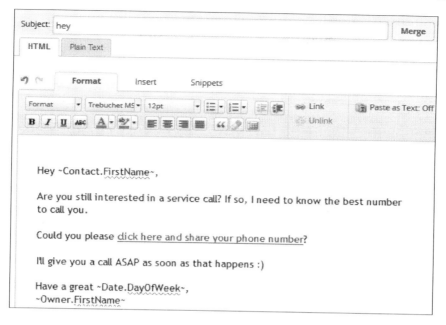

54. Make sure the link is using a hosted web form link:

55. Click on the **Draft** button in the upper-right side of the page to change the e-mail to **Ready**.
56. Click on **Back to Sequence** in the upper-left side of the page.
57. Click on the **Draft** button in the upper-right side of the page to change the sequence to **Ready**; click on **Back to Campaign** in the upper-left side of the page.
58. Publish the campaign.
59. Run the PPC ads to a landing page that uses that web form OR drive traffic directly to the hosted version.

How it works...

When someone clicks through the PPC ad, they can begin requesting a service call by submitting their name and e-mail. The next page asks for their phone number and the last page asks for their time of day preference. When someone goes through all three steps, a higher-priority task is created to show up on the calendar at either 8 am or 1 pm. If someone only provides a phone number, a task is created to call them. If someone doesn't submit their phone number initially, in 15 minutes a reminder e-mail automatically goes out driving them back to share their phone number.

There's more...

Although this recipe is functional, in real life we would intentionally design all forms/steps to match the brand and voice. Especially when it comes to a PPC ad, the look and feel of the ad image must match the first step's look and feel for optimal conversions. The visitor should have no doubt they are in the right place after clicking.

We built backwards in this recipe to minimize clicking back and forth between web forms.

Don't leave a dead end on the Step 3 thank-you page. This can easily be extended to an order form for a one-time offer, a social media nudge, or something like a newsletter opt-in.

We can add/remove form fields based on our needs but the first step should always just collect a name and e-mail as this is the minimum required for follow-up. We can collect all the other information we want in future forms. If anything, we can add a third question on the first step that begins segmenting the visitor, such as the service type request.

Track PPC and ROI by appending `?inf_field_LeadSourceId=xxx` to the end of the Step 1 form URL and adding a hidden lead source field; where `xxx` is the lead source ID for the specific ad. This only works with the JavaScript or hosted version of the form because the auto-populating code using URL queries is present in those versions.

Setting up web analytics

Infusionsoft has some built-in web tracking that creates anonymous visitor profiles per device. When someone opts in through a web form, if there is a visitor profile for that device, Infusionsoft will merge their visitor activity into the contact record. This allows us to dig deeper into the browsing behavior of our database.

This recipe shows how to find the web analytics tracking code so it can be placed on your website(s).

Getting ready

We need to be logged in to Infusionsoft and inside a specific account.

How to do it...

1. Hover over the Infusionsoft symbol in the upper-left side of the page, navigate to the **Marketing** column, and click on **Lead Generation**:

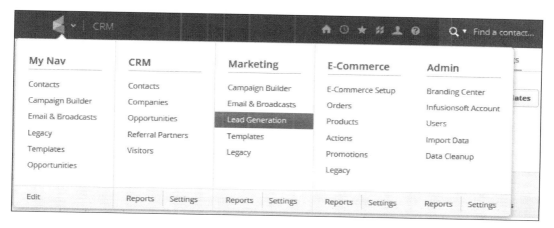

2. In the **Web Tracking** section, click on **Web Analytics**:

3. Click on the green **Get Tracking Code** button to display the web analytics tracking code:

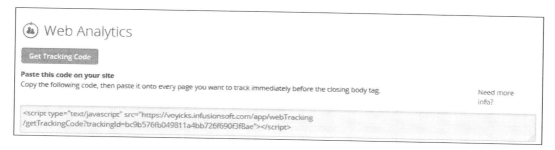

4. Copy and paste this code into the header of any page(s) we want Infusionsoft to track.

How it works...

When the tracking script is loaded on our website, Infusionsoft creates a visitor record and if someone opts in, that record is merged with the contact record.

There's more...

On the **Web Analytics** page is a visual report for web tracking that can be broken down based on page views, contacts, and so on.

4
Selling Products Online and Getting Paid

In this chapter, we will cover the following topics:

- ▶ Setting up your merchant account
- ▶ Creating products and subscriptions
- ▶ Building order forms
- ▶ Implementing an automated cart abandon follow-up
- ▶ Collecting failed automated billing attempts
- ▶ Creating a one-click upsell
- ▶ Building a one-click upsell or downsell chain

Introduction

The second phase of Lifecycle Marketing is *Sell*. This chapter concerns itself with different tactics to sell products and collect payments online.

Setting up your merchant account

The best way to collect payment for our goods and services using Infusionsoft is to connect a **merchant account**, so we can accept credit cards.

There are many different providers in the world, and Infusionsoft works with a handful of them. The setup is similar for all providers, and the only difference is the specific credentials each one uses. After completing this recipe, we will be able to collect payment through the shopping cart and order forms.

Getting ready

We need to be logged in to Infusionsoft and inside a specific account.

How to do it...

1. Hover over the Infusionsoft symbol in the upper-left corner of the page, navigate to the **E-Commerce** column, and click on **Settings**:

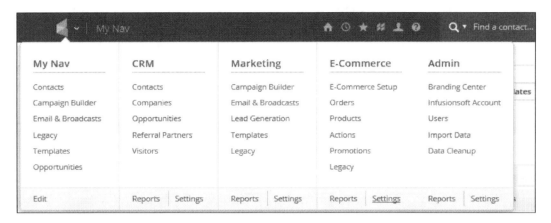

2. Click on **Merchant Accounts** in the menu on the left-hand side:

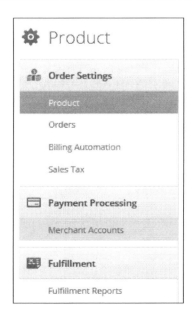

3. Select your merchant account provider from the dropdown to the right of the page; this will open a pop-up window:

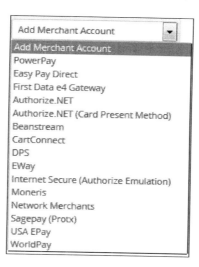

4. Input your account credentials and click on **Save**:

5. Hover over the Infusionsoft symbol in the upper-left corner of the page, navigate to the **E-Commerce** column, and click on **E-Commerce Setup**:

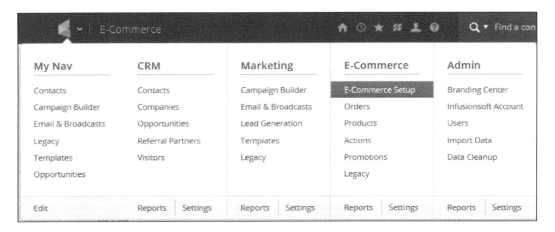

6. In the **Payment** section, click on **Payment Types**:

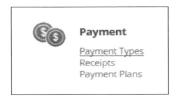

7. Check the box next to **Process Credit Card Payments**, as follows:

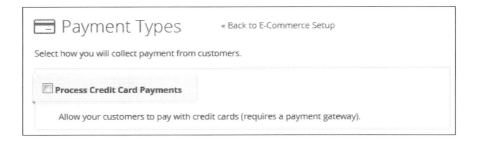

8. Select the merchant account we set up earlier from the dropdown and click on the green **Save** button in the lower-right corner of the page:

How it works...

When someone checks out using the shopping cart or an order form using this account, the merchant account will process their credit card payment.

There's more...

Remember to switch to **Live Mode** when we are done testing and want to begin transacting real currency.

It is recommended that you test the account credentials after step 4 by clicking on **Click Here** in the **Test account** column; this opens a pop-up window. This function attempts to charge a valid credit card 1 penny and then refund 1 penny. A success or fail message will be shown to indicate a proper setup: *Please note that not all merchant types support this small a test transaction, so this function may fail even with the proper credentials. In this case, running a test order for $1 should do the trick to test a proper setup:*

We can change the currency type by going to the same menu as we did in step 2 and selecting **Orders**. There is a **Billing** section where we can choose the local currency. This controls which currency symbol is displayed inside the application:

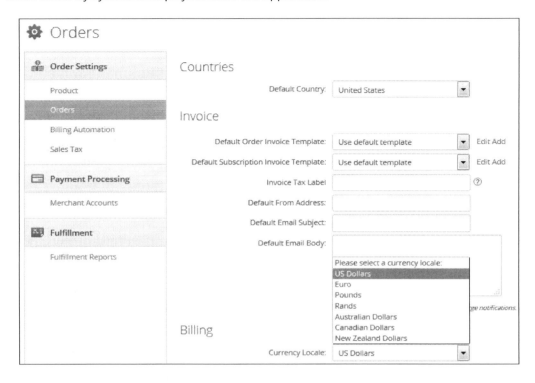

See Infusionsoft's **Help Center** for provider-specific setup instructions.

We can only use one merchant account with the shopping cart, but order forms can select which merchant account to use. This means multiple order forms can use multiple merchant accounts.

Certain merchant accounts have a **Transactional Email** setting. **Transactional e-mail** means it will send the *receipt* version of each payment via e-mail from the merchant. These e-mails are often plain text and visually boring.

We can also set up a PayPal account from the same screen we used in step 7.

Infusionsoft has its own **payment gateway**, which is fast and easy to set up from the same screen we used in step 7.

Creating products and subscriptions

Now that our merchant account is set up, we can lay the foundation for the different types of selling available. Whether we are selling products through the shopping cart, order forms, or opportunities, having the products and/or subscriptions configured unlocks the selling power of Infusionsoft.

This recipe has two versions. The first version is for a *single purchase product* such as a consumable, a one-off service, or a digital asset. The second version is for a *recurring purchase product* such as a program subscription or monthly service.

Getting ready

We need to be logged in to Infusionsoft and inside a specific account.

How to do it...

1. Hover over the Infusionsoft symbol in the upper-left corner of the page, navigate to the **E-Commerce** column, and click on **Products**.

2. Click on the green **Add a Product** button in the upper-right corner of the page:

3. Give the product/subscription a name, keep the product type as **Product**, and click on **Save**:

The single purchase version of this recipe

1. Add a short description and a price:

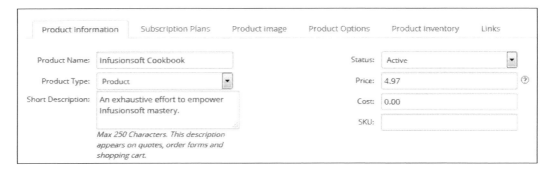

2. Scroll to the bottom of the page and click on **Save**.

The recurring purchase version of this recipe

1. Add a short description and set the price as the subscription price.

2. Click on the **Subscription Plans** tab, check the **Subscription Only** box, and click on the green **Save** button at the bottom of the page:

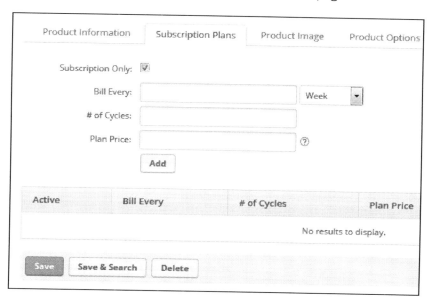

3. After the page reloads, click on the **Subscription Plans** tab again and set the subscription terms:

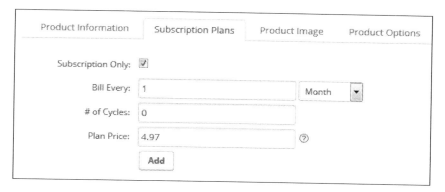

4. Click on **Add**, and once the plan displays at the bottom of the page, click on the green **Save** button:

How it works...

Anytime an order is created inside Infusionsoft, manual or automated, the line items for the purchase can make use of these different products.

There's more...

Setting the subscription cycles to 0 means there is no end date for the subscription; it will bill the customer until they cancel.

We can turn on inventory tracking and notifications in the main **E-Commerce | Settings** menu:

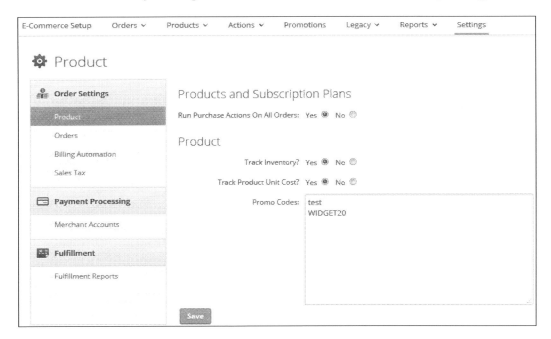

This setting enables a tab on products where we can set inventory levels and a low inventory notification:

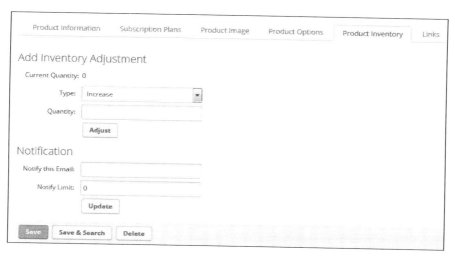

While we don't have to use products/subscriptions for manually created orders, in doing so, it also empowers per-product reporting and helps standardize our offerings. It also saves the end user time while creating the order's line items.

This recipe gives us a bare-bones product that can be used in an order form or the shopping cart. For a better customer experience, add a product image. These show up on order forms and in various places around the shopping cart:

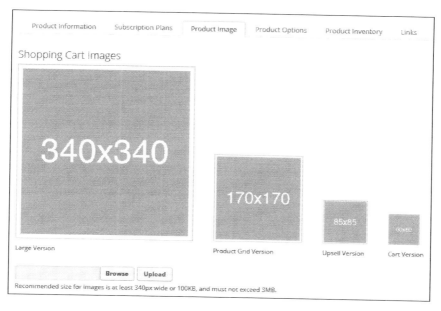

The long description of a product is only relevant if we are using the shopping cart function; order forms do not display this information.

Certain products may have different options that can be configured by the customer, for example, the text for a personalized monogram. There are two types of product options: *fixed* and *typed*. The first type is an option with fixed selections such as the size of a shirt. The second type is text like the previous monogram example. We can have no more than three options per product.

 Product options should only be used on shopping carts as a customer cannot select product options on an order form.

The following screenshot shows the various constraints for fixed product options:

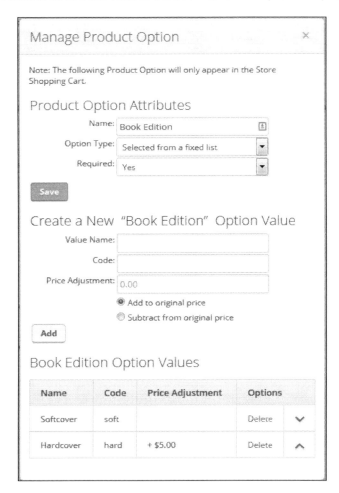

For typed product options, there is a significant amount of constraints that can be imposed to ensure proper submission types:

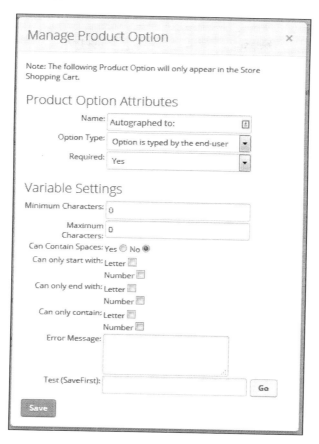

Categories are helpful to organize the storefront. They can also be used for discount promotions.

If we want to hide certain products from the shopping cart, because those products are only sold on an order form, we can hide a product from the product listings using the shopping cart options in the **Product Information** tab:

Clicking on the **Edit** button displays a menu where you can choose to hide this product listing from the storefront by checking the **Is hidden in cart** checkbox:

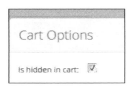

We can sell as a single-serve product or subscription using one listing; simply configure both those elements of the product. For example, the full price of a product can be $100 or there could be a two-month subscription for $50. This is similar in function to a payment plan, but there are some technical differences. Using a subscription version of a product as a payment plan will create multiple order records; one for each time a payment of the plan is charged. Using a formal pay plan will keep the product in one order. One final consideration when choosing between the two: a payment plan can natively bake in a finance charge, whereas this would have to be calculated and added to each cycle in a subscription version of a product.

We can have more than one subscription type per product (for example, annual or monthly). In that case, we set the price on the **Product Information** tab as what will be displayed in the storefront for the product:

Building order forms

An **order form** is a special type of web form that collects credit card information securely and, in most cases, processes a payment.

This recipe has two parts. First, we are going to create a theme for our order form. The theme is the visual skin of the order form. Next, we are going to create an order form using this theme.

Getting ready

We need to be logged in to Infusionsoft and inside a specific account. This recipe assumes that a merchant account has already been connected.

How to do it...

Part 1 – creating the order form theme

1. Hover over the Infusionsoft symbol in the upper-left part of the page, navigate to the **E-Commerce** column, and click on **E-Commerce Setup**, as shown in the following image:

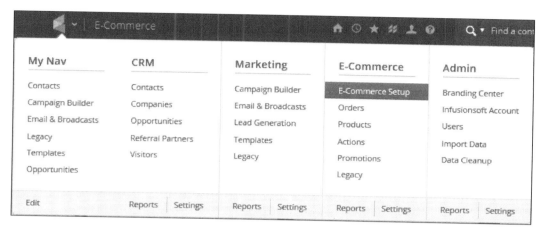

2. In the **Design** section, click on **Order Form Themes**:

3. Click on the green **Create a New Theme** button.

4. Select the **One Column** layout and click on **Use This theme** next to the starting theme we want to use; this will display a pop-up menu:

5. Give the new theme a name and click on **Save**:

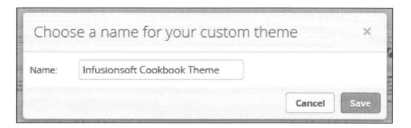

6. Click on the **Edit** button to update the default company image:

7. Click on **Browse** to upload the company logo and then click on the green **Save** button:

Part 2 – building the order form

1. Hover over the Infusionsoft symbol in the upper-left corner of the page, navigate to the **E-Commerce** column, and click on **E-Commerce Setup**.

2. In the **Checkout** section, click on **Order Forms**:

3. Click on the green **Create New** button in the upper-right corner of the page:

4. Give the order form a name and click on the green **Save** button:

5. Place your cursor in the **Product** section and begin typing the product name you wish to sell on this order form:

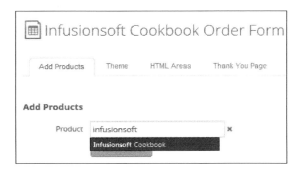

6. Click on the product name to select it and then click on the green **Add Product** button. This will add it to the **Products** on this **Order Forms** section at the bottom of the page:

7. Click on the **Theme** tab at the top of the page.

8. Scroll down and click on **Make Active** on the theme we want to use:

9. Click on the **Thank-you Page** tab at the top of the page.

10. Configure a confirmation message a customer will see upon successful order and click on the green **Save** button:

11. Click on the **Settings** tab at the top of the page.

12. In the **Notifications** section, check the box and enter an e-mail address that will receive successful order notifications; click on the green **Save** button at the bottom of the page, as shown in the following image:

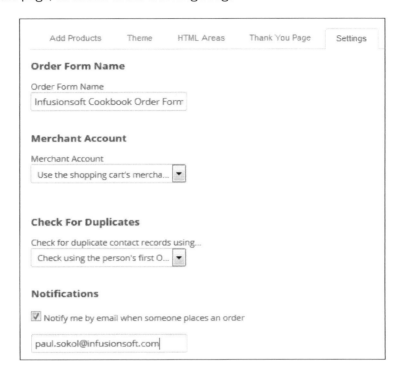

13. Click on the **Links** tab at the top of the page to get the order form's URL.

How it works...

When someone visits the order form and submits with correct billing information, a contact record is created with an order associated to the product(s) being sold and any relevant payments are attempted.

There's more...

We can save time in the future by starting at part 2 and using the previously created theme.

Certain order form themes support PayPal as well.

In part 1, we can preview the theme by hovering over the listing and clicking to preview:

Selecting a two-column layout in part 1 enables another custom HTML area to the right of the main order form themes.

If we are comfortable with CSS, we can heavily customize the order form's theme by using the **Edit CSS** tab in the theme setup:

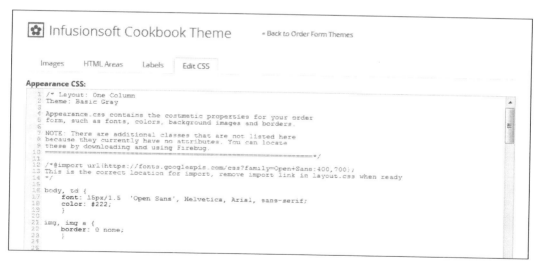

There is a setting on the order form to prevent people from adjusting item quantities. This can be useful while selling bundles or products that don't make sense to be sold in multiple quantities:

There is an option in the **Settings** tab to disable promo codes on the order form. This can allow us to prevent shopping cart promo codes from being used where they shouldn't be.

In the **Settings** tab, we can explicitly tell an order form to use a particular merchant account. By default, the shopping cart's configured merchant account is used.

The custom header HTML area of an order form is useful for holding the sales copy. This way, the order form can operate as a sales page in addition to the point of sale:

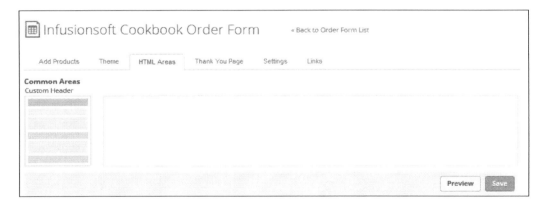

Any purchase goals associated with products being sold on the order form will be triggered upon successful purchase. This is how we can do automated follow-up based on the product purchase.

See also

To connect a merchant account, see the *Setting up your merchant account* recipe earlier in this chapter.

Implementing an automated cart abandon follow-up

When selling products online, people may fall out during the checkout process and not complete their order. This is just something that comes with the territory, which is similar to the fact that people will unsubscribe from your lists occasionally.

By implementing an automated follow-up when people fail to complete their purchase, we can recoup sales that would have otherwise never occurred.

Getting ready

We need to edit a campaign that is driving traffic to a live order form for a purchase.

In the context of this recipe, we are assuming that the campaign model starts off looking like this:

Main Sales Sequence   Purchase Widget A   Widget A Customer Welcome

How to do it...

1. Drag out a new link click goal, sequence it, and connect/rename it, as shown here:

2. Double-click on the link click goal and select all links in all sales e-mails that are pointing to the order form; click on **Back to Campaign**:

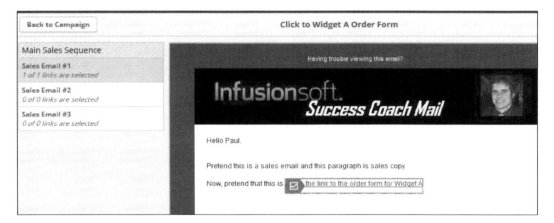

3. Double-click into the cart abandon sequence and connect a **Timer** and **Email** step, as shown here:

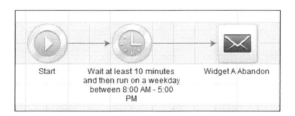

4. Double-click on the **Email** step and write a message to recover the sale:

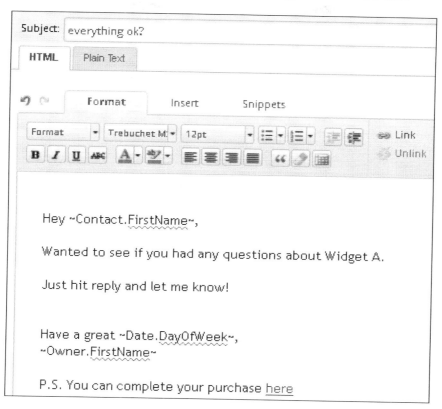

5. Mark the e-mail as **Ready** and click on **Back to Sequence** in the upper-left corner of the page.

6. Mark the sequence as **Ready** and click on **Back to Campaign** in the upper-left corner of the page.

7. Publish the campaign.

How it works...

When someone clicks the order form from any of the sales e-mails, the link click goal sees this behavior and adds them to the abandon sequence. If the purchase doesn't come through before the timer, the recovery e-mail is delivered.

There's more...

If we want to implement a cart abandon follow-up without stopping the primary sequence, we can autotag on a link click and use that to trigger the cart abandon follow-up:

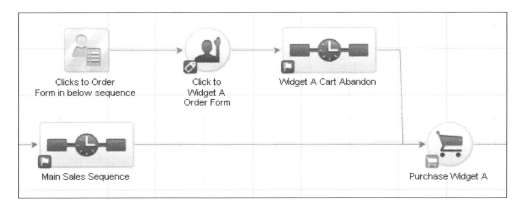

We can add extra e-mails to the abandon sequence if we want to extend the recovery process. In these e-mails, we can address common objections, add extra purchase bonuses, deliver a discount code, and so on.

While the recovery e-mail is automated, for best results, it shouldn't feel automated. Rather, it should "just happen" to show up at the perfect time. It is recommended to encourage people to reply, so we can close the sale individually for those who bubble up.

See also

For a template similar to this recipe, download the **Turn Abandoned Carts into Sales** campaign from the Marketplace.

Collecting failed automated billing attempts

When using payment plans or selling subscriptions, it is critical to have a *failed billing recovery* process in place to ensure that money isn't slipping through the cracks.

Infusionsoft has **billing triggers** available that can automate based on a failed payment attempt to streamline this process.

Getting ready

We need to be logged in to Infusionsoft and inside a specific account.

How to do it...

1. Hover over the main navigation menu and go to **E-Commerce | Settings**:

2. Click on **Billing Automation** in the menu on the left-hand side:

3. Using the **Triggers (by type)** drop-down menu, select **When a credit card autocharge attempt is made** and click on **Add Trigger**; this will open a pop-up window, as follows:

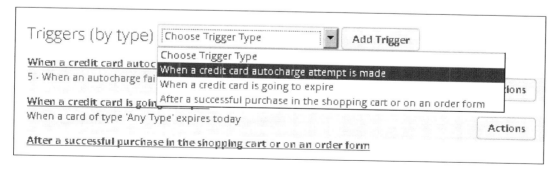

4. Configure the trigger as follows:

    ❑   Set the **When an autocharge** option to **Fails**

    ❑   In the **And this is** option, check **the LAST failure**

    ❑   Also, select the product we want to recover payment on

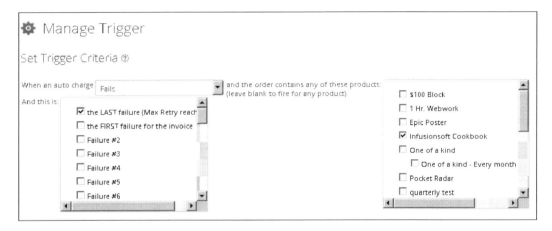

5. In the **Actions** section mentioned later, add an action to apply a failed billing tag that is specific to the product we want to recover payment on:

6. Click on **Save Trigger**.

7. Go to the **Campaign Builder** and add a new campaign.

8. Drag out a tag goal, note the template goal, and a sequence; connect as seen in the following image and rename accordingly:

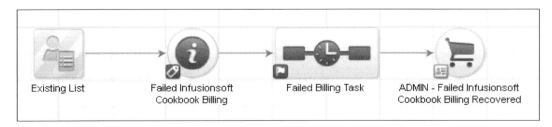

9. Double-click on the tag goal and configure it for the tag we applied in the billing trigger; click on **Save**:

10. Double-click on the note template and configure **Description** and **Creation Notes**; click on **Save**:

11. Double-click into the sequence, drag out a **Tag** step, a **Task** step, and connect as shown in the following image; rename accordingly:

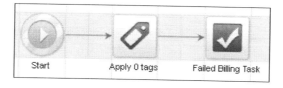

12. Double-click on the **Tag** step and configure it to remove the tag, which starts this recovery campaign; click on **Save**:

13. Double-click on the **Task** step and configure with instructions to recover the payment. Make sure that the exact name of the note template is present in the task body:

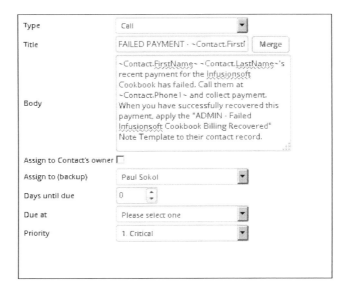

14. Mark the task as **Ready** and click on **Back to Sequence** on the upper-left side of the page.

15. Mark the sequence as **Ready** and click on **Back to Campaign** on the upper-left side of the page.

16. Publish the campaign.

How it works...

If the last payment attempt for the product fails, the billing automation trigger will apply the campaign tag, which creates a task for a user to recover the payment. The note template makes it easy to report on which payments are being recovered.

There's more...

We can add a failed payment notification e-mail into the recovery sequence to let the customer know about the situation and to expect a phone call.

While this recipe assumes that the final payment attempt has failed, we can easily create a unique billing fail tag for each attempt and build a cascading structure to try and recover each failed attempt. This can provide further insight into the effectiveness of our recovery process:

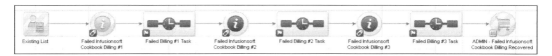

We can also set up a billing trigger for when a payment is successful and when the previous attempt failed. This can save man-hours in the instances where a card fails and then it becomes successful on future attempts:

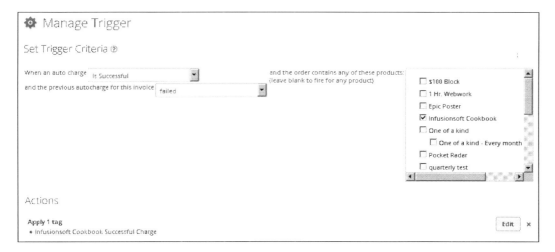

In this case, we want to end the recovery campaign with a successful payment tag:

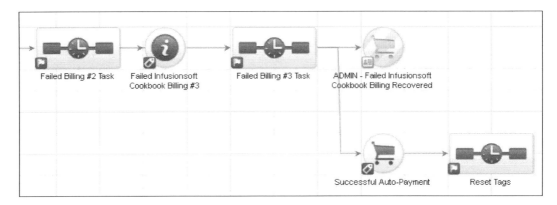

When setting up the billing trigger, if we do not select any product specifically, it will fire for a failed attempt on any product. However, it is always recommended to create a unique trigger and a recovery campaign because we can customize the messaging for that specific product. This also makes it easier to report on different product recovery initiatives.

Infusionsoft also has a membership site product named **CustomerHub**. One of the features is that customers can manage their own orders and subscriptions. This could be used to implement a similar recipe that is completely automated.

See also

For a template similar to this recipe, download the **Collect All Recurring Billings** campaign from the Marketplace.

Creating a one-click upsell

An easy way to boost revenue is to present another offer immediately after a successful purchase. When we allow that additional purchase to be made with a single click, it capitalizes on the excitement and momentum of their previous purchase; having the customer submit another form would introduce unnecessary friction.

For this recipe, we are going to first create a payment plan, then create an action set to generate the **upsell** product order, and finally connect it all within a campaign. Once this is done, we'll connect the one-click upsell to the order form.

Getting ready

In addition to being logged in to Infusionsoft and inside a specific account, we also need to have the following:

- ► Our merchant account setup
- ► An order form
- ► A product created for the upsell offering
- ► A web page for customers that decline the upsell offering

How to do it...

1. Hover over the main navigation menu and click on **E-Commerce Setup**:

2. In the **Payments** section, click on **Payment Plans**:

3. On the upper-right side of the page, click on **Add a Payment Plan**:

4. Provide a name and a description, as shown here:

5. Scroll down and configure the **Scheduling** and **Options** sections, as shown in the following screenshot:

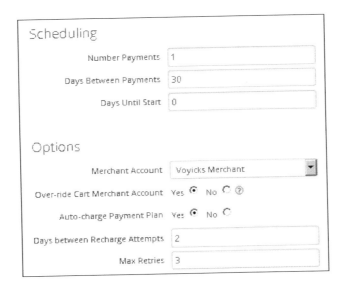

6. Click on the green **Save** button at the bottom of the page.

7. When the page reloads, scroll to the bottom and using the **Add Criteria** dropdown, select **Date Range Criteria**; this will open a pop-up window, as shown here:

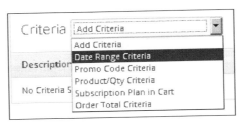

8. Set the **Start Date** and **End Date**, making sure that both are in the past; click on **Save** to close the window:

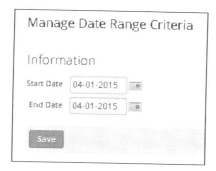

9. Hover over the main navigation menu and go to **Marketing | Settings**:

10. In the menu on the left-hand side, click on **Action Sets**:

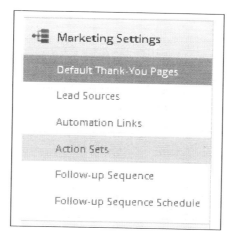

11. In the upper-right corner of the page, click on the green **Add an Action Set** button; this will open a pop-up window, as shown here:

12. Give the **Action Set** a name, and using the **Add New Action** dropdown, select **Create an Order**:

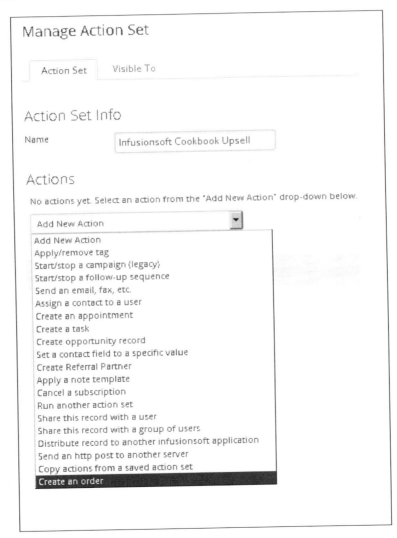

13. Next to the **Bundle** dropdown, click on the **Save this Action** link:

14. In the **Product** section, begin typing the name of the upsell product and click on it; this will change the red **X** to the right of the field into a green check:

15. Click on the **Add** button; this will populate the product in the section as given here:

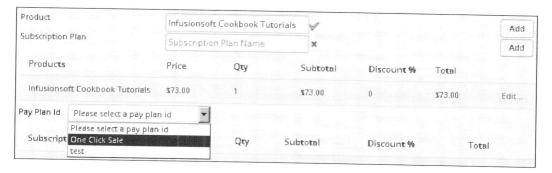

16. Using the **Pay Plan Id** dropdown, select the payment plan we created previously and click on the green **Save** button at the bottom of the page to save this **Create an Order** action:

17. Click on the green **Save** button at the bottom of the page to save **Action Set**; this will close the window.

18. Open a new campaign and drag out a **landing page** goal and a sequence; connect and rename, as shown in the following image:

19. Double-click on the landing page to edit it.

20. Delete all form fields.

21. Add a **Hidden** field snippet.

22. Select **Email** and leave the **Field Value** field empty; click on **Save**:

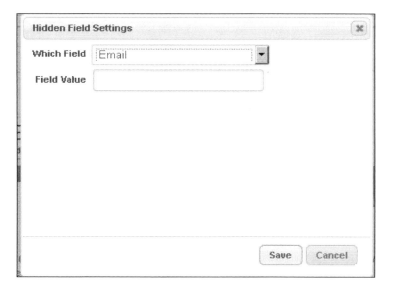

23. Design the rest of the page to present the one-click upsell offer:

> Congratulations! Your Infusionsoft Cookbook is on its way!
> But if you really want to implement faster than you ever imagined
> take advantage of this ONE-TIME ONLY offer and...
>
> ...Get Discount Access to
> Video Tutorials of EVERY RECIPE in the cookbook!!!!
>
> ➡ You get lifetime access, instantly which means you don't have to wait for the
> cookbook to arrive!
>
> ➡ Follow along with me as I build every recipe from scratch in real time so that you can
> be confident in YOUR implementation!
>
> *Hidden Field (Email)*
>
> Yes! Add This To My Order For Only $73!

24. Add a **Paragraph** snippet directly below the **Submit** button and create a link for customers that do not want the upsell offer; configure the link for the declined offer page:

> *Hidden Field (Email)*
>
> Yes! Add This To My Order For Only $73!
>
> No thanks Paul! If I need access to this in the future
> I'm ok spending the full $97 for the exact same video tutorials

25. Click on the **Thank-you Page** tab at the top and design a confirmation message for those who choose the upsell:

> Boom!
>
> You just saved $24 ~Contact.FirstName~, great choice :)
>
> Check your email right now for your username and password.

26. Click on the **Settings** tab at the top and verify that the **Auto-populate Form** has its option selected:

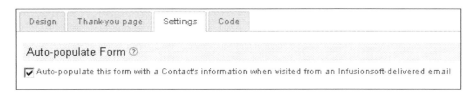

27. Mark the landing page as **Ready** and click on **Back to Campaign** in the upper-left corner of the page.

28. Double-click into the connected sequence, drag out an **Action Set (Legacy)** step, and rename appropriately:

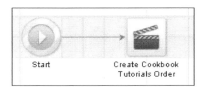

29. Double-click on the **Action Set (Legacy)** step.

30. Using the **Action Set** dropdown, select the action set we created previously; click on the green **Save** button:

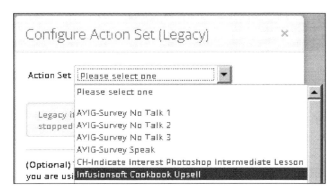

31. Set the sequence as **Ready** and click on **Back to Campaign** in the upper-left corner of the page.

32. Publish the campaign.

33. After the campaign has been published, open the landing page again and click on the **Code** tab.

34. Copy the landing page URL.

35. Exit **Campaign Builder** and go to the order form that is going to be used with this one-click upsell.

36. Click on the **Thank You Page** tab:

37. Using the **Thank You Page to Display** dropdown, select **Web Address**.

38. Paste in the landing page URL into the **URL** field and check the option to pass the contact's information:

39. Click on the green **Save** button in the upper-right corner of the page:

<h2>How it works...</h2>

When a customer successfully places an order using the order form, they are taken to the landing page, which presents the one-click offering. The hidden field on the landing page is being pre-populated because we are passing it from the order form's thank you page. If they accept the offer (also known as submitting the landing page), Infusionsoft will create another order for the upsell product for that contact.

There's more...

Don't forget to add any other fulfillment steps for the upsell order!

If we do not select a payment plan when setting up the action set, Infusionsoft doesn't know which merchant account to autocharge while creating the order. If this happens, the order will be created and the payment will have to be collected manually at a later time.

Orders created via the action set do not charge immediately but rather are run in batches every six hours or so. If we need to control access or fulfillment based on a successful payment, we can create a *billing automation* trigger that applies a tag to advance the campaign:

Setting the **Date Range Criteria** in the payment plan for dates in the past ensures that the plan will not display in the shopping cart or on order forms.

See also

- ▶ For help setting up a merchant account, see the first recipe in this chapter, *Setting up your merchant account*.
- ▶ For help creating the upsell product, see the *Creating products and subscriptions* recipe earlier in this chapter.
- ▶ For help creating an order form, see the *Building order forms* recipe earlier in this chapter.

Building a one-click upsell or downsell chain

Similar to the previous recipe, we can create a series of one-click offers for additional upsell or **downsell** opportunities. This is a great strategy when we have a variety of complementary products/services that enhance the original purchase.

Since this recipe is simply an extension of the previous recipe's strategy (and to avoid a needless duplication of steps), we are going to begin with that existing structure and build from there.

The strategic context of this recipe is to offer a payment plan on the initial upsell product if the customer declines the original upsell and offer a higher ticket item if they do choose the original upsell.

Getting ready

In addition to being logged in to Infusionsoft and inside a specific account, we also need to have the following:

- The previous recipe built
- An action set that creates an order for the downsell offering
- An action set that creates an order for the second upsell offering
- A web page for customers who decline the downsell offering
- A web page for customers who decline the second upsell offering

How to do it...

1. On the existing one-click upsell model, drag out two landing page goals, a web form goal, and two sequences; connect and rename, as shown in the following image:

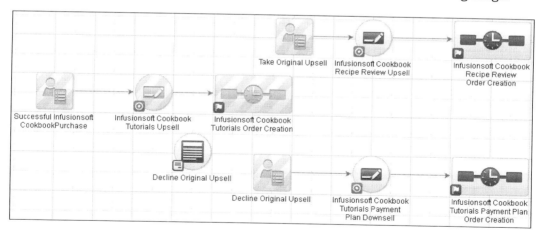

2. Double-click on the second upsell landing page to edit it.

3. Delete all form fields.

4. Add a **Hidden** field snippet.

5. Select **Email** and leave the **Field Value** field empty; click on **Save**.

6. Design the rest of the page to present the second one-click upsell offer.

7. Add a **Paragraph** snippet directly below the **Submit** button and create a link for customers that do not want the second upsell offer; configure the link for the declined second offer page:

Boom! You just saved money and got instant access to the videos!
But if **you want to be 100% confident in your implementation**
take advantage of this final offer and...

...Get A Personal Review of Your
Recipe Implementation by Paul Himself!!!!

I haven't done any one-on-one consulting since 2013, but
I'm making myself available at half my normal hourly rate of $997
just this one time because you are awesome
and I'm completely dedicated to YOUR business' success :)

 You get a one hour one-on-one personal consultant of your completed recipe!

 You'll also get a customized checklist of things you can do to further optimize your conversion rates!

Hidden Field (Email)

OMG Yes! Add A Personal Review To My Order For Only $498.50!

No thanks Paul! You're cool and all, but I think the videos will be just fine!

---

8. Click on the **Thank-you Page** tab at the top and design a confirmation message for those who choose the upsell:

Yeah buddy!

I'm excited to see what you end up building.

Check your inbox right now for instructions on how to schedule your consultation.

---

9. Click on the **Settings** tab at the top and verify that the **Auto-populate Form** option is selected.

10. Click on the **Code** tab at the top and copy the landing page URL.

11. Mark the landing page as **Ready** and click on **Back to Campaign** in the upper-left corner of the page.

12. Double-click into the sequence connected after this second upsell landing page, drag out an **Action Set (Legacy)** step, and rename appropriately:

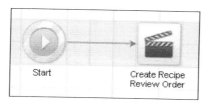

13. Double-click on the **Action Set (Legacy)** step.

14. Using the **Action Set** dropdown, select the action set that will create the second upsell order; click on the green **Save** button:

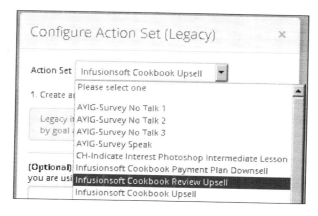

15. Set the sequence as **Ready** and click on **Back to Campaign** in the upper-left corner of the page.

16. Double-click into the first landing page (the one created in the previous recipe), and when it loads, click on the **Thank-you Page** tab.

17. Using the **Thank-you Page to Display** dropdown, select **Web Address**.

18. Paste in the URL of the second upsell landing page and check the **Pass contact's information...** option:

19. Click on **Back to Campaign** in the upper-left corner of the page.

20. Double-click on the downsell landing page to edit it.

21. Delete all form fields.

22. Add a **Hidden** field snippet.

23. Select **Email** and leave the **Field Value** field empty; click on **Save**.

24. Design the rest of the page to present the one-click downsell offer.

25. Add a **Paragraph** snippet directly below the **Submit** button and create a link for customers that do not want the downsell offer; configure the link for the declined downsell offer page:

$73 a bit too steep for you right now?
I'll cut you a deal so can still advantage of this ONE-TIME ONLY offer and...

**...Make Two Payments for Instant Access to
Video Tutorials of EVERY RECIPE in the cookbook!!!!**

➡ You get the same lifetime access, instantly which means you don't have to wait for the cookbook to arrive!

➡ You can still follow along with me as I build every recipe from scratch in real time so that you can be confident in YOUR implementation!

Hidden Field (Email)

Yes! Charge Me $36.50 Now and Another $36.50 in 30 Days!!

No thanks Paul! If I need access to this in the future
I'm still ok spending the full $97 for the exact same video tutorials

---

26. Click on the **Thank-you Page** tab at the top and design a confirmation message for those who choose the downsell offer, as follows:

You got it ~Contact.FirstName~!

I'll charge you $36.50 now and another 36.50 in 30 days.

Check your email right now for your username and password.

---

27. Click on the **Settings** tab at the top and verify that the **Auto-populate Form** option is selected.

28. Click on the **Code** tab at the top and copy the landing page URL.

29. Mark the landing page as **Ready** and click on **Back to Campaign** in the upper-left corner of the page.

30. Double-click into the sequence connected after this downsell landing page, drag out an **Action Set (Legacy)** step, and rename appropriately:

31. Double-click on the **Action Set (Legacy)** step.

32. Using the **Action Set** dropdown, select the action set that will create the downsell order; click on the green **Save** button:

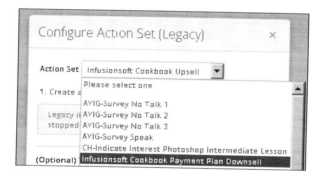

33. Set the sequence as **Ready** and click on **Back to Campaign** in the upper-left corner of the page.

34. Double-click into the **Decline Original Upsell** web form.

35. Delete all form fields.

36. Add a **Hidden** field snippet.

37. Select **Email** and leave the **Field Value** field empty; click on **Save**.

38. Update the **Submit** button text with a call to action that declines the original upsell offer (that was created in the previous recipe):

39. Using the **Thank-you Page to Display** dropdown, select **Web Address**.

40. Paste in the URL of the downsell landing page and check the **Pass contact's information...** option:

URL:

https://voyicks.infusionsoft.com/app/page/5906fbafe47d43024262ccc5ec17640a

☑ Pass contact's information to the thank-you page ⑦

41. Click on the **Settings** tab at the top and verify that the **Auto-populate Form** has its option is selected.

42. Click on the **Code** tab and copy the code from the **Javascript Snippet** option for the web form.

43. Mark the web form as **Ready** and click on **Back to Campaign** in the upper-left corner of the page.

44. Double-click on the original landing page created in the previous recipe.

45. Delete the original decline link beneath the **Submit** button.

46. Add an **HTML** snippet beneath the **Submit** button.

47. Paste in the code from the **Javascript Snippet** option for the decline web form and click on **Save**:

48. Publish the campaign.

How it works...

When a customer successfully places an order using the order form, they are taken to the first landing page, which presents the first one-click offering. The hidden e-mail field on the landing page is being prepopulated because we are passing it from the order form's thank you page. The decline button is actually a web form that also has its hidden e-mail field populated; we have embedded a second form within the landing page:

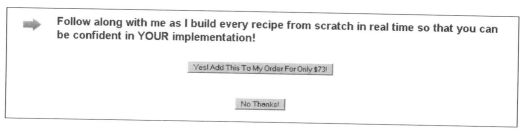

If they accept the offer (also known as submitting the landing page), Infusionsoft will create another order for the upsell product for that contact and redirect them to the second landing page (which has its hidden field populated). If they submit this second landing page, another order will be created.

If they decline the original upsell offer, they are actually submitting a web form, which will redirect them to the downsell landing page, that will also have the hidden e-mail field populated. If they choose the downsell offer, Infusionsoft will create another order for the downsell offering.

There's more...

Don't forget to add any other fulfillment steps for the second upsell order or the downsell order!

This strategy can be extended to create a chain of different upsell or downsell offers depending on the different offers a customer accepts or doesn't; there is no upper limit for how deep the offer chain can go. In this case, it is highly recommended to lay out the campaign model for clarity and to leave ourselves plenty of canvas notes for comprehension.

5
Selling with a Sales Team

In this chapter, we will cover:

- ▸ Setting up a sales pipeline
- ▸ Working sales opportunities
- ▸ Using round robins for sales teams
- ▸ Saving time with FAQ workflows
- ▸ Sending automated appointment reminders
- ▸ Merging custom opportunity fields into e-mails
- ▸ Setting up lead scoring
- ▸ Automating based on lead score achievement
- ▸ Building a long-term prospect nurture

Introduction

As we mentioned earlier, the second phase of Lifecycle Marketing is *Sell*. Whereas the previous chapter dealt with selling online, Infusionsoft is also a very powerful tool to sell with a sales team.

The campaign model in the final recipe, *Building a long-term prospect nurture*, could be used for either type of selling.

Setting up a sales pipeline

A **pipeline** is a clearly defined process flow with specific measureable milestones (or stages). A **sales pipeline** is a set of defined sales stages that sales reps can use to manage their leads/prospects.

Infusionsoft has a very easy to use pipeline module known as **Opportunities**. Although the sales milestones will vary from business to business, for this recipe, we are going to be building a sales pipeline with the following sales stages:

▶ **New Opportunity**: Lead has been identified as someone who should be contacted

▶ **Contacting**: Sales rep has made one attempt to get voice-to-voice communication, but did not reach the lead

▶ **Engaging**: Sales rep has established conversation but the lead has not yet been determined as qualified to proceed down the pipeline

▶ **Qualified**: Sales rep has determined that the lead has a budget and authority to spend it; lead is now a prospect

▶ **Quote Sent**: Sales rep has delivered the prospect a quote for the potential sale

▶ **Quote Finalizing**: Sales rep is adjusting the details of the quote with the prospect

▶ **Quote Accepted**: Prospect has given verbal or written acceptance of the proposed quote

▶ **Deposit Secured (Win)**: Prospect has paid the initial deposit and is now a paying customer

▶ **Lost**: Lead/prospect is not going to become a customer at this time

This recipe contains two main parts. First, we are going to build the sales stage definitions. Then we are going to configure the pipeline settings for the stages that were just created.

Getting ready

We must be logged in to Infusionsoft and inside a specific account.

How to do it...

1. Hover over the main navigation and in the **CRM column**, click on **Settings**:

2. In the **Sales Settings** menu on the left of the page, click on **Sales Pipeline**:

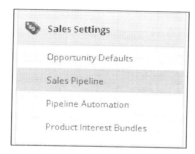

3. In the **Stage** section at the top, populate the fields as shown in the following screenshot; click on **Save**:

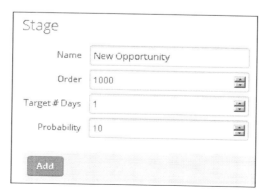

4. Repeat the previous step for each of the following sales stages:

Stage	Order	Target # Days	Probability
Contacting	1100	7	25
Engaging	1200	7	35
Qualified	1300	7	50
Quote Sent	1400	7	60
Quote Finalizing	1500	7	75
Quote Accepted	1600	7	95
Deposit Secured (Win)	1700	0	100
Lost	1800	0	0

5. Scroll down to the bottom of the page and verify the pipeline stages have been configured properly:

Edit...	New Opportunity	1	10	1000	Checklist...	Delete
Edit...	Contacting	7	25	1100	Checklist...	Delete
Edit...	Engaging	7	35	1200	Checklist...	Delete
Edit...	Qualified	7	50	1300	Checklist...	Delete
Edit...	Quote Sent	7	60	1400	Checklist...	Delete
Edit...	Quote Finalizing	7	75	1500	Checklist...	Delete
Edit...	Quote Accepted	7	95	1600	Checklist...	Delete
Edit...	Deposit Secured (Win)	0	100	1700	Checklist...	Delete
Edit...	Lost	0	0	1800	Checklist...	Delete

6. If everything looks OK, scroll back to the top of the page and click on **Opportunity Defaults** in the left menu:

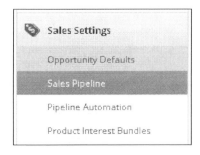

7. In the **Active Sales Stages** section, select all stages except the win/loss stage from the **Active Sales Stages** list box.

8. Using the **Default Stage** dropdown, select **New Opportunity**:

9. In the **Win & Loss Stages** section, select the **Win Stage** and **Loss Stage** respectively; we also should add some win/loss reasons for future reporting:

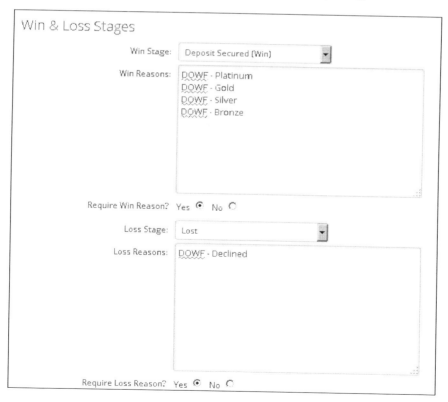

10. Scroll to the bottom of the page and click on **Save**.

How it works...

This recipe lays down the foundation for any pipeline by first declaring the sales stages and then configuring the key sales milestone options. The stages and options configured here will control how users interact with opportunity records.

There's more...

When creating a pipeline stage, the order determines how the stages displayed in the dropdown present to a sales rep working inside an opportunity.

When creating a pipeline stage, **Target # Days** is helpful for the sales rep when working inside an opportunity to see how soon they should be trying to advance a lead/prospect:

When creating a pipeline stage, the probability is used to determine weighted revenue forecast reporting. In effect, it is the chance a lead/prospect has of becoming a customer based on the sales stage they are currently in. For example, if we set the probability of a stage as 50, this means a prospect in that stage who is considering a $1,000 dollar product has a weighted revenue of $500 (50 percent of $1,000).

After a pipeline stage has been created, we can click on the **Checklist** link to open a pop-up menu:

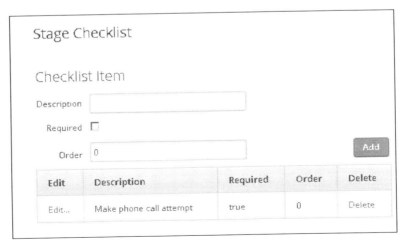

This allows us to create stage-specific steps that display when a person is in that opportunity stage. Be wary as there is no automation available for steps or *searchability*:

The only way to look at these is through the **Sales History** tab at the bottom of an opportunity record.

For sales that have an involved or complex fulfillment process (for example, solar panel installation), we can add extra stages after the win stage to manage the customer fulfillment experience.

We can create custom fields for opportunity records to store critical information or data that needs to be reported.

Win or loss reason is an available search option for opportunities. This is great for tracking trends and innovating. Requiring the win/loss reason forces the user to choose a reason when moving to a win or loss stage and setting the **Win & Loss Stages** empower certain types of sales reports.

In order for a user to be assigned opportunities, they must be part of the group chosen in the first dropdown of the **Viewing Opportunities** options toward the bottom of the **Opportunity Defaults** page. Users can be added to different groups through the **Users** menu in the main navigation:

See also

For help learning how to properly work an opportunity, see the next recipe, *Working sales opportunities*.

Working sales opportunities

No matter what kind of process pipeline has been created, the act of "working" an opportunity record is the same every single time. By building this workflow into our habits, it ensures that nobody slips through the cracks and that there is a very clear digital paper trail of the actions taken to work the opportunity.

Getting ready

In addition to being logged into Infusionsoft and inside a specific account, we need to be looking at an opportunity record.

How to do it...

1. Beneath the **Next follow-up action:** section, click on the **+ Add a note about your last action link**:

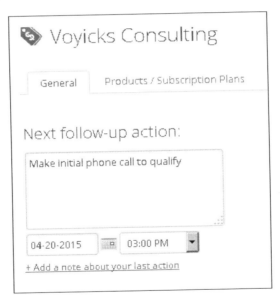

2. In the **What did you do?** section, leave concise notes about the action that was taken to forward the opportunity:

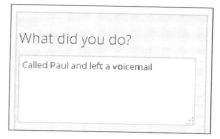

3. Check the **Do you want to change it?** box beneath the notes we just left.

4. Leave notes for our future self about what needs to occur next. The more detail and context we can provide the better:

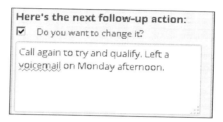

5. Using the calendar dropdown, select the date we plan to perform the action we just declared:

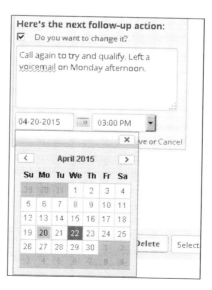

6. Using the dropdown, select the time we plan to perform that action; click on the blue **Save** button at the bottom of the workflow box:

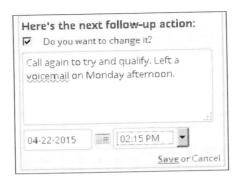

7. If it is appropriate, using the **Sales Stage** dropdown in the middle of the page, select another stage that reflects the current status of the opportunity; click on the green **Save** button:

How it works...

When a user performs this recipe on an opportunity record, the system will:

▶ Update the opportunity's entry on the assigned user's calendar

▶ Leave a note in the contact record

▶ Run any automation associated with a stage move (if a stage change is saved)

There's more...

An opportunity will show up on the assigned user's calendar at **next action date and time**. It will also show up in the **Calendar Items** widget on the following dashboard:

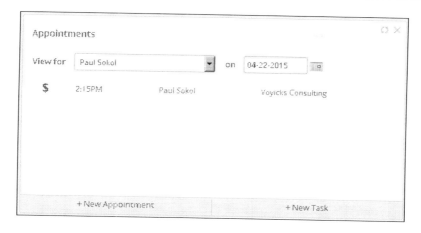

The note created in the contact record allows us to track what happened and what was supposed to happen. This is why leaving impeccable and highly contextual notes in the next action is recommended:

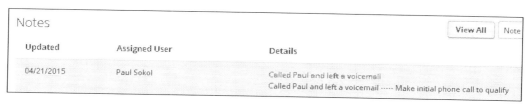

To use revenue forecast reporting, the products and/or subscriptions being sold must first exist as products in the **E-Commerce** section already. From there, two things must occur:

▸ The user must select a closing date on the **General** tab; the **Commit to Forecast?** checkbox is optional and can be used to filter forecast reports:

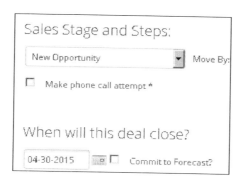

▶ The user must add items using the **Product / Subscription Plans** tab; this will add an opportunity value in the header next to the title:

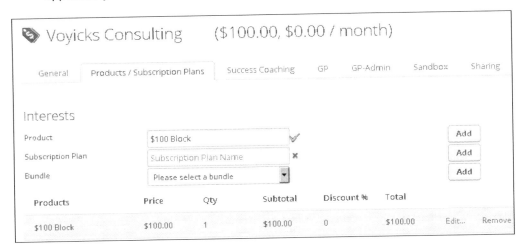

If we are tracking the products/subscriptions being sold, we can also generate an order directly from within an opportunity:

▶ Using the dropdown next to the green button group, select **Create an Order**:

▶ In the pop-up menu that displays, click on **Process**; if a merchant account is also set up, we can choose a credit card (or add a new one) to immediately run the charge:

This will create an order record for the products/subscriptions listed on the opportunity record. If no credit card is used to process the order, Infusionsoft will create an order with a balance due.

If the shopping cart is set up with a merchant account, a user can send the prospect a unique link via e-mail for them to check out for the items listed in the **Products / Subscriptions** tab. This is known as a **Buy Now** link:

  ▶ Using the dropdown next to the green button group, select **Send Buy Now**:

  ▶ This will open a pop-up window with a pre-populated link in an e-mail that can be customized

Clicking on a Buy Now link and purchasing through it are both available automation triggers. These can be found in **CRM Settings** under **Opportunity Defaults**. Use these to create highly relevant automation such as sending the sales rep a **Super Hot Lead, call right now** e-mail if they don't buy in 15 minutes or some other type of follow-up:

For faster next action date selection, it is recommended to get familiar with the date shortcut keys. For users who work mainly in the opportunity record, the habit of using these can greatly increase productivity. If we place our cursor in a date field and press *I* on the keyboard, it will display a list of shortcut keys. There is a reasonable amount of logic behind each key press so feel free to study up. For example, adding a month to the date is *M* and subtracting a month is *H* because the last letter of *month* is *h*. Also, the lower-left corner of the QWERTY keyboard is Monday through Friday.

The following is a list of quick date keys:

Quick Date Keys

t: Set date to today
= : Add one day
+ : Subtract one day
w : Add one week
k : Subtract one week
y : Add one year
e : Subtract one year
m : Add one month
h : Subtract one month
q : Clear the date
f : Go to the first day of the month
l : Go to the last day of the month
z : Go to Monday of the week selected
x : Go to Tuesday of the week selected
c : Go to Wednesday of the week selected
v : Go to Thursday of the week selected
b : Go to Friday of the week selected

OK

See also

- For help configuring a merchant account, see the *Setting up your merchant account* recipe at the beginning of the *Chapter 4, Selling Products Online and Getting Paid*

- For help creating products and subscriptions to use for revenue forecasting, see the *Creating products and subscriptions* recipe in *Chapter 4, Selling Products Online and Getting Paid*

- To do weighted revenue forecasting, a stage must have a probability. See the *Setting up a sales pipeline* recipe earlier in the chapter to learn how to set closing probabilities

Using round robins for sales teams

Anytime there is more than one user working opportunities, creating a **round robin** can assist in the automated assignment of new opportunities.

For this recipe, we are going to build a round robin for two sales reps that automatically assigns new opportunities one at a time when someone has submitted a web form on our website.

Getting ready

In addition to being logged in to Infusionsoft and inside a specific account, we need:

- ▸ Both sales reps' user accounts created
- ▸ A campaign with the website's web form

How to do it...

1. Hover over the main navigation and click on **Settings** in the **CRM** column:

2. In the left menu, click on **Round Robins**:

3. In the upper-right of the page, click on the **Add Round Robin** button:

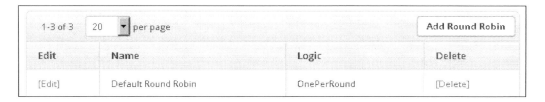

4. Give the round robin a name, click on the **One record per round** option, and click on the green **Save** button:

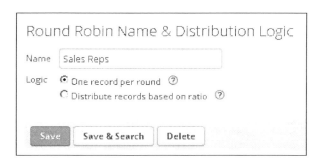

5. Type 1 next to the two sales reps who are in this round robin; click on the green **Save** button:

6. Navigate to the campaign containing the web form on our website and open the sequence connected after the web form goal:

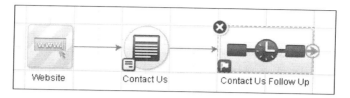

7. Connect a **Create Opportunity** step; rename appropriately:

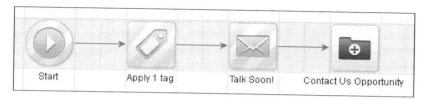

8. Double-click on the **Opportunity** step.

9. Configure the **Starting Stage**.

10. Using the second dropdown on the far right, select the round robin we just created:

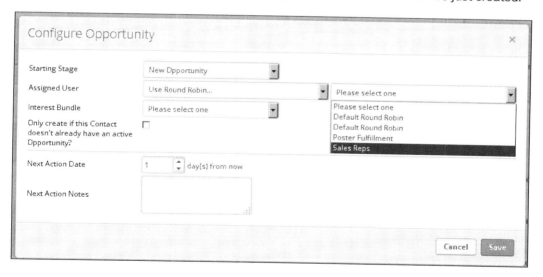

11. Finish configuring the opportunity's **Next Action Date** and **Next Action Notes** options with the proper context for the sales rep to take action; click on the green **Save** button:

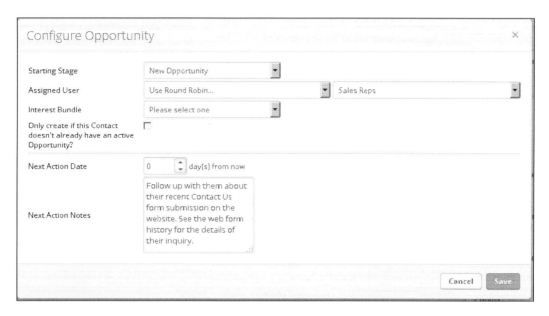

12. Mark the sequence as **Ready** and publish the campaign.

How it works...

When someone fills out the *Contact Us* form on the website, Infusionsoft will create a new opportunity assigned to the first user in the `Sales Reps` round robin. The next time someone fills out the form, it will go to the second user.

There's more...

Be careful about automatically assigning opportunity owners using a round robin. In order for the user to actually view the record, they must be in the **user group** that is configured inside the **Opportunity Defaults** in the **CRM** settings.

There is a second logic option for a round robin that is based on ratio. This allows for a "weighted" assignment giving more new opportunities to users than others:

To streamline the sales process, opportunities can be created with certain products and/or subscriptions pre-populated as the possible sale. These **interest bundles** can be configured in the **CRM** settings:

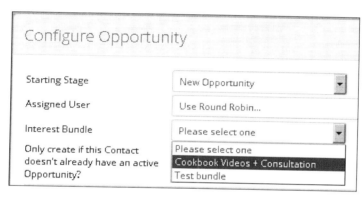

The option beneath the **Interest Bundle** dropdown can be used to prevent duplicate opportunities from being created. An opportunity is considered *active* if one exists in the stages defined as so in the **CRM** settings. If this is checked, a new opportunity will only be created if another opportunity doesn't already exist in one of those active stages:

Since an opportunity record will display on the user's calendar, we can use **Next Action Date** to empower future sales automatically; leads will magically "appear" in a sales rep's pipeline. We could have also used a **Delay Timer** of 60 days then created the opportunity with **Next Action Date** of 0 for the same effect. The difference would be having the opportunity hit their pipeline immediately with a future date, or having the opportunity hit their pipeline at day 60:

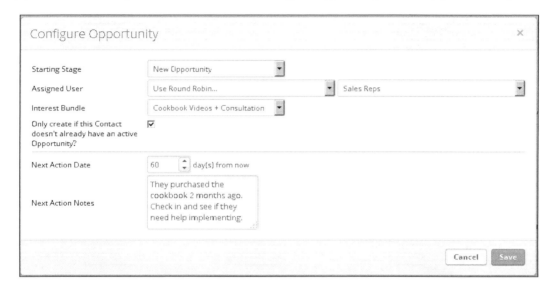

See also

▶ For help with user groups and opportunity assignment, see the *There's more...* section of the *Setting up a sales pipeline* recipe

▶ For help with active opportunity stage declaration, see the *Setting up a sales pipeline* recipe

▶ For how to work an opportunity record, see the previous recipe, *Working sales opportunities*

▶ For a basic *Contact Us* form for your website, see the *Creating a Contact Us form* recipe at the beginning of *Chapter 3, Attracting Leads and Building Your List*

Saving time with FAQ workflows

Quite often in business, there are **Frequently Asked Questions** (**FAQs**) that must be answered. A novel way to save time, get organized, and grow sales is by automating those types of e-mails.

Normally, each time one of those questions is asked, someone has to manually type the answer and send it. A savvier business may have a swipe file of common answers that can be copied/pasted to save time.

This recipe leverages the power of a note template to automatically trigger a pre-authored e-mail answering a common question.

Getting ready

We need to be logged into Infusionsoft, inside a specific account, and inside the campaign builder.

How to do it...

1. Drag out a new note template goal, a new sequence, and connect; rename accordingly:

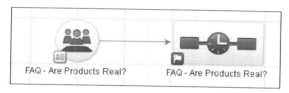

2. Double-click on the note template goal and configure with the appropriate context; click on the green **Save** button:

3. Double-click into the sequence and drag out a new **Email** step; rename accordingly:

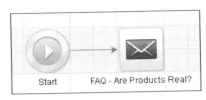

4. Double-click into the e-mail and write the answer to the frequently asked question:

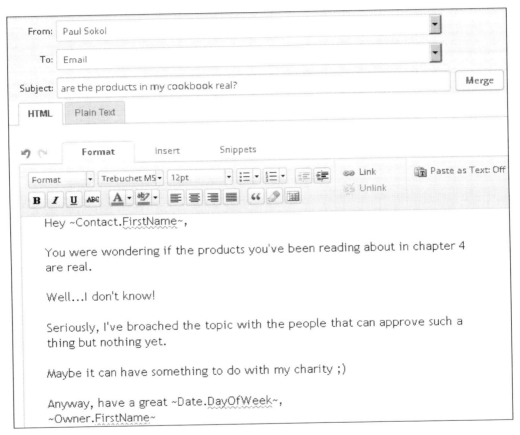

5. In the upper-right of the page, click on **Draft** to change the e-mail to **Ready**; click on **Back to Sequence**.

6. In the upper-right of the page, click on **Draft** to change the sequence to **Ready**; click on **Back to Campaign**.

7. Publish the campaign.

How it works...

When someone asks the frequently asked question, a user can simply apply the **FAQ** note template to automatically send the e-mail and save time while also leaving a clean digital paper trail.

There's more...

There may be certain times where following up on an FAQ can be beneficial, but also a very low-priority to-do. If there are any links within the automated e-mail, we can leverage a link click goal to provide a world-class experience:

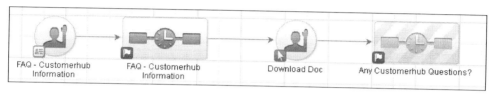

The name of the note template goal will display for the end user. To group similar note template types, use prefixes so they are easy to find:

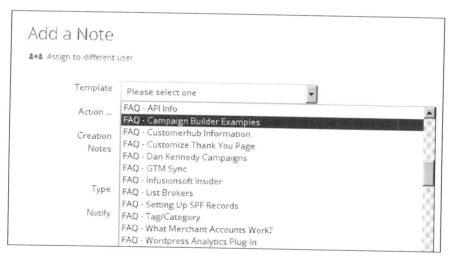

The **Action** and **Type** dropdown options available when setting up the note template can be configured in the **CRM** settings. This can be useful for reporting on certain note behavior.

By default, the user who applies the note template is credited as applying the note in the contact record. However, we can change who the note is assigned to in the note template configuration. The same functionality exists within a **Note** step inside a sequence as well:

When configuring a note template, we can also trigger an e-mail notification to a user every time the note template is applied:

Think of a note template as a big red automation *button*. When we need something automated that we know Infusionsoft can do (send an e-mail, HTTP Post, and so on) but aren't quite sure *HOW* to trigger the automation, a note template is a quick fix.

Although this recipe is for an FAQ specifically, this tactic can be used for any type of common automation. Some common prefixes for names are:

- ▸ **ADMIN** - : For notes related to administrative automation
- ▸ **CUSTOMER** - : For notes related to customer automation
- ▸ **FINANCE** - : For notes related to financial automation
- ▸ **LEAD** - : For notes related to lead development automation
- ▸ **SALES** - : For notes related to sales automation

See also

For how to apply the note template to a contact, see the *Using note templates for workflow* recipe in *Chapter 2, Critical Tools for Mastery*.

Sending automated appointment reminders

Scheduling an appointment with someone is useless unless the appointment actually occurs. We can improve our chances of the appointment occurring by sending automated reminders leading up to the appointment date.

This recipe is about building a workflow tool that can easily be operated after a user has put the scheduled appointment in their appropriate system of existence (online calendar, offline calendar, mobile device, and so on).

Getting ready

We need to be logged into Infusionsoft and inside a specific account. Also, inside the campaign builder we should have:

- A custom **Date** type field for the scheduled appointment
- A custom **Text** type field for the appointment time

How to do it...

1. Drag out a new internal form goal, a new sequence, and connect; rename accordingly:

Existing Lead   LEAD - Schedule Appointment   Appointment Confirmation & Reminders

2. Double-click on the internal form goal to edit it.

3. Ensure the internal form has at least the **First Name** and **Email** field and that both are required.

4. Add a **Title** and **Paragraph** snippet above the fields; provide some context for the end user submitting the form:

> **LEAD - Schedule Appointment**
> Use this form to send automated reminders
> leading up to a scheduled appointment.
>
> First Name *   [   ]
>
> Email *   [   ]

5. Using the **Field Snippets** tab, add an **Other** snippet; this will open a configuration menu.

6. Using the **Which Field** dropdown, select the **Date** type field that is storing the appointment date.

7. Make sure the field is marked as **Required** and click on **Save**:

8. Using the **Field Snippets** tab, add another **Other** snippet.

9. Using the **Which Field** dropdown, select the **Text** type field that is storing the appointment time.

10. Make sure the field is marked as **Required** and click on **Save**:

11. Mark the form as **Ready** and click on **Back to Campaign**:

12. In the upper-right of the page, click on **Draft** to change the e-mail to **Ready**; click on **Back to Sequence**.

13. In the upper-right of the page, click on **Draft** to change the sequence to **Ready**; click on **Back to Campaign**.

14. Double-click into the connected sequence.

15. Drag out two **Email** steps and a **Field** timer; connect as shown in the following screenshot and rename accordingly:

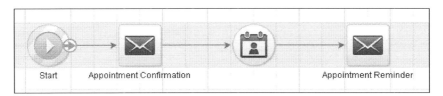

16. Double-click into the first e-mail and write an appointment confirmation:

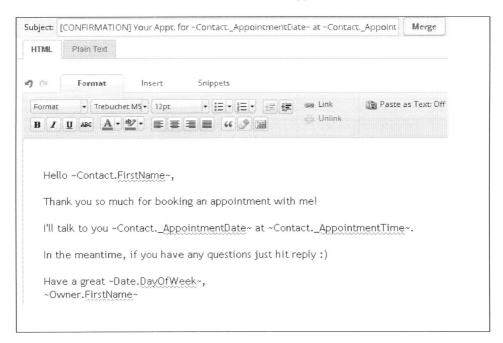

17. In the upper-right of the page mark the e-mail as **Ready** and then click on the **Back to Sequence** button in the upper-left corner of the page.

18. Double-click on the **Field** timer and configure it to wait 1 day before the contact's appointment date and run at 8 am; click on **Save**:

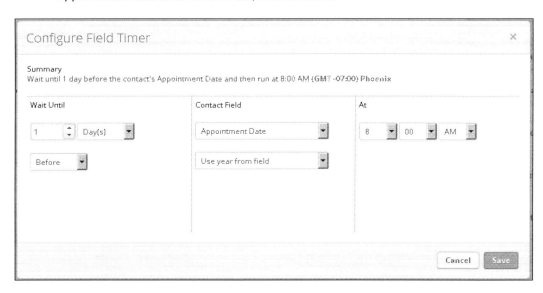

19. Double-click into the second e-mail and write an appointment reminder:

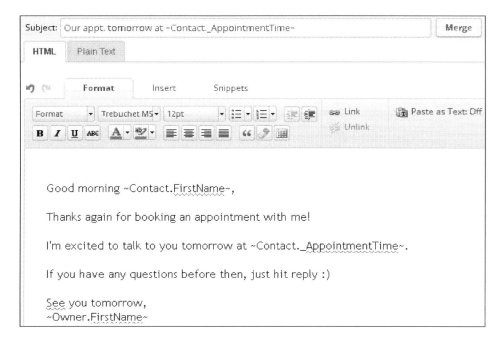

20. In the upper-right of the page mark the e-mail as **Ready** and then click on the **Back to Sequence** button in the upper-left corner of the page.

21. Mark the sequence as **Ready** and publish the campaign.

How it works...

When someone submits the **LEAD - Schedule Appointment** internal form, the system will send an immediate confirmation e-mail and then schedule an e-mail reminder for the morning before the appointment.

There's more...

As of this writing, a custom **Date/Time** field is not usable in a **Field** timer; this is why we needed to separate the appointment date and time into two custom fields.

Although it won't work in all cases, keeping a low-key friendly tone for these e-mails can encourage a conversation before the appointment. If the e-mails look or sound too automated it won't be an enjoyable experience.

To help with appointment stick rates, include appointment-specific instructions or other resources that would be helpful in the initial confirmation e-mail. We can get really fancy by tracking click behavior on those resources with a link click goal and provide a more intimate pre-appointment experience:

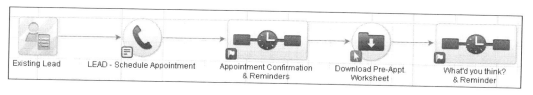

Voice broadcasts can also help with appointment stick rates if used strategically. They can also be a very handy reminder when someone needs to bring certain items to a meeting:

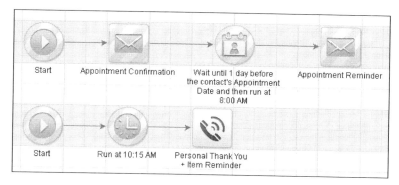

As long as the date is stored within the contact record, this tactic can be extended for sending reminders around any critical date. The system comes out of the box with a *birthday* and *anniversary* date on the contact record that can be used to provide world-class customer experiences.

Although it doesn't display in the form builder, with the **Date** type field for appointment, the end user will have a calendar picker available and all the keyboard shortcuts work.

To minimize wasted time from missed appointments, we can include an **I need to reschedule** link in the reminder e-mail and use a link click goal to create a task to reschedule. For a great end user experience, include the exact name of the internal form that needs to be submitted upon a successful reschedule in the task body:

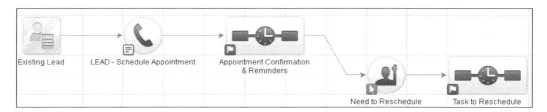

There are certain third-party plugins that can generate a "humanized" date to merge into communications besides the formal MM/DD/YYYY presentation. These plugins can be found in the Infusionsoft Marketplace.

See also

> ▸ For how to submit an internal form for a contact, see the *Using internal forms for workflow* recipe in *Chapter 2, Critical Tools for Mastery*

> ▸ For a list of available **Date** field keyboard shortcuts, see the *See More* section of the *Working sales opportunities* recipe earlier in this chapter

Merging custom opportunity fields into e-mails

It is possible to merge opportunity field information into an e-mail communication.

For the context of this recipe we are assuming a sales pipeline with a stage named **Appointment Scheduled** and we are going to send an e-mail with the opportunity's next action date and time when a prospect is moved into that stage.

Getting ready

We need to be logged into Infusionsoft, inside a specific account, and have the sales stage created.

How to do it...

1. Hover over the main navigation and at the bottom of the **CRM** column, click on **Settings**:

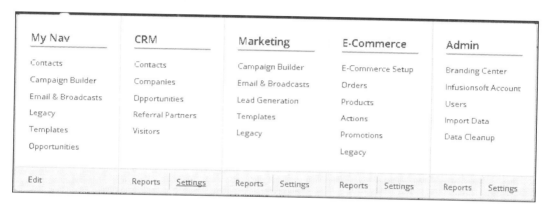

2. In the **Sales Settings** menu on the left of the page, click on **Pipeline Automation**:

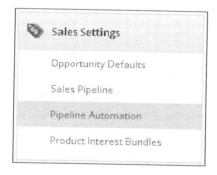

3. Using the **Choose Trigger Type** dropdown at the top of the page, select **When moving from one stage to another** and click on the **Add Trigger** button; this will open a popup:

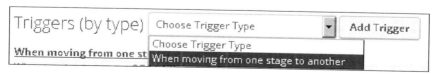

4. In the **Set Trigger Criteria** section, configure for when moving into the **Appointment Scheduled** stage:

5. Using the **Add New Action** dropdown, select **Send an email, fax, etc.**:

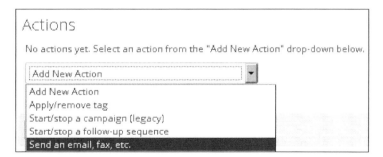

6. Using the **Please select an activity** dropdown, select **Email**:

7. To the right of the **Configuration** options, click on the **Add** button; this will open another popup:

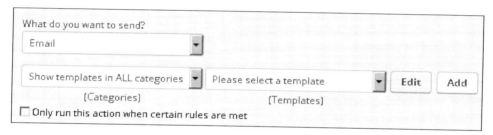

8. In the **Template Options** section, give this new e-mail template a meaningful name:

9. At the top of the **Compose Email** section, make sure the e-mail is coming from the owner and that there is an appropriate subject line:

10. Just below the subject line, click on the **Edit Email Body** button to open the **Email Builder**:

11. Compose the message until we need to merge in an opportunity field and leave the cursor where the field needs to be inserted.

12. Click on the **Insert** tab in the top ribbon and then click on **Merge Fields**:

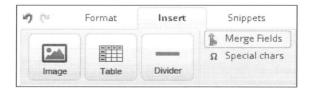

13. Scroll to the bottom of the **Merge Fields** menu to find the opportunity fields; click on **Opportunity fields**.

14. Click on the **Merge Fields** option to populate the merge field value:

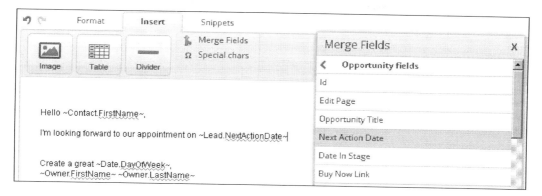

15. Finish composing the e-mail message and click on the *floppy disk* icon at the top-left of the page to save the e-mail; click on **Close Builder**.

16. Scroll down to the bottom of the **Manage Email Template** page and click on **No** to mark the e-mail as **Ready**:

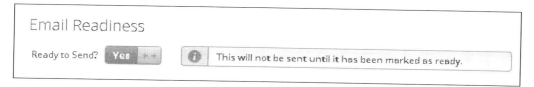

17. Click on the green **Save** button.

18. In the **Manage Trigger** window, click on the green **Save** button:

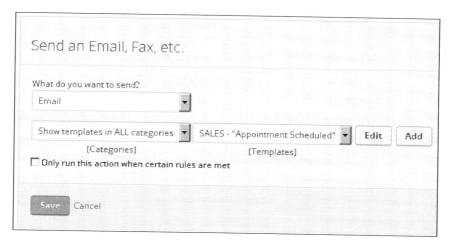

19. Click on the **Save Trigger** button:

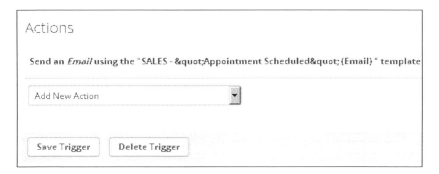

How it works...

When a sales rep moves an opportunity into the **Appointment Scheduled** stage, Infusionsoft will immediately send an e-mail merging in any inserted opportunity information from that specific opportunity record.

There's more...

The **Pipeline Automation** trigger will fire every time the stage move conditions are met. For this recipe, every time the prospect is put in the **Appointment Scheduled** stage from some other stage, the e-mail will be sent.

This functionality can be handy when using custom opportunity fields to store critical information about the potential sale or complex fulfillment data.

Although it won't work in all cases, keeping a low-key friendly tone for these e-mails can encourage a digital conversation between voice-to-voice interactions. If the e-mails look or sound too automated, it won't be a good experience.

We can also automate when someone moves out of a pipeline stage. This can be useful for controlling automated campaigns. For example, turning off a long-term nurture campaign when someone leaves an *In Long Term Nurture* stage. The recommended tactic is to set up a Pipeline Automation trigger that applies a functional tag associated with a tag goal in the long-term nurture campaign.

Someone can have multiple sales opportunities throughout the course of their lifetime, hence a contact record can potentially have more than one opportunity associated with it. The Pipeline Automation triggers are able to pull information from the opportunity that triggered it, no matter how many opportunities exist. This is also why we cannot merge opportunity information into a campaign builder communication. The campaign builder operates at the level of contact record and, as of this writing, is not able to distinguish which opportunity specifically triggers a **stage move goal**.

This recipe can be used to easily send a branded Buy Now e-mail because that is an available opportunity merge field. In that case, we would need to set up a sales stage for the purpose of triggering a Buy Now e-mail.

If we create a new e-mail template from the **Billing Automation** triggers, we have credit card information that can be merged into an e-mail. This is primarily used to provide credit card update functionality. The **Update** merge fields operate similar to a Buy Now link except the link will drive to a page where the recipient can update a Credit Card record:

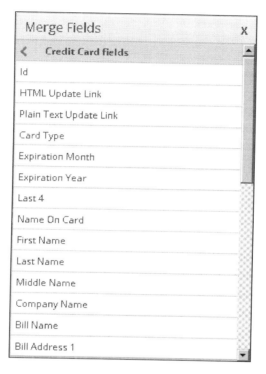

If we create a new e-mail template from the **Invoice** options in **Order Settings**:

We also have order **Merge Fields**. This can be very handy when needing a custom invoice:

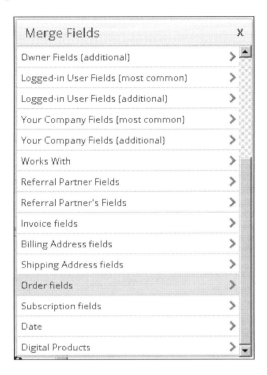

See also

▸ For how to create custom opportunity fields, see the *Creating custom fields* recipe in *Chapter 2, Critical Tools for Mastery*

▸ For how to create a sales stage, see the *Setting up a sales pipeline* recipe earlier in this chapter

▸ For more information on Buy Now e-mails, see the *Working sales opportunities* recipe earlier in this chapter

▸ For more information on Billing Automation triggers, see the *Collecting failed automated billing attempts* recipe in *Chapter 4, Selling Products Online and Getting Paid*

▸ For a recipe that uses the Credit Card merge fields, see the *Updating a soon-to-be-expired credit card automatically* recipe in *Chapter 7, Wowing Existing Customers with Great Experiences*

Setting up lead scoring

For organizations that are opportunity heavy, it can sometimes be hard for sales reps to know whom they should reach out to first. This is especially true when a sales rep has a large number of opportunities with a next action date for today.

To help identify which prospects are the most engaged, and so should be reached out to first, Infusionsoft has the ability to do lead scoring.

For the context of this recipe, we want to be scoring leads based on the following activity:

- ▸ Form submissions
- ▸ E-mail opens
- ▸ Link clicks
- ▸ E-mail unsubscribes

Getting ready

We need to be logged in to Infusionsoft and inside a specific account.

How to do it...

1. Hover over the main navigation and at the bottom of the **CRM** column, click on **Settings**.

2. In the **Contact & Company Settings** menu on the left of the page, click on **Scores**:

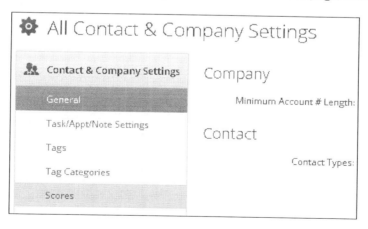

3. In the **Name & Status** section, give our lead scoring rules a name and make sure lead scoring is turned on:

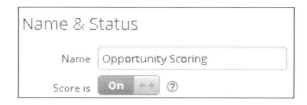

4. Set a value of 50 for how many points equals 5 flames:

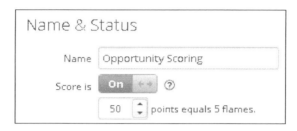

5. In the **Rules** section at the bottom, click the options to configure a rule for if a contact's activity contains **Web Form Submission**; award 25 points:

6. Hover to the right of the row containing the rule and click on the **+** sign to add a new rule:

7. Configure this new rule for if a contact's activity contains **Email Open**; award 5 points:

8. Click on the **+** sign to add another rule and configure it for if a contact's activity contains **Link Click**; award 10 points:

9. Click on the **+** sign to add another rule and configure it for if a contact's activity contains **Email Unsubscribe**; award -100 points; click on the green **Save** button at the bottom of the page:

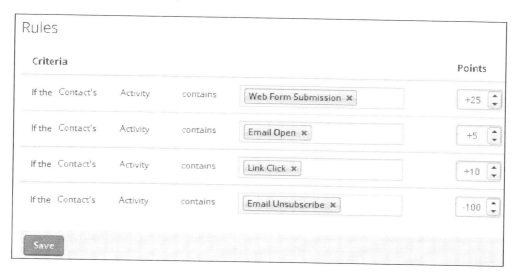

How it works...

As a contact engages with our marketing through different types of behavior, Infusionsoft will award points based on the rules outlined. The total number of points is then weighted against the value set for 5 flames to determine a contact's lead score. For example, since the maximum points in this recipe is set to 50, if a lead has 30 points, they will display 3 flames on their record. Looking at this contact's record, in the upper-right of the **General** tab it will look like this. The **Score** is also displayed in the right side of the page when looking at an opportunity record:

There's more...

Web Form Submission, **Email Open**, and **Link Click** award lead score points for each unique instance of that action. For example, if someone opened two different e-mails, they would receive twice the points. However, if they opened the same e-mail multiple times, they would only receive points for the first open of that e-mail.

When designing your lead scoring rules, be sure to leverage negative engagement types (like we did with the **Email Unsubscribe**) to push weak leads to the bottom. This is where tag-based lead score rules can become very handy.

We can also assign lead scores based on specific tags being applied. Multiple tags in a rule are using **OR** logic:

In other words, it doesn't matter if someone has one or more of the potential tags as they will only receive the lead score points once. If we need points for each tag, we would need to create a unique rule for each tag.

For **dynamic lead scoring** (sometimes known as a **decaying lead score**), we can have lead score points expire after a certain number of weeks:

The name we configure at the beginning of this recipe is how it will display when filtering contact or opportunity records:

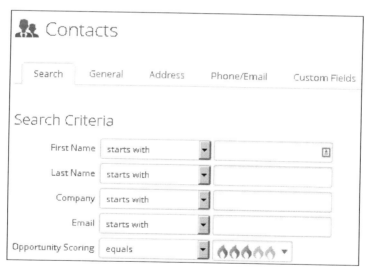

The **Update recent activity** option enables lead score transitions to be shown in the **Recent Activity** widget on a user's dashboard:

See also

For how to automate based on a certain lead score being achieved, see the next recipe, *Automating based on lead score achievement*.

Automating based on lead score achievement

Once we have lead scoring set up, we can also automate based on a contact achieving a certain lead score.

For this recipe, we are going to send the opportunity owner, in this case a sales rep, an e-mail notification when one of their leads achieves the highest lead score possible (5 flames).

Getting ready

We need to be logged in to Infusionsoft, inside a specific account, and inside a new campaign.

How to do it...

1. Drag out a lead score goal and a sequence; connect as shown in the following image and rename accordingly:

2. Double-click on the lead score goal to configure it.

3. Configure the goal for when the score increases to 5 flames; click on the green **Save** button:

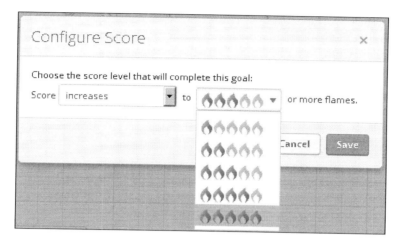

4. Double-click into the sequence and add a new e-mail step; rename accordingly:

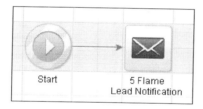

5. Double-click into the e-mail to edit it.

6. Configure the e-mail to come from a no-reply address and to the owner using the available merge fields:

7. Compose a message with information that the sales rep needs to act upon immediately:

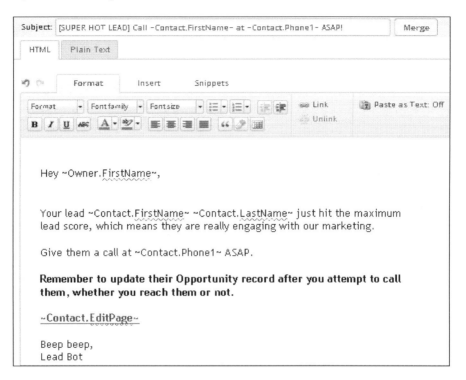

8. In the upper-right of the page, click on **Draft** to change the e-mail's status to **Ready**; click on the **Back to Sequence** button in the upper-left of the page.

9. In the upper-right of the page, click on **Draft** to change the sequence's status to **Ready**; click on the **Back to Campaign** button in the upper-left of the page; publish the campaign.

How it works...

As a contact engages with our marketing through different types of behavior, Infusionsoft will award points based on the rules outlined. When the contact reaches the lead score configured in the lead score goal, the assigned user will receive an immediate e-mail with instructions to reach out to the contact.

There's more...

The ~Contact.EditPage~ merge field used in the preceding example will populate as a link to the contact's record. Upon clicking, the user will need to log in if they are not already, and be taken right to the person's record. This allows for proper pipeline management even on the go.

If we are using expiring lead score points, a contact's score may fluctuate up and down over time. If we need to make the lead score automation happen repeatable with a looping structure that sandwiches a sequence between two lead score goals, configure with the same settings:

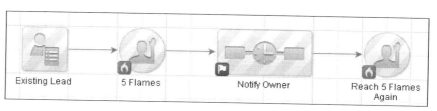

We can also configure a decreasing lead score goal for early risk detection and re-engagement:

For more advanced lead score automation, we can develop a pyramid-shaped model that ascends up to 5 flames, and then descends down to none. This way, we can create a personalized experience as someone's lead score fluctuates up and down. Jordan Hatch, a world-renowned Infusionsoft expert, is credited with discovering this particular structure.

The left side of the pyramid is modeled as follows:

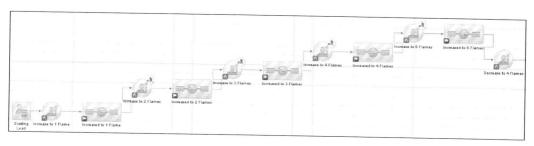

And the right side of the pyramid is modeled as:

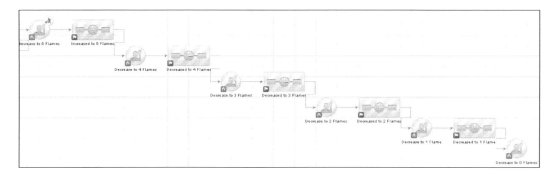

See also

  ▸ For how to set up lead scoring, see the previous recipe, *Setting up lead scoring*

  ▸ For a campaign template similar to this model, download the **Focus on Your Hottest Leads** campaign from the free Marketplace

Building a long-term prospect nurture

To close out this chapter on selling with Infusionsoft, we are going to implement a strategy ensuring that if someone is not ready to buy now, they don't slip through the cracks and become a totally lost prospect. After all, just because they don't buy now, doesn't mean they can't in the future.

The high-level strategy behind a long-term prospect nurture is to reach out every once in a while with a small bit of value and make it easy for the person to request a phone call.

For the context of this recipe, we are going to be building a six-month nurture that delivers three quality online resources. Of course, this recipe is easy to extend longer depending on the nature of our customer's buying cycle.

Getting ready

We need to be logged in to Infusionsoft, inside a specific account, and inside a new campaign. In addition to this, we are assuming:

  ▸ An *In Long Term Nurture* stage exists

  ▸ We have three URLs, one for each nurture resource

How to do it...

1. Drag out two stage move goals, a link click goal, and two sequences; connect as shown in the following image and rename accordingly:

2. Create a campaign merge field for the title of each nurture resource:

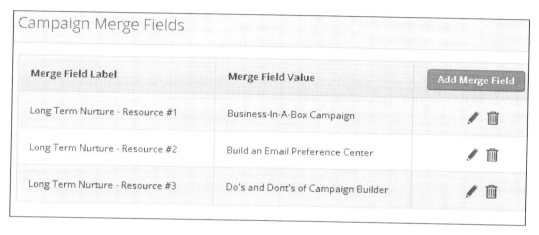

3. Create a campaign link with the URLs of each nurture resource:

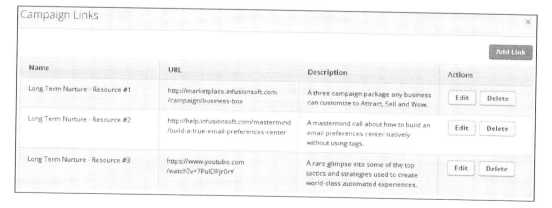

4. Double-click on the first stage move goal and configure for when moving into the *In Long Term Nurture* stage; click on the green **Save** button:

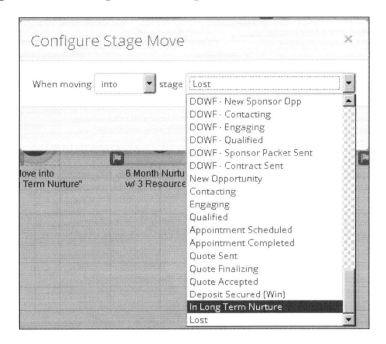

5. Double-click into the nurture sequence and add four new e-mail steps and four **Delay Timers**; connect and rename accordingly:

6. Double-click into the first e-mail to edit it.

7. Write a low-impact message addressing that a buying decision wasn't made now and that we'll keep in touch with valuable resources in the future:

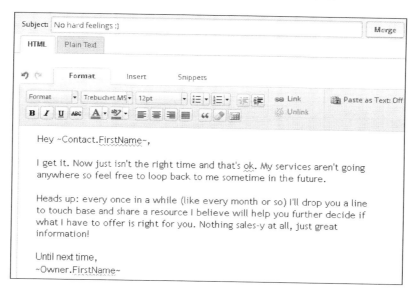

8. In the upper-right of the page, click on **Draft** to change the e-mail's status to **Ready**; click on the **Back to Sequence** button in the upper-left of the page.

9. Double-click the first **Delay Timer** and configure it to wait two months and then send on a weekday at 8 am; click on **Save**:

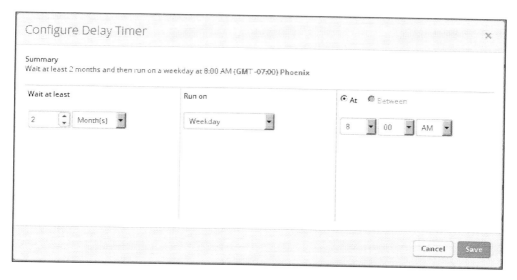

10. Double-click into the second e-mail to edit it.

11. Write a message delivering the first nurture resource that uses the campaign merge field and link for `resource #1`:

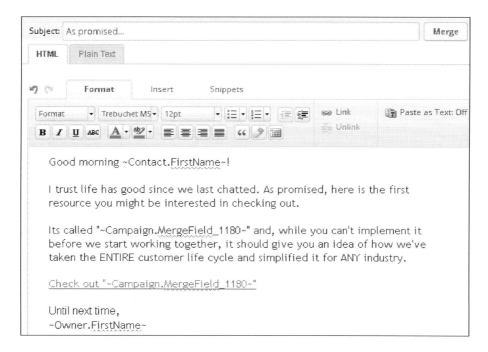

12. In the *P.S.* of the message, write a call to action for someone to click if they are ready to chat again:

13. Highlight the call to action text in the *P.S.* and click on the **Link** button in the toolbar at the top of the editor:

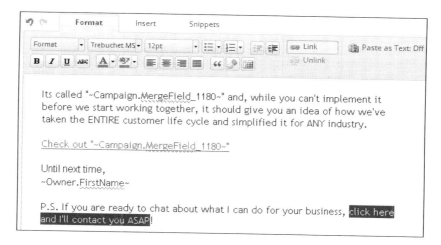

14. Using the **Link to:** dropdown, select **Thank-you page**; click on the **Edit thank-you page** link that appears to open a popup:

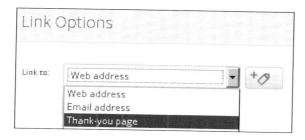

15. Write a brief confirmation message letting the re-engaged prospect know what to expect:

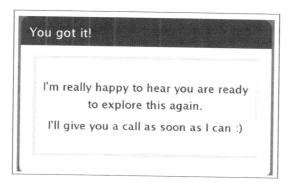

16. At the bottom of this window, click on the **Save & Close** button.

17. Click on the green **Insert/Update** button to save the link:

> Its called "~Campaign.MergeField_1180~" and, while you can't implement it
> before we start working together, it should give you an idea of how we've
> taken the ENTIRE customer life cycle and simplified it for ANY industry.
>
> Check out "~Campaign.MergeField_1180~"
>
> Until next time,
> ~Owner.FirstName~
>
> P.S. If you are ready to chat about what I can do for your business, click here
> and I'll contact you ASAP!

18. In the upper-right of the page, click on **Draft** to change the e-mail's status to **Ready**; click on the **Back to Sequence** button in the upper-left of the page.

19. Double-click the second **Delay Timer** and configure it to wait 2 months and then send on a weekday at 8 am; click on **Save**.

20. Double-click into the third e-mail to edit it.

21. Write a message delivering the second nurture resource that uses the campaign merge field and link for resource #2. Be sure to include the call to action in the *P.S.* To save time, clone the nurture resource #1 e-mail:

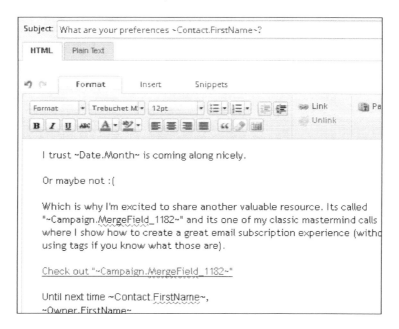

22. In the upper-right of the page, click on **Draft** to change the e-mail's status to **Ready**; click on the **Back to Sequence** button in the upper-left of the page.

23. Double-click the third **Delay Timer** and configure it to wait two months and then send on a weekday at 8 am; click on **Save**.

24. Double-click into the fourth e-mail to edit it.

25. Write a message delivering the third nurture resource that uses the campaign merge field and link for `resource #3`. Be sure to include the call to action in the *P.S.* To save time, clone a previous e-mail in the chain:

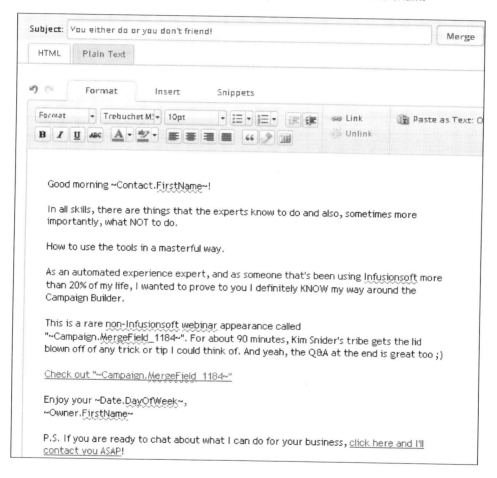

26. In the upper-right of the page, click on **Draft** to change the e-mail's status to **Ready**; click on the **Back to Sequence** button in the upper-left of the page.

27. Double-click the fourth **Delay Timer** and configure it to wait 2 months and then send on a weekday at 8 am; click on **Save**:

28. In the upper-right of the page, click on **Draft** to change the sequence's status to **Ready**; click on the **Back to Campaign** button in the upper-left of the page.

29. Double-click the link click goal.

30. Using the menu on the left of the page, select each nurture e-mail and select the link in the *P.S.* on the right of the page. Make sure all e-mails with a *P.S.* are being tracked and click on **Back to Campaign**:

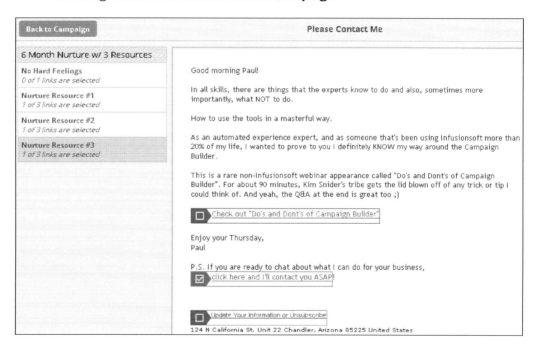

31. Double-click the notify owner sequence and add a new e-mail step; rename accordingly:

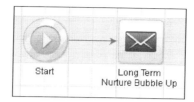

32. Double-click into the e-mail and configure the e-mail to come from a no-reply address and to the owner using the available merge fields:

33. Compose a message with information that the sales rep needs to act upon immediately:

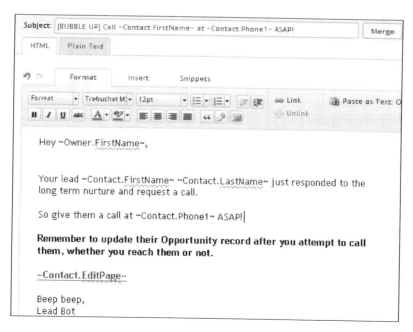

34. In the upper-right of the page, click on **Draft** to change the e-mail's status to **Ready**; click on the **Back to Sequence** button in the upper-left of the page.

35. In the upper-right of the page, click on **Draft** to change the sequence's status to **Ready**; click on the **Back to Campaign** button in the upper-left of the page.

36. Double-click on the second stage move goal and configure for when moving out of the *In Long Term Nurture* stage; click on the green **Save** button:

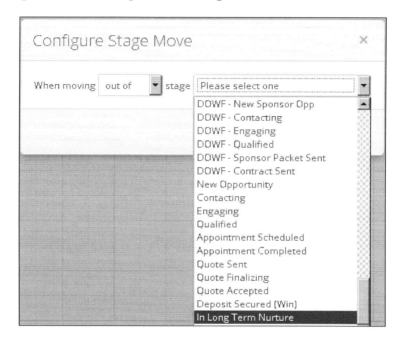

37. Publish the campaign.

How it works...

When a user moves a prospect's opportunity into the *In Long Term Nurture* stage, the prospect automatically receives communications for the next six months. In each communication, the sales rep is providing them with something of extreme value while also making it easy for the prospect to request a call. If the prospect requests a call by clicking the link in the *P.S.* of each e-mail, the sales rep is automatically notified and can continue working the opportunity. To ensure a great customer experience, whenever their opportunity stage is moved the nurture sequence is automatically stopped.

There's more...

Add a **P.P.S.** link to allow people to drop out if they are no longer interested:

> P.S. If you are ready to chat about what I can do for your business, click here and I'll contact you ASAP!
>
> P.P.S. And listen, if you *really* aren't considering me anymore, save us both time and click here. No hard feelings :)

Use a link click goal to track this behavior so we can notify the owner to move the opportunity:

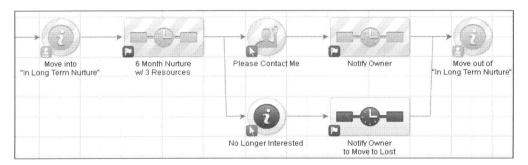

If we can, mix up the types of resources we share. Different people respond to different kinds of content so make sure we have a healthy mix of written word, spoken word, videos, and presentations.

Mix up the time of day you deliver the resources. Feel free to experiment with sending on weekends since these e-mails should be pure valuable content. Remember, the high-level strategy is to make it easy for people to bubble up. It is entirely possibly that your offering would only be seen when they check their e-mail over the weekend because they are overwhelmed during the week.

Mix up the communication channels. As long as the **Return On Investment** (**ROI**) is there, we can send direct mail pieces at certain steps in the nurture. In that case, make sure there is still an easy mechanism for the prospect to respond to the mail piece.

This strategy can also be initiated from other mechanisms besides opportunity stage moves. An internal form, a note template, an API goal, or a tag goal can just as easily trigger this nurture campaign.

This strategy can also be expanded for customer nurture as well. In that case, we may also choose to use a purchase goal to trigger the campaign.

See also

For an explanation of the ~Contact.EditPage~ merge field, see the *There's more...* section of the *Automating based on lead score achievement* recipe in this chapter.

6
Wowing New Customers with Great Experiences

In this chapter, we will cover the following:

- ▸ Segmenting by last purchase date
- ▸ Building a new customer welcome campaign
- ▸ Creating a customer satisfaction survey
- ▸ Asking for testimonials automatically
- ▸ Setting up a birthday collection mechanism
- ▸ Building automated *Happy Birthday* messages

Introduction

The third phase of lifecycle marketing is *Wow*. This chapter concerns itself with different tactics to *Wow* your new customers.

There is a general flow to the recipes and, while each can stand by itself, a new business would be advised to start at the top and work their way down.

If a small business were to implement every recipe in this chapter, I feel very strongly that their business would not only earn more per customer, but the costs to acquire a customer would go down because the automated systems would support a completely delightful experience—an experience they would surely tell their friends about.

Segmenting by last purchase date

When we can segment our customer database based on someone's most recent purchase, it unlocks an entire world of automation potential.

This information can be used to plan promotions, automatically switch paths, or simply enhance an existing report for a deeper layer of insight.

This type of segmentation cannot easily be performed retroactively, so the sooner a business implements this recipe, the sooner they begin building their lake of data.

Getting ready

We need to be logged in to Infusionsoft, inside a specific account and in a new campaign. We also need to have:

▸ The shopping cart configured or a live order form

▸ The last purchased segments we want to track created as tags, for example

    ❑   Last purchased -> within 30 days

    ❑   Last purchased -> within 30-90 days

    ❑   Last purchased -> within 90-180 days

    ❑   Last purchased -> within 180 days-1 year

    ❑   Last purchased -> over 1 year ago

How to do it...

1. Drag out two purchase goals and a sequence; connect and rename them accordingly:

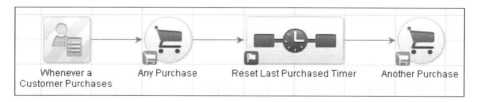

2. Double-click on the first purchase goal and configure it for **Any Purchase**; click on **Save**:

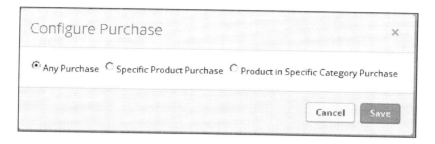

3. In the lower-left corner of the second Purchase goal, click on the green symbol to open the goal settings.

4. Using the **This goal can be achieved by...** dropdown, select **Any Contact**; click on **Save**:

5. Double-click on the second purchase goal and configure it for **Any Purchase**; click on **Save**:

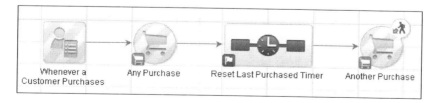

6. Double-click into the sequence and add two **Tag** steps:

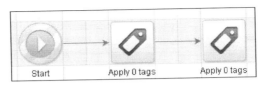

7. Double-click into the first **Tag** step and configure it to apply the first purchase segment tag; click on **Save**:

8. Double-click into the second **Tag** step and configure it to remove all the other purchase segment tags; click on **Save**:

9. Drag out a new **Start Timer**, **Delay Timer**, and two **Tag** steps.

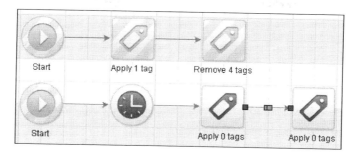

10. Double-click on the timer and configure it to wait as long as the first segment and then run on any day at 12 AM; click on **Save**:

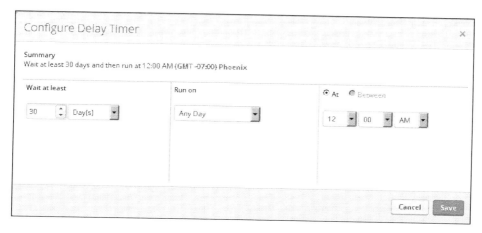

11. Double-click into the first **Tag** step and configure it to remove the first purchase segment tag; click on **Save**:

12. Double-click into the second **Tag** step and configure it to apply the second purchase segment tag; click on **Save**:

 At this point, we may want to leave canvas notes to track the different segments.

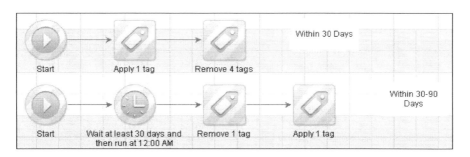

13. Repeat this **Start** - **Delay** - **Tag** switching structure for each of the remaining purchase segments:

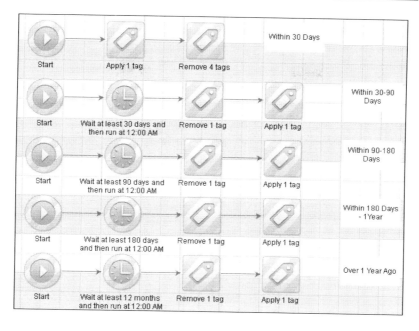

14. In the upper-right corner of the page, click on **Draft** to mark the sequence as **Ready**.

15. In the upper-left corner of the page, click on **Back to Campaign** and publish the campaign.

How it works...

The first time someone makes a purchase, they are tagged with the first purchase segment and then the tags switch as time passes. If they make another purchase, the second purchase goal will pull them out of the sequence and then the first purchase goal will add them back into the sequence. When this happens any previously applied tags will be removed and the first purchase segment tag is reapplied. To ensure that this always happens, we set the second purchase goal as an entry point.

There's more...

This timer is tracking any purchase. We can easily modify this model to time-specific product purchases and re-purchases.

The magic of this recipe lies in the fact that we can sandwich a sequence between two of the same goals and create a looping effect. We can also create loops with:

- ▶ Lead score goals
- ▶ Opportunity stage move goals
- ▶ Tag goals
- ▶ API goals

For example, if we wanted to create a timer based on a user logging in to an app:

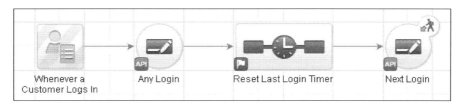

See also

For a similar resettable timer model that uses tags, see the *Tracking e-mail engagement levels* recipe in *Chapter 8, Administrative - Conquer Internal Chaos*.

Building a new customer welcome campaign

Anytime a customer receives their product or is delivered a service, we have an opportunity to make them feel appreciated and increase the chances of future business. By making that appreciation known over time, we greatly increase the chances of future business.

While a welcome campaign can use many different communication channels, for this recipe, we are only going to be contacting the customer via e-mail.

Getting ready

We need to be logged in to Infusionsoft, inside a specific account and in a new campaign. We are also assuming the following:

▸ The product or service is being sold via the shopping cart or order form (see the *There's more...* section if this is not the case)

▸ The business has an active social media profile

How to do it...

1. Drag out a purchase goal and a sequence; connect and rename accordingly:

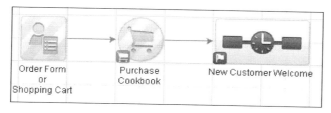

2. Double-click on the first purchase goal and configure it for the specific product or service being sold; click on **Save**:

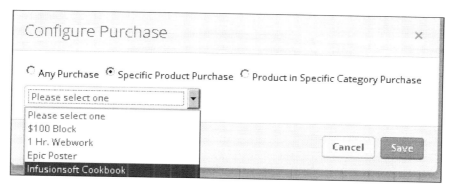

3. Double-click into the sequence. Add three e-mail steps and two **Delay Timers**; connect and rename accordingly:

4. Double-click into the first e-mail step and write a message thanking the new customer and making them feel appreciated:

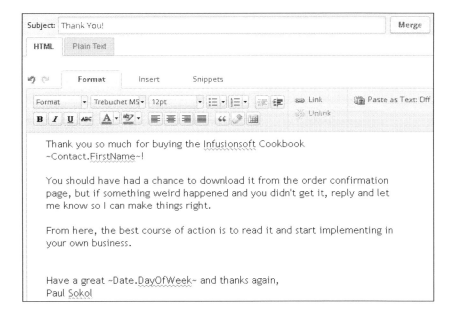

5. In the upper-right corner of the page, click on **Draft** to mark the e-mail as **Ready**; in the upper-left corner of the page, click on **Back to Sequence**.

6. Double-click on the first timer and configure it to wait 7 days and then run on any day at 8 AM; click on **Save**:

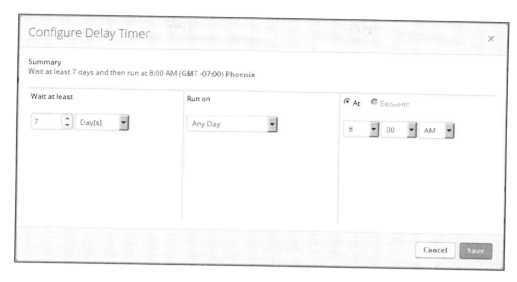

7. Double-click into the second e-mail step and write a message thanking the customer again and providing additional resources if they need assistance:

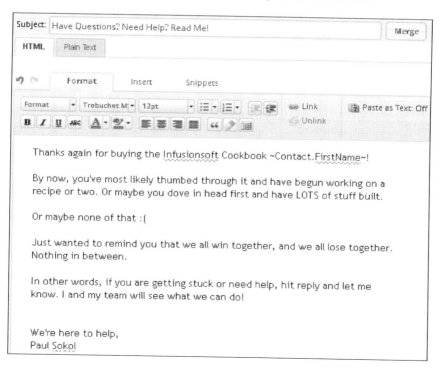

8. In the upper-right corner of the page, click on **Draft** to mark the e-mail as **Ready**; in the upper-left corner of the page, click on **Back to Sequence**.

9. Double-click the second timer and configure it to wait 23 days and then run on any day at 8 AM; click on **Save**:

10. Double-click into the last e-mail step and write a message inviting the customer to follow you on a social media channel:

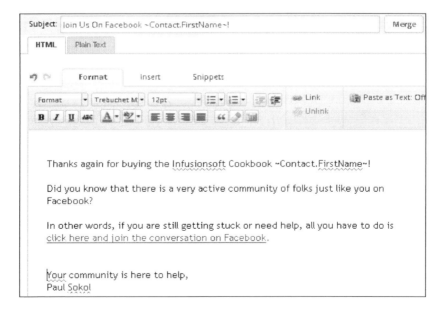

11. In the upper-right corner of the page, click on **Draft** to mark the e-mail as **Ready**; in the upper-left corner of the page, click on **Back to Sequence**.

12. In the upper-right corner of the page, click on **Draft** to mark the sequence as **Ready**.

13. In the upper-left corner of the page, click on **Back to Campaign** and publish the campaign.

How it works...

When a customer makes a purchase through the shopping cart (or using an order form), they receive an immediate thank you e-mail. One week later, they get another e-mail with more resources, and one month after their purchase, they are invited to follow on a social channel.

There's more...

Don't forget to add any Tag steps to switch out a contact's tags! For example, we may want to remove specific prospect tags and apply customer tags.

Don't forget to include any necessary fulfillment information in the initial welcome e-mail or fulfillment tasks in the sequence. For example, if there is a physical product being shipped, we may want to include some expectations around estimated delivery times.

Depending on the specific business, we may want to communicate at different frequencies than this recipe. For example, an annual service may wait a full quarter after the initial welcome e-mail.

This recipe is a generic new customer welcome that will work for a majority of products/services. For maximum effectiveness, add extra steps based on the company's strategic objectives. For example, a business that relies heavily on repeat purchases could have a welcome that lasts a year and provides a special offer or discount for another purchase. Or, for a business that relies heavily on word-of-mouth referrals, we might introduce a social invitation much earlier.

If our business is not using the shopping cart or order forms, we can trigger this campaign manually with a note template.

See also

For a potential extension to this recipe, see the next recipe *Creating a customer satisfaction survey*.

Creating a customer satisfaction survey

When we understand how satisfied (or not) a customer is, we can adjust the customer experience to ask for a testimonial/referral or take steps to make things right. One way to acquire this information is with a customer satisfaction survey.

A customer satisfaction survey can be requested for each purchase, after a general period of time (for example annually) or a customer interaction. It all depends on the specific business.

For the context of this recipe, we are creating a survey for a recently purchased product.

Getting ready

We need to be logged in to Infusionsoft, inside a specific account and in a new campaign.

How to do it...

1. Drag out a web form goal and three sequences; connect and rename accordingly. The decision node will appear after connecting the form to more than one sequence:

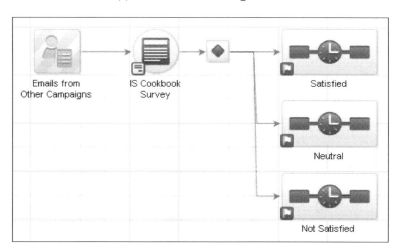

2. Double-click on the web form goal.
3. Delete all visible fields.
4. Add a **Hidden** field snippet.

5. Configure it for the **Email** field. Make sure that the value is left empty, and click on **Save**:

6. Add a **Logo** snippet and a **Title** snippet; update the **Title** snippet text with customer instructions:

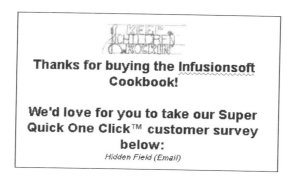

7. Using the **Field Snippets** tab, add a **Radio** snippet.

8. Change the label to ask the survey question:

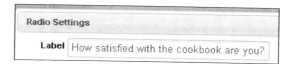

9. Click on the *plus* sign next to the options to get one more field; we want a total of three options as shown in the following image:

10. Fill in the field values and select the option next to **Neutral**; click on **Save**:

11. Click on the **Submit** button to edit the call to action.

12. Change the button label and set the alignment to **Center**; click on **Save**:

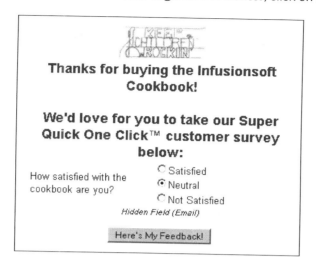

13. Click on the **Thank-you Page** tab at the top of the page.

14. Configure the page with a friendly thank you message:

15. Click on the **Settings** tab at the top of the page and make sure that the **Auto-populate** has its option selected:

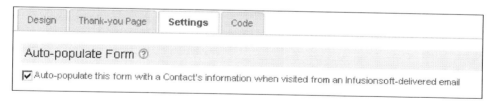

16. In the upper-right corner of the page, click on **Draft** to mark the web form as **Ready**, and in the upper-left corner of the page, click on **Back to Campaign**.

17. Double-click into the decision node.

18. Configure the logic so that each radio option directs the contact into the appropriate sequence; click on **Back to Campaign** in the upper-left corner of the page:

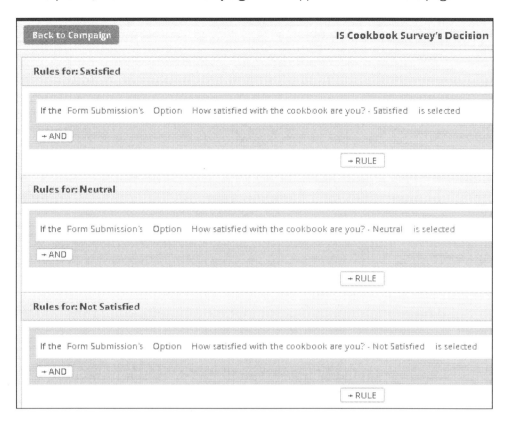

19. Double-click into the **Satisfied** sequence. Add one e-mail step and rename accordingly:

20. Double-click into the e-mail step and write a message thanking the customer for their feedback and asking for a testimonial as shown in the following image:

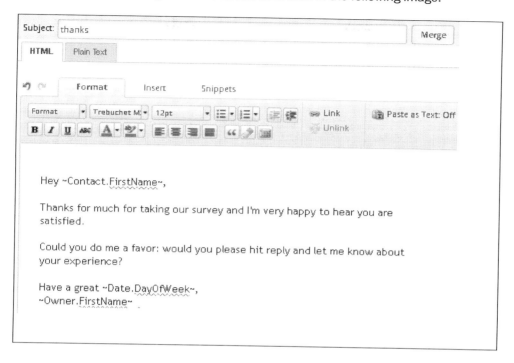

21. In the upper-right corner of the page, click on **Draft** to mark the e-mail as **Ready**; in the upper-left corner of the page, click on **Back to Sequence**.

22. In the upper-right corner of the page, click on **Draft** to mark the sequence as **Ready**.

23. Click on **Back to Campaign** and then double-click into the **Neutral** sequence.

24. Add one e-mail step and rename accordingly:

25. Double-click into the e-mail step and write a message thanking the customer for their feedback and asking what could have been done better:

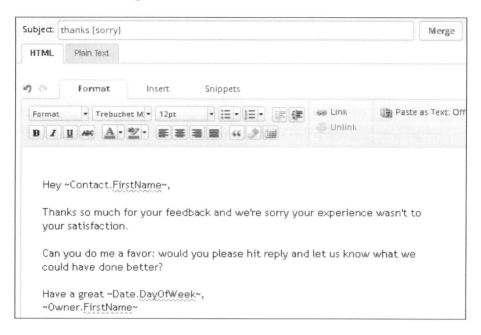

26. In the upper-right corner of the page, click on **Draft** to mark the e-mail as **Ready**; in the upper-left corner of the page, click on **Back to Sequence**.

27. In the upper-right corner of the page, click on **Draft** to mark the sequence as **Ready**.

28. Click on **Back to Campaign** and then double-click into the **Not Satisfied** sequence.

29. Add one **Task** step and rename accordingly:

30. Double-click into the task and configure for an outbound customer call to make things right:

31. In the upper-right corner of the page, click on **Draft** to mark the task as **Ready**; in the upper-left corner of the page, click on **Back to Sequence**.

32. In the upper-right side of the page, click on **Draft** to mark the sequence as **Ready**.

33. In the upper-left side of the page, click on **Back to Campaign** and publish the campaign.

How it works...

When a customer clicks through to the web form from an e-mail, their e-mail address will prepopulate in the hidden field, so when they submit their feedback, Infusionsoft knows who is submitting the form. If they are satisfied, we automatically ask for a testimonial. If they are neutral, we automatically inquire into what wasn't working. If they are not satisfied, someone is tasked with contacting the customer to make things right.

There's more...

We can easily drive traffic from other campaign e-mails to this survey using **Hosted web form** links:

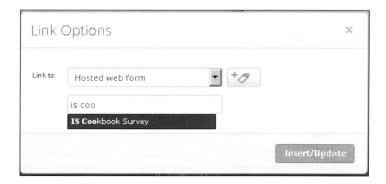

We can add-on an invite sequence that is triggered via tag to standardize how surveys are administered. This makes it easy to request a survey from any campaign; just apply the functional tag when it is time to ask for feedback:

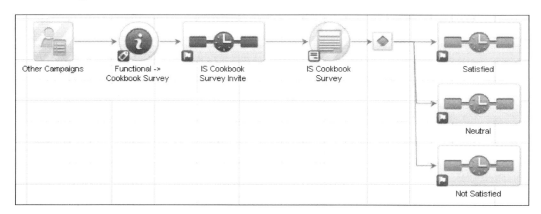

We can also use a full landing page instead of a web form for a richer survey experience.

Rather than providing a dead end, use the momentum from a form submission to drive customers somewhere on the thank you page:

For a more human experience, add a **Delay Timer** before any of the automated e-mails:

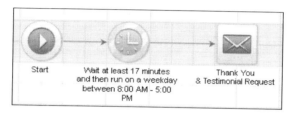

The logo shown in the preceding example is one of the select special characters supported by the form builder. They can be accessed from the **Insert** tab at the top of the toolbar.

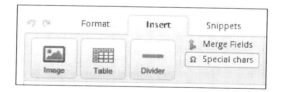

Add an internal form after the **Not Satisfied** sequence to track the resolution of unsatisfied customers:

We may choose to add tags for their current satisfaction status. Tagging can create more robust automation experiences by providing an opportunity for campaign switching using decision nodes looking for certain tags. However, if the satisfaction-level tagging is only being done for reporting, we can keep the database lean and use campaign reporting instead:

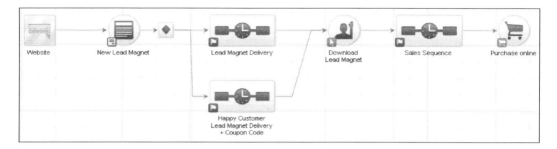

We can add a general survey link into the footer of our standard customer e-mail template to create a steady stream of feedback over time.

Asking for testimonials automatically

Social proof is one of the most persuasive tools for marketing. When potential customers can read about another customer's experience in their own words, it greatly increases trust in our products or services.

Having a system to automatically ask for testimonials can provide us with a steady stream of social proof that can be used throughout our marketing efforts.

Getting ready

We need to be logged in to Infusionsoft, inside a specific account and in a new campaign. In addition to this, we also want to have a functional tag created to trigger the testimonial request.

How to do it...

1. Drag out a tag goal, a web form goal, and one sequence; connect and rename them accordingly:

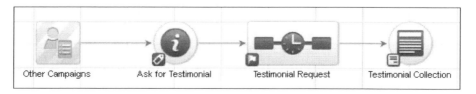

2. Double-click on the web form goal.

3. Delete all visible fields.

4. Add a **Hidden** field snippet.

5. Configure it for the **Email** field. Make sure that the value is left empty and click on **Save**.

6. Add a **Logo** snippet and a **Title** snippet; update the **Title** snippet text with customer instructions:

7. Using the **Field Snippets** tab, add an **Other** snippet.

8. Using the **Which Field** dropdown, scroll to the bottom and select **Append to Person Notes**:

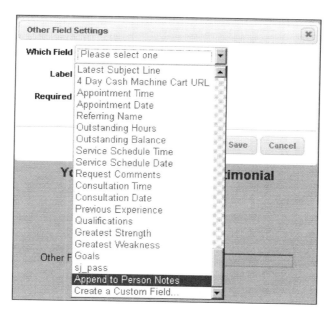

9. Change the label to read **Write your testimonial**, mark the field as **Required** and click on **Save**:

10. Click on the **Submit** button to edit the call to action.

11. Change the button label and set the alignment to **Center**; click on **Save**:

12. Click on the **Thank-you Page** tab at the top of the page.

13. Configure the page with a friendly thank you message:

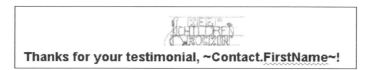

14. Click on the **Settings** tab at the top of the page and make sure that the **Auto-populate** has its option selected.

15. In the upper-right corner of the page, click on **Draft** to mark the web form as **Ready** and then in the upper-left corner of the page, click on **Back to Campaign**.

16. Publish the campaign so the **Testimonial Collection** form is live. After it has published, in the upper-left side of the page, click on the **Edit** tab.

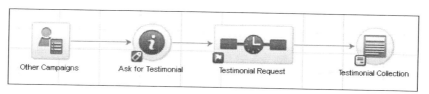

17. Double-click on the tag goal and configure it for the functional tag that will start the campaign; click on **Save**:

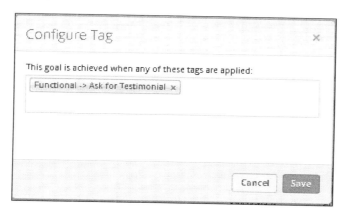

18. Double-click into the **Testimonial Request** sequence. Add two e-mail steps, a **Delay Timer** and rename accordingly:

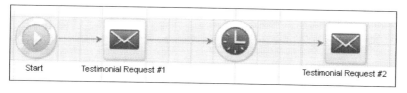

19. Double-click into the first e-mail step and write a message thanking the customer and asking for a testimonial:

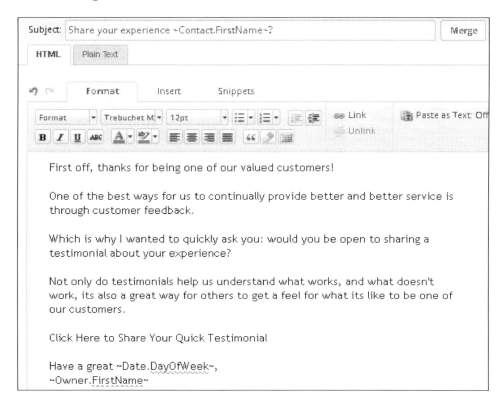

20. Highlight the call to action and click on the **Link** button at the top of the toolbar:

21. Using the **Link To:** dropdown, select **Hosted web form**:

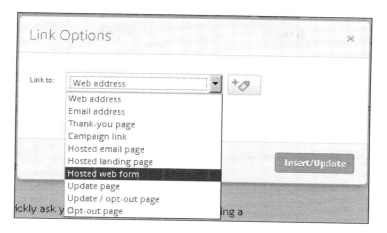

22. Place your cursor in the field that appears below and begin typing the name of the testimonial form.

23. Click on the name of the form, and click on **Insert/Update**:

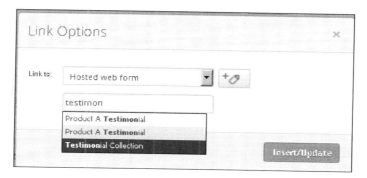

24. In the upper-right corner of the page, click on **Draft** to mark the e-mail as **Ready**; in the upper-left corner of the page, click on **Back to Sequence**.

25. Double-click on the **Delay Timer** and configure it to wait 7 days and then send on any day at 8 AM; click on **Save**:

26. Double-click into the second e-mail step and write a message thanking the customer and asking for a testimonial again:

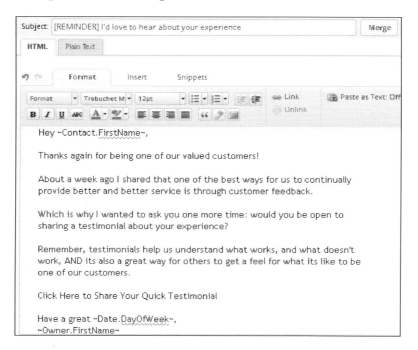

27. Highlight the call to action, and click on the **Link** button at the top of the toolbar:

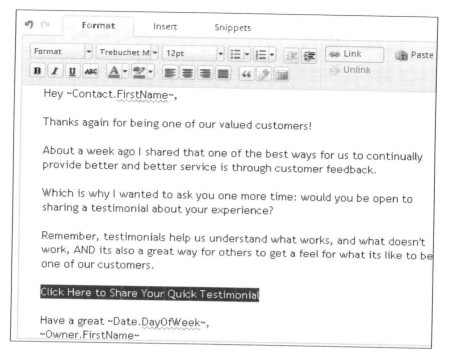

28. Using the **Link To:** dropdown, select **Hosted web form**.

29. Place your cursor in the field that appears below and begin typing the name of the testimonial form.

30. Click on the name of the form and click on **Insert/Update**.

31. In the upper-right corner of the page, click on **Draft** to mark the e-mail as **Ready**; in the upper-left corner of the page, click on **Back to Sequence**.

32. In the upper-right corner of the page, click **Draft** to mark the sequence as **Ready**.

33. In the upper-left corner of the page, click on **Back to Campaign** and publish the campaign.

How it works...

When another campaign applies the functional starting tag, the customer receives two e-mails asking for a testimonial. If someone provides a testimonial from the first e-mail, the second request e-mail will not be delivered.

There's more...

We can use a custom **Text Area** field, which provides a larger space to write:

Include a checkbox, so people can opt-out of having their testimonial published:

Use this checkbox to segment which testimonials are okay to use in your marketing and follow up accordingly:

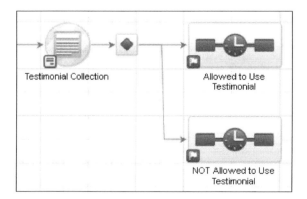

We can also use a full landing page instead of a web form for a richer testimonial collection experience.

Rather than provide a dead end, use the momentum from a form submission to drive customers somewhere on the thank you page:

Out of the box, this recipe will only ask for a testimonial once unless the functional tag is automatically removed. This automated removal means another campaign could trigger the sequence again in the future.

Setting up a birthday collection mechanism

When we have a person's birthday on file, it enables us to build goodwill by providing timely birthday messages. Combined with other data it can be used to provide a more targeted experience. For example, if we have the birthday of someone who is not yet a customer, we might send them a birthday discount in an attempt to get that first purchase.

Getting ready

We need to be logged in to Infusionsoft, inside a specific account and in a new campaign. In addition to this, we also want to have a functional tag created to trigger the birthday collection and another tag to track people with a birthday on file.

How to do it...

1. Drag out a tag goal, a web form goal, and two sequences; connect and rename accordingly:

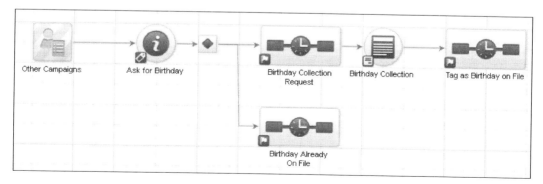

2. In the lower-left corner of the web form, double-click on the purple *goal* icon.

3. Configure the goal to be achieved by any contact and click on **Save**:

4. Double-click on the web form goal.

5. Delete all visible fields.

6. Add a **Hidden** field snippet.

7. Configure it for the **Email** field. Make sure that the value is left empty and click on **Save**.

8. Add a **Logo** snippet and a **Title** snippet; update the **Title** snippet text with instructions:

9. Using the **Field Snippets** tab, add an **Other** snippet.

10. Using the **Which Field** dropdown, select **Birthday**, mark the field as **Required**, and click on **Save**:

11. Add a **Paragraph** snippet beneath the **Birthday** field and provide formatting instructions.

12. Click on the **Submit** button to edit the call to action.

13. Change the button label and set the alignment to **Center**; click on **Save**:

14. Click on the **Thank-you Page** tab at the top of the page.

15. Configure the page with a friendly thank you message:

16. Click on the **Settings** tab at the top of the page and make sure that the **Auto-populate** has its option selected.

17. In the upper-right corner of the page, click on **Draft** to mark the web form as **Ready** and then in the upper-left corner of the page, click on **Back to Campaign**.

18. Double-click into the **tag as birthday on file** sequence.

19. Add a new **Tag** step.

20. Double-click on the **Tag** step and configure it to add the **Birthday on File** tag; click on **Save**:

21. In the upper-right corner of the page, click on **Draft** to mark the sequence as **Ready** and then in the upper-left corner of the page, click on **Back to Campaign**.

22. Publish the campaign, so the *Birthday Collection* form and tagging sequence are live. After it has been published, in the upper-left corner of the page, click on the **Edit** tab:

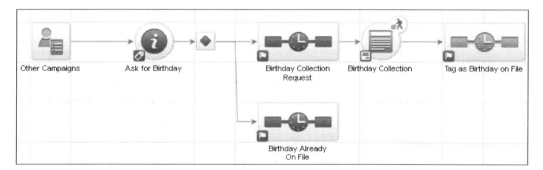

23. Double-click on the tag goal and configure it for the functional tag, which will start the campaign; click on **Save**:

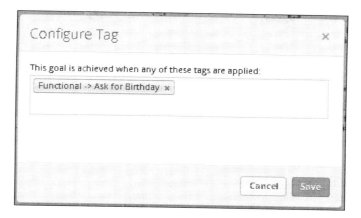

24. Double-click on **Decision Diamond** to configure the rules.

25. In the **Rules for: Birthday Collection Request** section, click on the **+ RULE** button to add a new rule as follows:

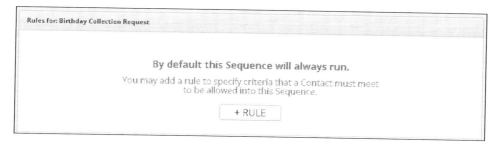

26. Configure a rule for **If the Contact's Tags doesn't contain** the **Birthday on File** tag:

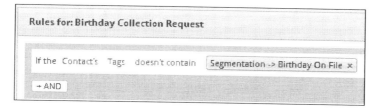

27. In the **Rules for: Birthday Already on the File** section, click on the **+ RULE** button to add a new rule.

28. Configure a rule for **If the Contact's Tags Contains** the **Birthday on File** tag; click on **Back to Campaign**.

29. Double-click into the **Birthday Collection Request** sequence. Add two e-mail steps, a **Start Timer**, an **Add/Remove Tag** step, and a **Delay Timer**; connect and rename accordingly:

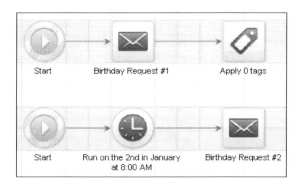

30. Double-click into the first e-mail step and write a message asking for their birthday:

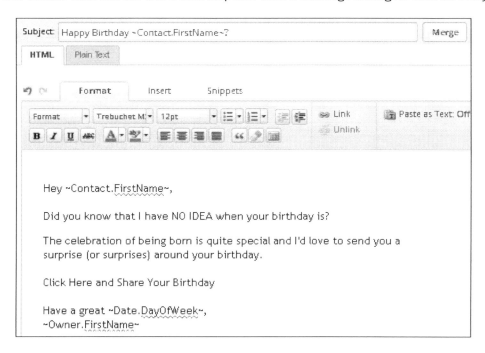

31. Highlight the call to action and click on the **Link** button at the top of the toolbar:

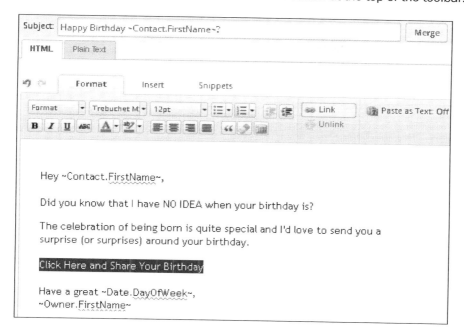

32. Using the **Link To:** dropdown, select **Hosted web form**:

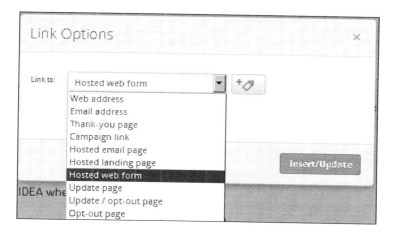

33. Place your cursor in the field that appears below and begin typing the name of the *Birthday Collection* form.

34. Click on the name of the form and click on **Insert/Update**:

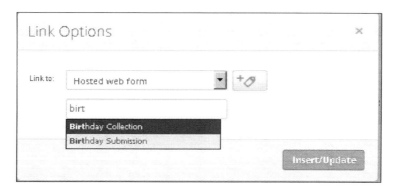

35. In the upper-right corner of the page click on **Draft** to mark the e-mail as **Ready**; in the upper-left corner of the page, click on **Back to Sequence**.

36. Double-click on the **Add/Remove Tag** step and configure to remove the functional tag; click on **Save**:

37. Double-click on the **Delay Timer** and configure it to not wait, then run on January 2 at 8 AM; click on **Save**:

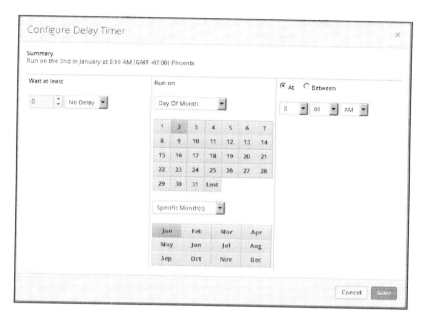

38. Double-click into the second e-mail step and write a message wishing them a wonderful new year and asking for their birthday again:

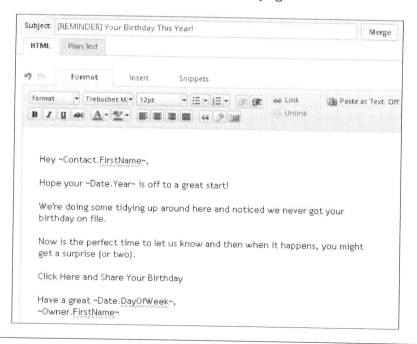

39. Highlight the call to action and click on the **Link** button at the top of the toolbar:

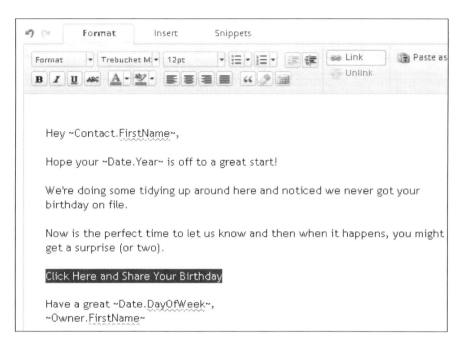

40. Using the **Link To:** dropdown, select **Hosted web form**:

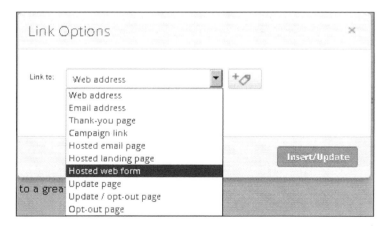

41. Place your cursor in the field that appears below and begin typing the name of the birthday collection form.

42. Click on the name of the form and click on **Insert/Update**:

43. In the upper-right corner of the page, click on **Draft** to mark the e-mail as **Ready**; in the upper-left corner of the page, click on **Back to Sequence**.

44. In the upper-right corner of the page, click on **Draft** to mark the sequence as **Ready**:

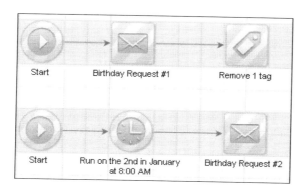

45. In the upper-left side of the page, click on **Back to Campaign**.

46. Double-click into the **Birthday Already On File** sequence.

47. Drag out a new **Add/Remove Tag** step:

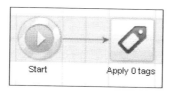

48. Double-click on the **Add/Remove Tag** step and configure to remove the functional tag; click on **Save**.

49. In the upper-right side of the page, click on **Draft** to mark the sequence as **Ready**.

50. In the upper-left side of the page, click on **Back to Campaign** and publish the campaign.

How it works...

When another campaign applies the functional starting tag and a birthday isn't on file, the customer receives two e-mails asking for their birthday. If they haven't provided their birthday by the beginning of the New Year, at the start of the next year, they receive a reminder to share it. When someone does provide their birthday, they are tagged accordingly, so this data can be leveraged to segment in other areas, such as a campaign or a report.

There's more...

We can also use a full landing page instead of a web form for a richer birthday collection experience.

Rather than providing a dead end, use the momentum from a form submission to drive customers somewhere on the thank you page:

Ok ~Contact.FirstName~! Forget you did this and enjoy any surprises that might come your way :)

Click here to find out about personal 1-on-1 consulting

See also

▶ For a recipe that schedules an automated birthday e-mail, see the next recipe *Building automated Happy Birthday messages*

▶ For a similar campaign, see the **Birthday Collection** campaign in the free Marketplace

Building automated Happy Birthday messages

Once we have someone's birthday on the file, it is very easy to schedule an automated message around their birthday each year.

For this recipe, we are going to build a mechanism that schedules an automated birthday e-mail annually.

Getting ready

We need to be logged in to Infusionsoft, inside a specific account and in a new campaign. In addition to this, we also want to have a functional tag that will be used to schedule an annual message.

How to do it...

1. Drag out two tag goals, a note template goal, and a sequence; connect and rename accordingly:

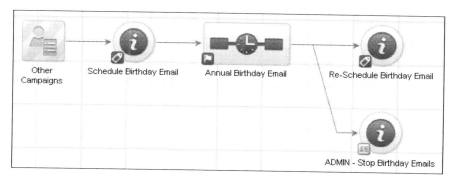

2. Double-click on the first tag goal and configure it for the functional tag, which will start the campaign; click on **Save**:

3. In the lower-left corner of the second tag goal, double-click on the small purple icon:

4. Configure the goal to be achieved by **Any Contact**; click on **Save**:

5. Double-click on the second tag goal and configure it for the same functional tag as the first tag goal; click on **Save**:

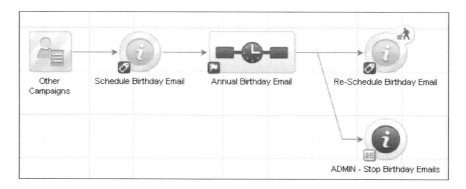

6. Double-click into the **Annual Birthday Email** sequence.

7. Add a two **Field Timers**, two **Tag** steps, and an **Email** step; connect and rename accordingly:

8. Double-click on the first **Field Timer** and configure it to wait until the contact's **Birthday** and then run at 8 AM; click on **Save**:

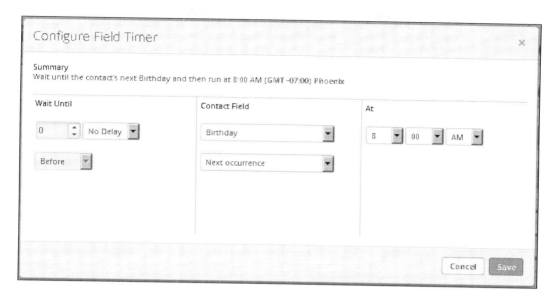

9. Double-click into the first **Tag** step and configure it to remove the functional tag; click on **Save**:

10. Double-click into the e-mail step and write a message wishing them a happy birthday:

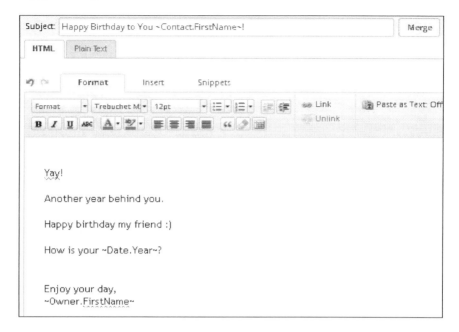

11. In the upper-right corner of the page, click on **Draft** to mark the e-mail as **Ready**; in the upper-left corner of the page, click on **Back to Sequence**.

12. Double-click on the second **Field Timer** and configure it to wait until one day after the contact's **Birthday** and then run at 12 AM; click on **Save**:

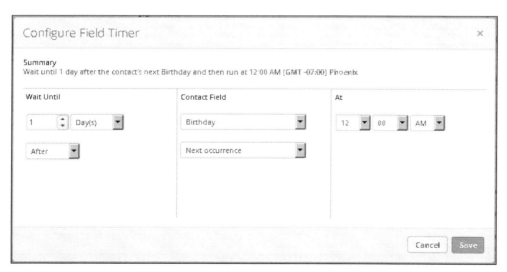

13. Double-click into the second **Tag** step and configure it to apply the functional tag; click on **Save**:

14. In the upper-right corner of the page, click on **Draft** to mark the sequence as ready:

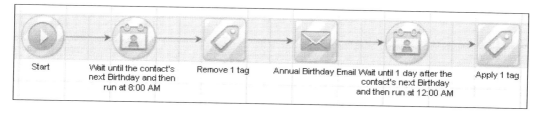

15. In the upper-left side of the page, click on **Back to Campaign**.

16. Double-click on the note template goal and configure with appropriate context; click on **Save**:

17. Publish the campaign.

How it works...

When another campaign applies the functional tag, the person will receive an e-mail on the morning of their birthday every year. At any point, a user may apply the note template to cancel any scheduled birthday messages.

There's more...

The removal and reapplication of the functional tag fires both tag goals at the same time. However, due to the mechanics of the builder, the second tag goal will trigger the first tag goal (the stopping goal), which will take them out of the sequence as **Done**. Next, the first goal will trigger (the start goal) and, since they are **Done** with the sequence, they will re-enter and thus be scheduled for next year's birthday e-mails.

We reapply the tag one day later. Otherwise, if we tried in the same day, the sequence steps would be skipped because the "next birthday" would be in the past and the loop would only run once.

This recipe can be an easy extension to the previous birthday collection recipe. Simply apply the birthday schedule tag in the post web form sequence:

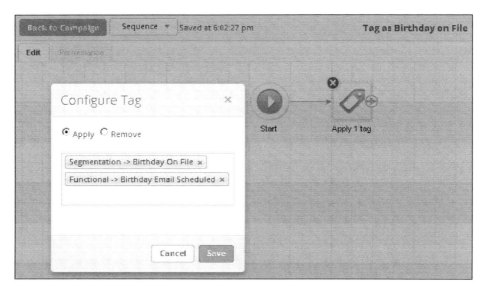

To create a more unique experience, do birthday promotions at odd times. For example, we can do a low-cost half-birthday gift:

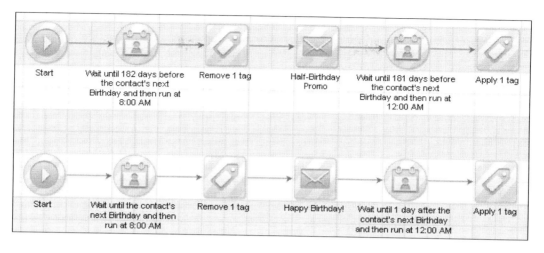

Use the last purchase tags for a highly targeted birthday e-mail experience:

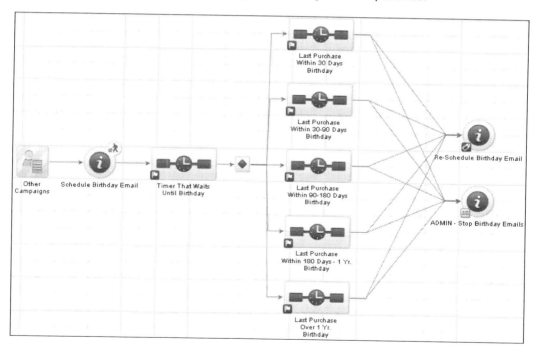

We can also choose to remove the functional tag if a user applies the note template; just add a sequence after it and remove the tag. This recipe leaves the tag on to prevent other campaigns from adding them again in the future. A **tag apply** step will not fire a tag goal if the contact already has the functional. Removing the functional tag creates the possibility that someone will be re-added to the birthday e-mails after we manually stopped them.

See also

- For a recipe that collects birthdays from your database, see the previous recipe *Setting up a birthday collection mechanism*

- For a similar campaign, see the **Birthday Reminders** campaign in the free Marketplace

- For a recipe that segments the database by last purchased, see the first recipe in this chapter *Segmenting by last purchase date*

7

Wowing Existing Customers with Great Experiences

In this chapter, we will cover the following:

- ▶ Updating a soon-to-be-expired credit card automatically
- ▶ Re-engaging inactive e-mails in your database
- ▶ Building a Vaynerchuk opt-out
- ▶ Setting up a basic referral partner program
- ▶ Building a referral partner sign-up form

Introduction

This chapter concerns itself with different tactics to *Wow* your existing customers.

There are two main reasons you want to completely to blow your existing customers socks off. First, it is much cheaper to make another sale to an existing customer compared with acquiring a brand new customer. Second, and similarly related, is that customers tell their friends about your customer experience no matter what. Their experience will come into conversation organically at some point in their life. You might as well do your best to ensure that when they inevitably talk to their friends, they only have the finest things to say about your business.

Updating a soon-to-be-expired credit card automatically

Collecting overdue payments can be expensive and time consuming. An innocent reason for the card on file to fail is simply that it has expired. By automatically giving customers the opportunity to update a card, we can provide a better customer experience and lower operating costs.

This recipe is primarily intended for companies that sell using subscriptions or payment plans.

Getting ready

We need to be logged in to Infusionsoft and inside a specific account.

How to do it...

1. In the upper-left corner of the page, hover over the navigation and in the **E-Commerce** column, click on **Settings**:

2. In the **Order Settings** menu on the left, click on **Billing Automation**:

3. Using the **Choose Trigger Type** dropdown, select **When a credit card is going to expire** and click on **Add Trigger** to open a pop-up window, as shown in the following image:

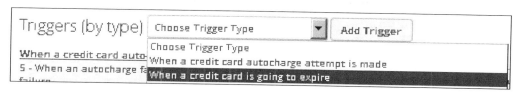

4. In the **Set Trigger Criteria** area, configure for the following:

   ❑ Card type: **Any Type**

   ❑ Card expires in: 30 days

   ❑ Set radio button to **No**

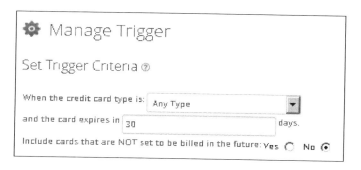

5. In the following **Actions** section, using the **Add New Action** dropdown, select **Send an email, fax, etc.:**

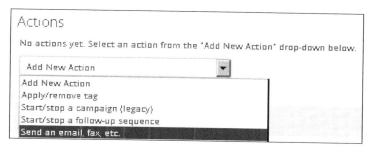

6. Using the **Please select an activity** menu that appears, select **Email**:

7. To the right of the dropdown fields, click on **Add** to open another popup as follows:

8. Give the new e-mail a title and configure the **From**, **To**, and **Subject** fields. Credit card merge fields are available in the **Merge** menu:

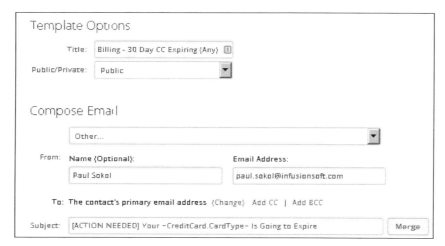

9. Beneath the subject line, click on **Edit Email Body**.

10. We can access the **Merge** menu using the **Insert** tab:

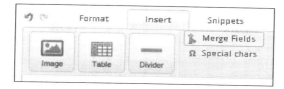

11. Write an e-mail notifying the customer that their card is about to expire and include the **Plain Text Update Link** merge field:

> Hello ~Contact.FirstName~,
>
> Sorry for the harsh subject line, but your ~CreditCard.CardType~ ending in ~CreditCard.Last4~ is going to expire soon.
>
> To prevent any headaches, if you could please take a minute right now to update the card on file, that would really help me out :)
>
> ~CreditCard.PlainTextUpdateLink~
>
> Have a great ~Date.DayOfWeek~,
> Paul

12. In the upper-left corner of the page, click on the **Save** icon and then click on **Close Builder** to close the window.

13. Scroll down to the bottom of the **Manage Email Template** window and click on **No** to mark the e-mail as **Yes** (ready to send); click on the green **Save** button to close the window:

14. Click on the green **Save** button under the **Actions** menu:

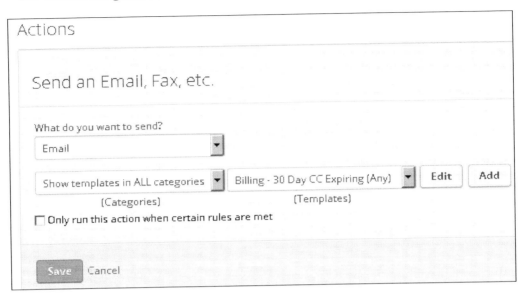

15. Click on the **Save Trigger** button under the actions:

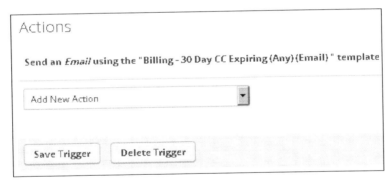

How it works...

When a customer has a card on file that is scheduled to be billed in the future, 30 days before that card's expiration an e-mail will be sent. The update link in the e-mail allows the customer to update the credit card record on their own and prevent automated billing interruptions.

There's more...

Credit card merge fields are available because we are editing an e-mail within the context of a credit card expiring trigger:

The billing trigger considers the card's official expiration date as the first day of the following month after expiration. For example, if a card expires in January 2015, and the trigger is set for 7 days, it will be delivered 7 days before February 1st.

We can also apply a tag in the expiration trigger to trigger a campaign:

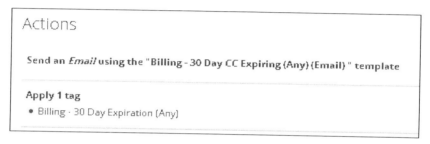

Since billing triggers deal with e-commerce experiences, Infusionsoft knows which credit card record it should be pointing to through the update link. However, the campaign builder is not able to discern which credit card record caused the tag to be applied. This means the update links will fail if manually typed into a campaign builder e-mail; any follow-up should be using other channels:

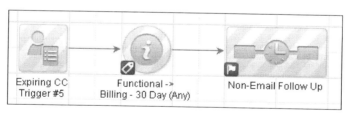

There are some esoteric yet very powerful automation triggers available to track update e-mail interactions. In the **E-Commerce** settings, under the **Order Settings** menu, there is an **Orders** section:

Just above the **Notifications** section midway through the page, we have an automation trigger for when someone clicks on an update link and when someone successfully updates their card:

If we configure those triggers to apply a tag, we can automatically control card expiration campaigns:

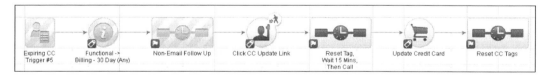

We can create a follow-up sequence using more than one billing trigger or tag. In this case, we want to make sure to remove any functional tags immediately, so the campaign will always fire for any expiring card:

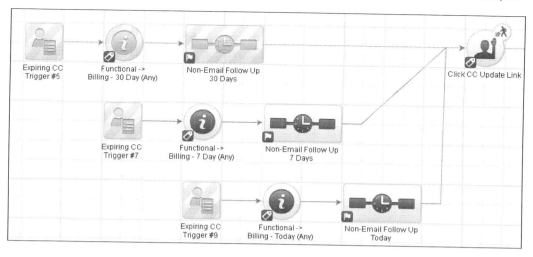

See also

For a recipe that leverages other billing trigger types, see the *Collecting failed automated billing attempts* recipe in *Chapter 4, Selling Products Online and Getting Paid*.

Re-engaging inactive e-mails in your database

Just as a gardener is used to trimming away leaves from their flowers, list attrition is part of the e-mail marketing game. There are lots of people that say, *The money is in the list.* While this is partially true, the money is actually in the relationship with the list.

When we are talking about an e-mail list, especially if that is the main communication channel, it is critical to regularly find inactive e-mail addresses and attempt to get them engaging again.

This is important for two reasons. First, it obviously helps the bottom line to have an active e-mail list. Second, it helps with inbox placement with the major ISPs. Spam filters are getting more advanced and when lots of e-mails are sent but never opened or clicked (among other things), it can cause a high junk folder placement.

For the context of this recipe, we are targeting people on the general newsletter list who haven't clicked anything in the past 120 days.

Getting ready

We need to be logged in to Infusionsoft, inside a specific account, and in a new campaign. We also need to have a functional tag created to trigger the re-engagement; we are also assuming a tag for the newsletter segment of the database exists.

How to do it...

1. Drag out a tag goal, a link click goal, and three sequences. Connect and rename accordingly The decision node will appear after connecting the form to the second sequence:

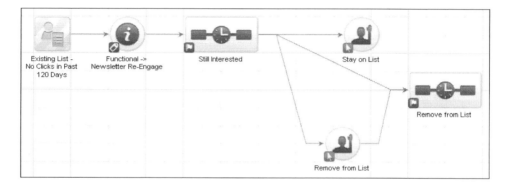

2. Double-click on the tag goal.
3. Configure it for the functional tag and click on **Save**:

4. Double-click into the **Still Interested** sequence.
5. Add a tag step, three **Email** steps, and three **Delay Timers**. Connect and rename them accordingly:

6. Double-click into the **Tag** step and configure it to remove the functional tag. Click on **Save**:

7. Double-click into the first e-mail step and write a message thanking the person for being on the newsletter, addressing their lack of activity and then asking them to indicate if they want to continue or not:

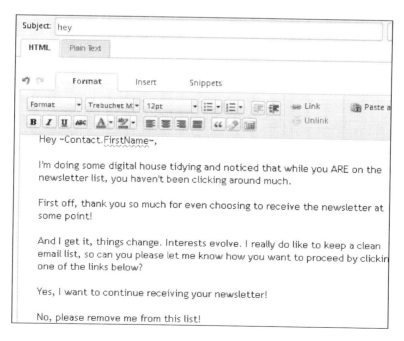

8. Highlight the first response option and click on **Link**:

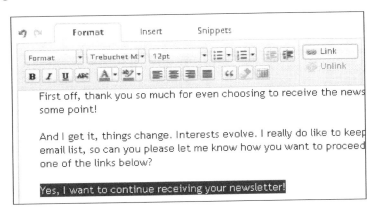

9. Using the **Link to:** dropdown, select **Thank-you Page**. Click on the **Edit Thank-you Page** link that appears to open a pop-up window:

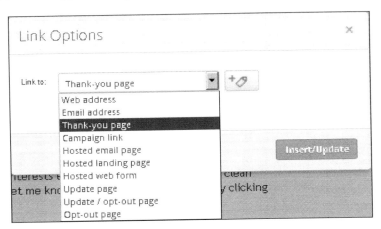

10. Write a friendly message thanking the person in order to choose to stay on the newsletter; click on **Save & Close** at the bottom of the page to close the window:

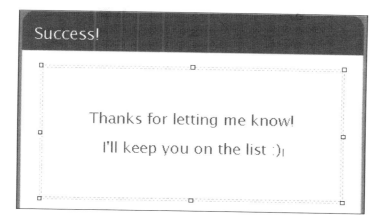

11. In the **Link Options** menu, click on the green **Insert & Save** button.

12. Repeat steps 8 to 11 for the second response option:

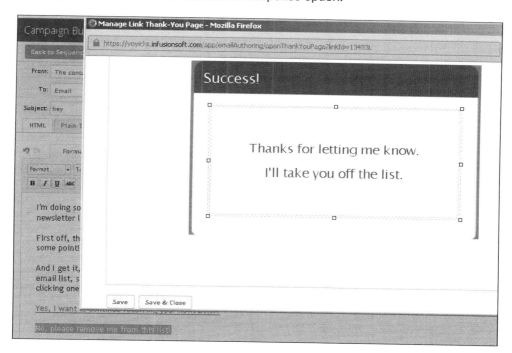

13. In the upper-right corner of the page, click on **Draft** to mark the e-mail as **Ready**; in the upper-left corner of the page, click on **Back to Sequence**.

14. Double-click on the first **Delay Timer** and configure it to wait one week and then run on a weekday at 8 AM. Click on **Save**:

15. Double-click into the second e-mail step and write a message thanking the person for being on the newsletter, addressing their lack of activity again, and asking them to indicate if they want to continue or not. We also need to configure the two thank-you page links, as we did in steps 8 to 12:

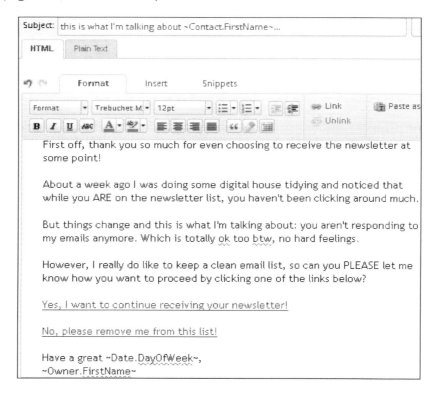

16. In the upper-right corner of the page, click on **Draft** to mark the e-mail as **Ready**; in the upper-left corner of the page, click on **Back to Sequence**.

17. Double-click on the second **Delay Timer** and configure it to wait one week and then run on a weekday at 4 PM; click on **Save**:

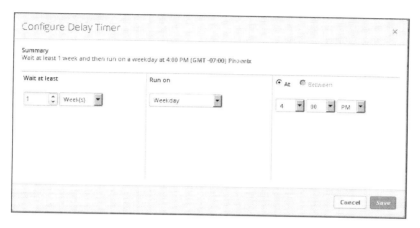

18. Double-click into the third e-mail step and write a message addressing their lack of activity again, alerting them that we will automatically remove them and then asking them one last time to indicate if they want to continue or not. We also need to configure the two thank-you page links, as we did in steps 8 to 12:

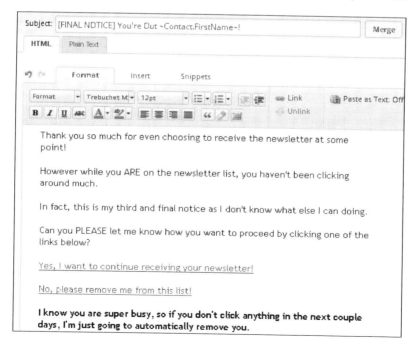

19. In the upper-right corner of the page, click on **Draft** to mark the e-mail as **Ready**; in the upper-left corner of the page, click on **Back to Sequence**.

20. Double-click on the third **Delay Timer** and configure it to wait 3 days and then run on a weekday at 8 AM; click on **Save**:

21. In the upper-right corner of the page, click on **Draft** to mark the sequence as **Ready**.

22. In the upper-left corner of the page, click on **Back to Campaign**.

23. Double-click on the **Stay on List** goal.

24. Using the list of e-mails on the left, click into each e-mail and select the appropriate links in each e-mail; click on **Back to Campaign**:

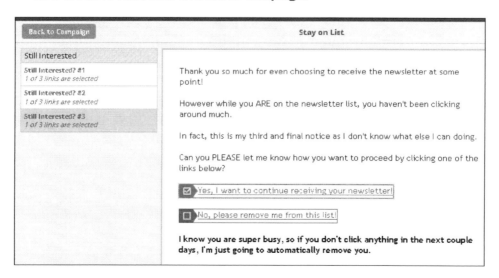

25. Double-click on the **Remove from List** goal.

26. Using the list of e-mails on the left, click into each e-mail and select the appropriate links in each e-mail; click **Back to Campaign**:

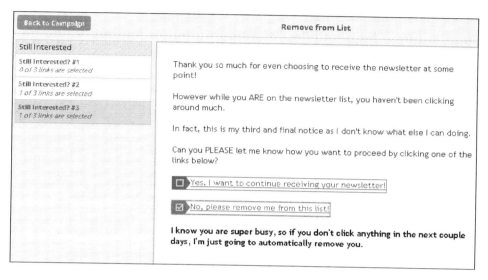

27. Double-click into the **Remove from List** sequence.

28. Add a new **Tag** step:

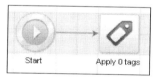

29. Double-click on the **Tag** step and configure it to remove the newsletter tag; click on **Save**:

30. In the upper-right corner of the page, click on **Draft** to mark the sequence as **Ready**.

31. In the upper-left corner of the page, click on **Back to Campaign** and publish the campaign.

How it works...

When the functional tag is applied to a contact, they are added into a three e-mail re-engagement campaigns that run over 3 weeks. If they never click on anything, at the end of those 3 weeks, they will automatically have the newsletter tag removed. If they click on any of the options, they will immediately stop receiving those e-mails.

There's more...

This campaign can be run manually by a user for a group of contacts periodically, or it can be used in conjunction with other campaigns that are timing inbox engagement.

If possible, we would want to segment out prospects from customers and deliver a slightly different message to each group:

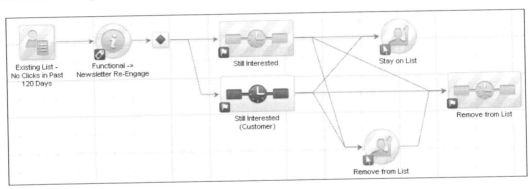

See also

For a similar campaign model, download the **Clean Your Contact List** campaign from the Infusionsoft Marketplace.

Building a Vaynerchuk opt-out

The strategy behind this recipe was inspired by a gentleman named Gary Vaynerchuk; hence, his name is used.

His idea was, after people have opted out from e-mails, to call them on the phone, apologize, and listen. This kind of experience, when done properly, can actually have people ask to re-join the list.

It is very easy to build a mechanism like this using Infusionsoft.

Getting ready

We need to be logged in to Infusionsoft and inside a specific account.

How to do it...

1. In the upper-left corner of the page, hover over the navigation, and in the **Marketing** column, click on **Settings**:

My Nav	CRM	Marketing	E-Commerce	Admin
Contacts	Contacts	Campaign Builder	E-Commerce Setup	Branding Center
Campaign Builder	Companies	Email & Broadcasts	Orders	Infusionsoft Account
Email & Broadcasts	Opportunities	Lead Generation	Products	Users
Legacy	Referral Partners	Templates	Actions	Import Data
Templates	Visitors	Legacy	Promotions	Data Cleanup
Opportunities			Legacy	
Edit	Reports Settings	Reports <u>Settings</u>	Reports Settings	Reports Settings

2. In the **Template Settings** menu on the left, click on **Email Defaults**:

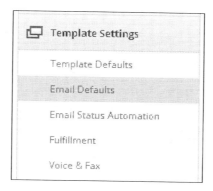

3.

3. In the **Email** section, next to the **When Someone Opts Out of All Email Marketing:** option, click on **Actions** to open a pop-up window, as shown in the following image:

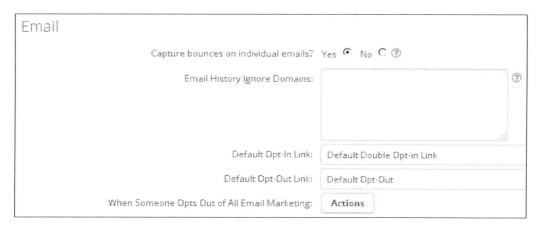

4. Using the **Add New Action** dropdown, select **Create a Task**:

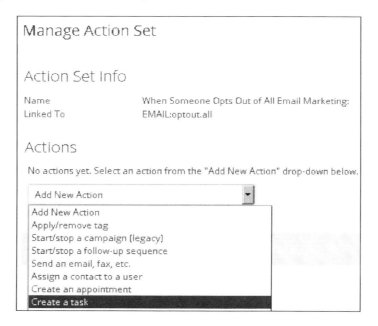

5. To the right of the dropdown fields, click on **Add** to open another popup:

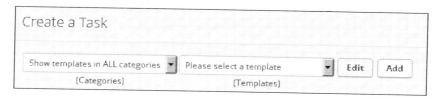

6. Give the new task a title:

7. Configure the task title and body to make a phone call to apologize for having them opt-out, listening, and seeing if anything can be done to make things better:

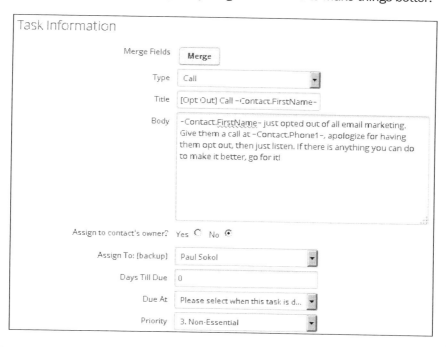

8. Scroll down to the bottom of the window and click on **No** to mark the task as **Yes** (ready to send); click on the green **Save** button to close this window:

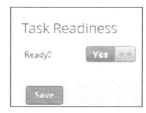

9. Check the box underneath the dropdown options to display the rules options:

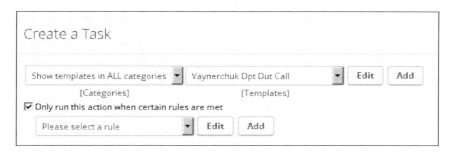

10. Click on the **Add** to the right of the **Please select a rule** dropdown; this will open a pop-up window.

11. Give the rule a name and click on **Create**:

12. In the **Rules Set Parameters** window using the dropdown, select **None**:

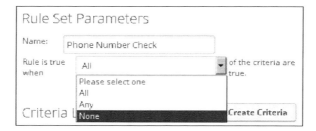

13. Click on the **Create Criteria** button.

14. Create a rule for the following:

    ❑ For the **Select Contact Field:** dropdown, select **Contact - phone & fax** and in the dropdown next to it, select **Phone 1 Number**

    ❑ For the **Criteria:** dropdown, select **Is Empty**

15. Click on **Save Criteria**.

16. Click on **Save & Close** to close the window:

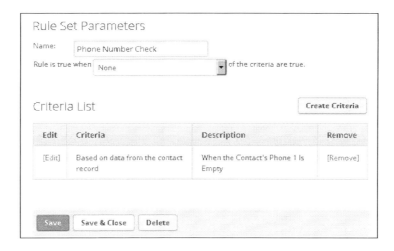

17. Click on the green **Save** button:

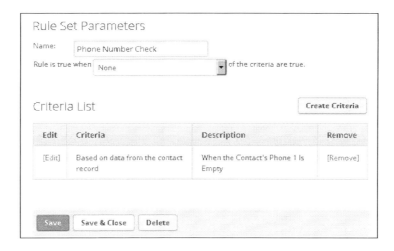

18. Click on the green **Save** button to save the automation trigger:

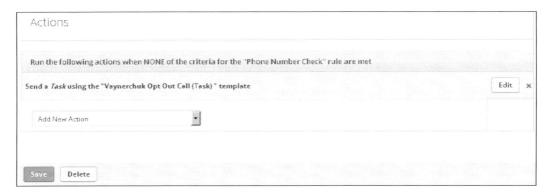

How it works...

When someone opts-out from the database entirely and they have a phone number on file, Infusionsoft will create a task for someone to call that person and find out what happened.

There's more...

We are using inverse logic to check for the presence of a phone number. In plain English, the rule says if there are *NO* empty fields, run the actions.

Take this experience to the next level by creating an internal form that users should complete after making the call. This can empower further segmentation based on the different outcomes, such as rejoining the list or provided valuable feedback.

Setting up a basic referral partner program

Infusionsoft has a built-in referral partner (affiliate) module on certain versions of the software. This makes it easy for a business to track who is referring whom. Also, if orders are being recorded inside Infusionsoft as well, it empowers the automatic calculation of commissions.

There are two components that must be set up before we start adding referral partners:

- ▶ **Commission program**: This is where we tell Infusionsoft how much to pay out for specific products and subscriptions
- ▶ **Referral tracking links**: This is where we can set up different URLs for our referral partners to promote

Getting ready

We need to be logged in to Infusionsoft and inside a specific account. For this recipe, we are also assuming the following:

▸ We already have a product created that we want to pay 50 percent commission on

▸ We have at least one URL that referral partners can drive traffic towards

How to do it...

1. In the upper-left corner of the page, hover over the navigation and in the **CRM** column, click on **Referral Partners**:

2. When the page loads, hover over **Referral Partners** in the menu and click on **Commission Programs**:

3. Towards the right of the page, click on the green **Add a Commission Program** button:

4. Give the commission program a name, notes, and click on the green **Save** button:

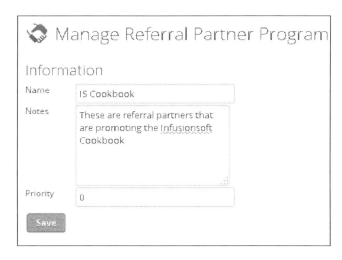

5. Scroll towards the bottom of the page and in the text field next to **Product Commissions**, type the product we need commissions for and select it when it appears; use the **Subscription Plan** section if we are paying commissions on a recurring product:

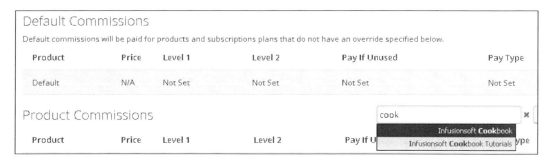

6. Click on the **Create Override** button next to the selected product:

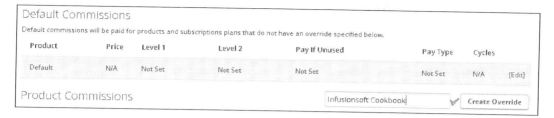

7. Using the **Payout Type** dropdown, select **Credit On Customer Payment**:

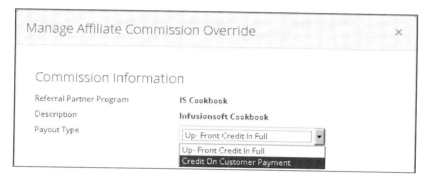

8. Set the **Level 1** sales commissions to 50 and click on the green **Save** button:

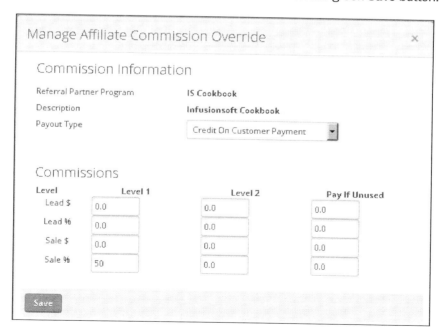

9. We should now see the new commission override listed; click on the green **Save** button:

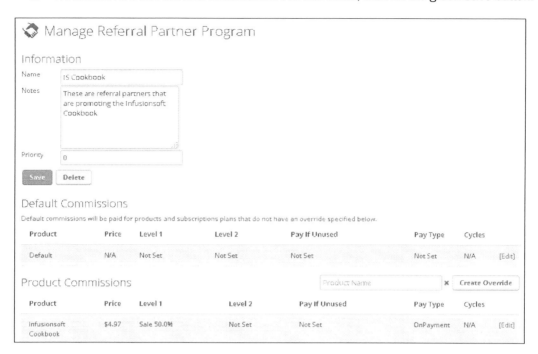

10. Hover over **Referral Partners** in the menu and click on **Referral Tracking Links**:

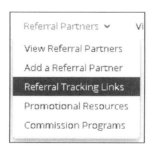

11. Towards the right of the page, click on the green **Add a Referral Tracking Link** button:

12. Give the link the following:

    ❑   A name; this will be visible to referral partners

    ❑   A short code

    ❑   The web address where referral traffic should redirect to

    ❑   Select the programs that can use this particular link

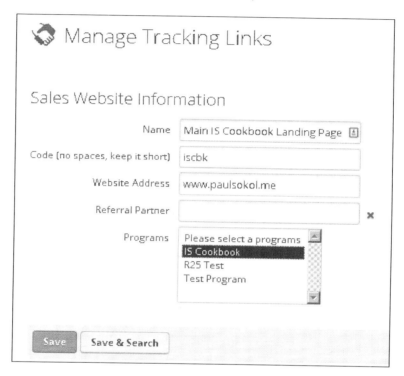

13. Click on the green **Save** button.

How it works...

When a referral partner is added to the IS Cookbook program, two things will happen. First, when they log in to the referral partner backend, they will be able to generate their own trackable link to the landing page provided. Second, if someone clicks through that link and eventually purchases through an order form or the shopping cart, the referral partner will receive commissions for that order.

There's more...

For most business models, we only want to pay a referral partner for traffic they provide towards a certain product (or family of products). There are certain instances where we would want to pay the referral partner for anything we sell to someone. In these cases, we can set the default commissions:

Certain products and subscriptions warrant a full commission payout even if there is a payment plan. For example, a high-priced consumer good that gets paid over 6 months. In these cases, we have an option when setting a commission override to award commission as soon as the order is created, regardless of when the actual payments arrive:

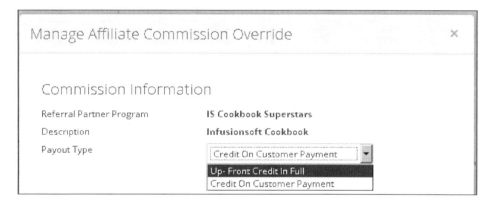

Since a referral partner can be in multiple commission programs, the priority helps determine the commissions when a referral partner is getting paid for the same product in two different programs. For example, if a referral partner receives 50percent of Widget A sales in one program, but 25 percent of Widget A sales in another program, the program with the highest priority is what gets paid out. In this case, the lower the priority number, the higher it is (that is, a program priority of 1 will pay out over a program priority of 3):

As a business grows its network of referral partners, it is entirely possible for someone to click through more than one partner's links. In this case, who gets the sale credit? The answer to this question is actually a **CRM** setting. Under the **Referral Partner Defaults** submenu, there is a dropdown where you can assign which referral partner gets credit in these situations:

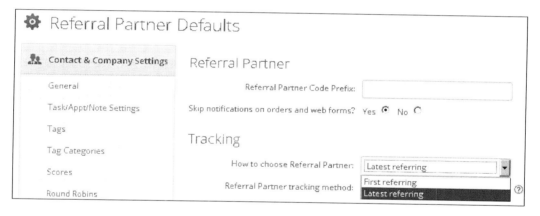

Just under this **First referring** and **Latest referring** setting, there is a setting that empowers an extra tab of information on the contact record:

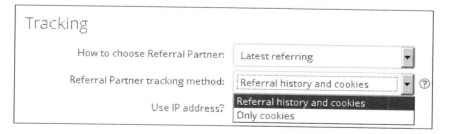

When we select **Referral history and cookies** and save the page, this adds another tab to the second row of the contact record:

Infusionsoft supports a nested referral partner network up to grandparent level. In other words, with three levels, if a referral partner can recruit another partner, and *THAT* partner gets someone under them too, the original partner can potentially receive commissions:

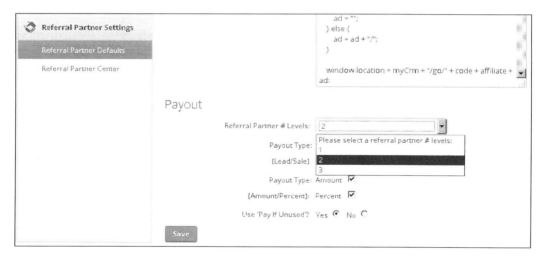

Promotional Resources are optional. If configured, they will display when the referral partner is logged in to the backend portal. This allows us to provide to our referral partners prewritten e-mails which can be used for promotions, banner ads, and pages inside the backend portal that can contain nearly anything. For example, we could create an e-mail template, a related banner ad and then create a page explaining how the referral partner should structure those resources for maximum effectiveness:

See also

For help creating a product or subscription, see the *Creating products and subscriptions* recipe early in *Chapter 4, Selling Products Online and Getting Paid*.

This recipe simply lays the groundwork for a referral partner program. While we can manually add referral partners, the next recipe, *Building a referral partner sign-up form*, allows people to add themselves to our programs and effectively automate the process.

Building a referral partner sign-up form

Once our referral partner commissions and links are set up, we can begin manually adding referral partners and sending them their login information.

However, we will save a bunch of time if we give people a web form where they can sign themselves up to be a referral partner.

Getting ready

We need to be logged in to Infusionsoft, inside a specific account, and in a new campaign. We are also assuming that a commission program has been created already.

How to do it...

1. Drag out a web form goal and a sequence; connect and rename accordingly:

2. Double-click on the web form goal.

3. Add a **Logo** snippet, a **Title** snippet, a **Paragraph** snippet, **Divider**, and another **Paragraph** snippet. Update the snippet text with instructions:

4. Using the **Field Snippets** tab, add required fields for:

    ❑ **First Name** and **Last Name**

    ❑ **Phone Number**

    ❑ **Email**

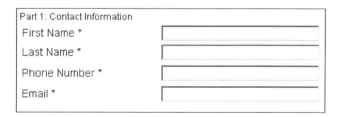

5. Add another **Divider**, a **Paragraph** snippet, and update the snippet text.

6. Using the **Field Snippets** tab, add in the required billing address fields:

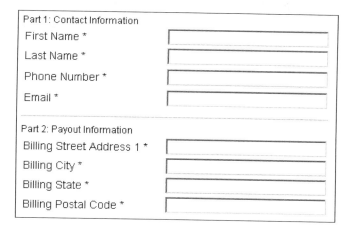

7. Add an another **Divider** and a **Paragraph** snippet; update the snippet text:

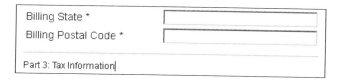

8. In the **Field Snippets** tab, add an **Other** snippet.

9. Using the **Which Field** dropdown, select **SSN**, update the label, and make it **Required**. Click on **Save**:

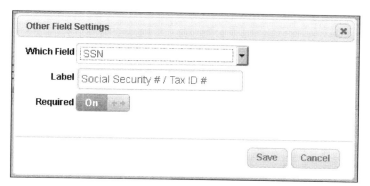

10. Add an another **Divider**, a **Paragraph** snippet, and update the snippet text:

11. Using the **Field Snippets** tab, add a **Partner** snippet.

12. Configure the **Referral Partner Settings** and click on **Save**:

   ❑ Adding to the proper commission program

   ❑ Set notification of **On New Lead** to **No**

   ❑ Set notification of **On Sale** to **No**

   ❑ Set **Referral Cookie Expires After** to 0 days

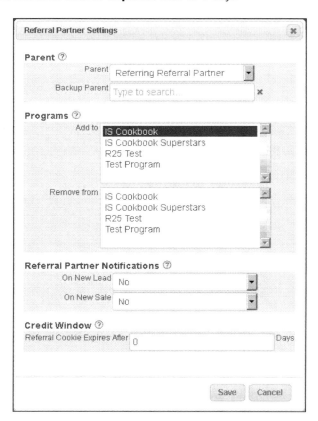

13. Click on the **Submit** button to edit the call to action.

14. Change the button label and set the alignment to **Center**. Click on **Save**:

15. Click on the **Thank-you Page** tab at the top of the page.

16. Configure the page with a friendly thank you message:

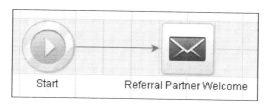

17. In the upper-right corner of the page, click on **Draft** to mark the web form as **Ready** and then in the upper-left corner of the page, click on **Back to Campaign**.

18. Double-click into the sequence and add one e-mail step. Connect and rename it accordingly:

19. Double-click into the e-mail step and write a message welcoming the new referral partner. Use the **Referral Partner** merge fields to merge in their code and password:

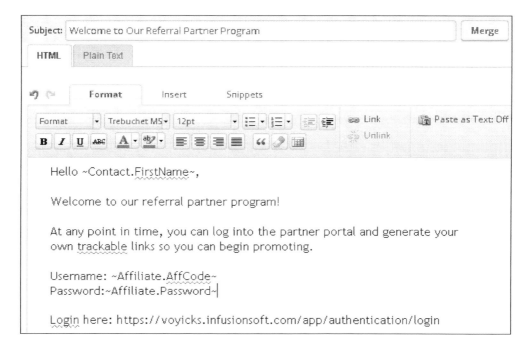

20. In the upper-right corner of the page, click on **Draft** to mark the e-mail as **Ready**; in the upper-left corner of the page, click on **Back to Sequence**.

21. In the upper-right corner of the page, click on **Draft** to mark the sequence as **Ready**.

22. In the upper-left corner of the page, click on **Back to Campaign** and publish the campaign.

How it works...

When someone signs up to be a referral partner through the web form, Infusionsoft creates a **Referral Partner** record and connects it to their contact record. When the system sends the welcome e-mail, it will merge in the information from this **Referral Partner** record.

There's more...

The login URL is the same for all Infusionsoft customers, we just have to make sure the subdomain is the correct app name.

The login URL is `https://APPNAME.infusionsoft.com/Affiliate/`.

We collect the social security or tax ID number to make taxes easier. If we want, we can include an extra paragraph snippet that explains why we are collecting this sensitive information.

See also

For how to create our commission programs and trackable links, see the previous recipe _Setting up a basic referral partner program._

8
Administrative - Conquer Internal Chaos

In this chapter, we will cover the following:

- ▸ Reconciling hard bounced e-mail addresses
- ▸ Tracking e-mail engagement levels
- ▸ Filtering out new hire applicants
- ▸ Creating a true e-mail preference center
- ▸ Using lead sources to track ROI
- ▸ Managing campaign model variations with versioning
- ▸ Adding groups of contacts to a campaign sequence
- ▸ Checking for duplicate contact records
- ▸ Cleaning up duplicate contact records
- ▸ Collecting W-9 forms from referral partners automatically

Introduction

Infusionsoft isn't only great for taking someone from a new lead and turning them into a raving fan, but it can also be used for different administrative functions.

The recipes in this chapter are very helpful for maintaining a clean organized database and systematizing critical business processes.

Reconciling hard bounced e-mail addresses

When an e-mail bounces, this means it was not delivered for one reason or another. There are different kinds of bounces for different situations. A hard bounce means the e-mail address flat out doesn't exist. Think of it like a *Return to Sender* when trying to send something in the post to an address that doesn't exist.

There are many reasons why a once-valid e-mail address stops working. However, just because an e-mail stops working doesn't mean that we shouldn't try and continue a relationship with the person.

Unfortunately, most businesses don't place a high priority on contacting and recovering a working e-mail address. This can result in false list statistics. For example, if we have 100 people but 15 are hard bounced, we really only have 85 people who can be reached via e-mail. Not only does this bad data throw off reporting, it can also lead to a bloated and, effectively, useless database.

The good news is that with Infusionsoft, we can automatically catch e-mails when they hard bounce and assign a task to someone to contact the person to collect a working e-mail.

Getting ready

We need to be logged in to Infusionsoft, inside a specific account, and in a new campaign. We also need to have a functional tag created.

How to do it...

1. Drag out a tag goal, an internal form goal, and a sequence; connect and rename them accordingly:

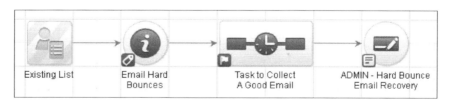

| Existing List | Email Hard Bounces | Task to Collect A Good Email | ADMIN - Hard Bounce Email Recovery |

2. Double-click on the tag goal and configure it for the functional tag; click on **Save**, as follows:

3. Double-click into the sequence and add a task and a **Tag** step:

4. Double-click into the **Task** step and configure it with instructions for someone to contact the person and collect a working e-mail address:

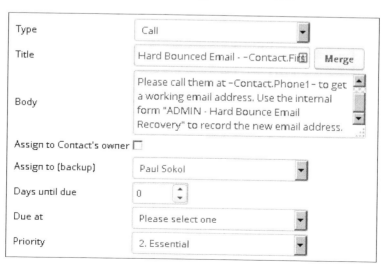

5. In the upper-right corner of the page, click on **Draft** to mark the task as **Ready** and click on **Back to Sequence** in the upper-left corner.

6. Double-click into the first **Tag** step and configure it to remove the functional tag; click on **Save**:

7. In the upper-right corner of the page, click on **Draft** to mark the sequence as **Ready**.

8. In the upper-left corner of the page, click on **Back to Campaign**.

9. Double-click into the internal form.

10. Add a **Title** snippet and provide some instructions for the user who will be submitting the form.

11. Remove all fields except for an **Email** field:

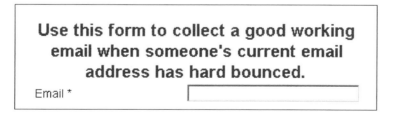

12. In the upper-right corner of the page, click on **Draft** to mark the internal form as **Ready**.

13. In the upper-left corner of the page, click on **Back to Campaign** and publish the campaign.

14. After the campaign has been published, in the upper-left corner of the page, click on **Back to List**.

15. Hover over the main navigation menu and in the **Marketing** column, click on **Settings**:

16. In the **Template Settings** menu on the left-hand side, click on **Email Status Automation**, as follows:

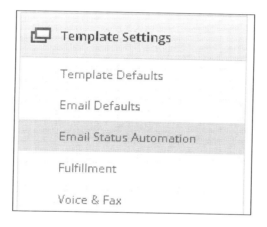

17. Using the **Choose Trigger Type** dropdown, select **When an email bounces** and click on **Add Trigger**. This will open a pop-up window, as shown in the following image:

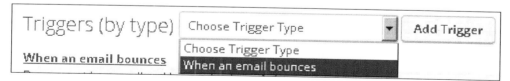

18. Configure the trigger for **when the bounce type is** field to **hard bounce** and set the **and the email has bounced** dropdown to **at least** 1 time:

19. Using the **Actions** dropdown beneath the trigger criteria, select **Add/remove tag**:

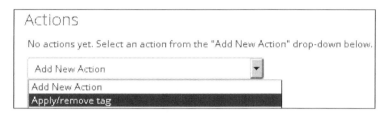

20. Configure the action to apply the functional tag and click on the green **Save** button:

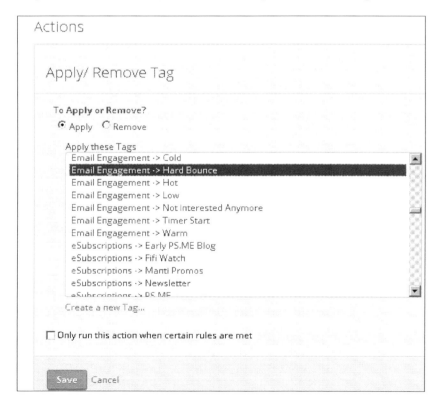

21. Click on the **Save Trigger** button to close the window, as shown here:

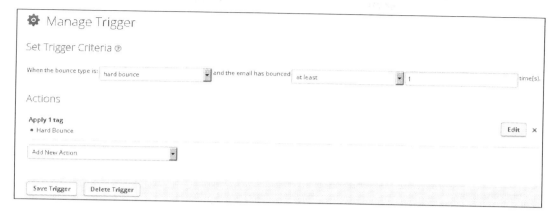

How it works...

Whenever Infusionsoft sends an e-mail and it returns as a hard bounce, the functional tag will automatically be applied, which triggers the recovery campaign. When a user submits the internal form to update the e-mail address, the bad e-mail on file will be overwritten.

There's more...

There are many different bounce types, and we can create different experiences depending on the situation:

Not all contacts will have a phone number on file. To make sure we don't waste time, we can make the functional tag application based on a rule that checks for the presence of a phone number:

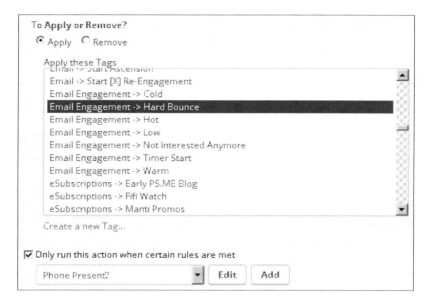

The rule itself would need the following configuration:

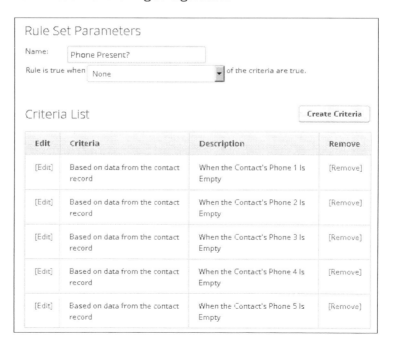

For a similar model, download the **Hard Bounce Recovery** campaign from the Marketplace.

Tracking e-mail engagement levels

When we can segment our database based on someone's engagement with your e-mails, it unlocks an entire world of automation potential.

This information can be used to plan promotions, automatically switch paths, or simply enhance an existing report for a deeper layer of insight.

This type of segmentation cannot easily be performed retroactively, so the sooner a business implements this recipe, the sooner they begin building their pool of data.

Getting ready

We need to be logged in to Infusionsoft, inside a specific account, and in a new campaign.

We also need to have some tags created:

▸ Three tags to track the engagement levels: hot, warm, and cold

▸ One functional tag that will trigger/reset the previously mentioned engagement tags

How to do it...

1. Drag out two tag goals and a sequence; connect and rename them accordingly:

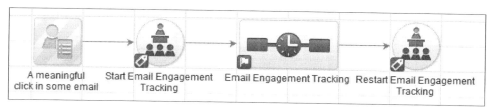

A meaningful click in some email   Start Email Engagement Tracking   Email Engagement Tracking   Restart Email Engagement Tracking

2. Double-click on the first tag goal and configure it for the functional tag, which will start the tracking; click on **Save**:

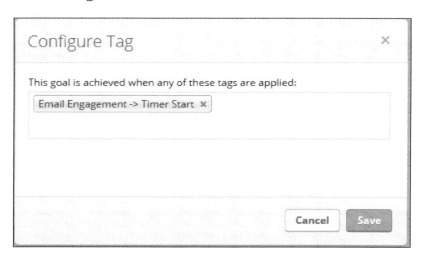

3. In the lower-left corner of the second tag goal, click on the purple symbol to open **Goal Settings**.

4. Using the **This goal can be achieved by...** dropdown, select **Any Contact** and click on **Save**:

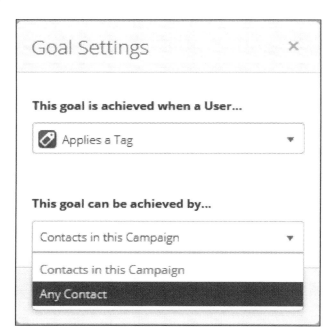

5. Double-click on the second tag goal and configure it for the same functional tag as the first tag goal; click on **Save**:

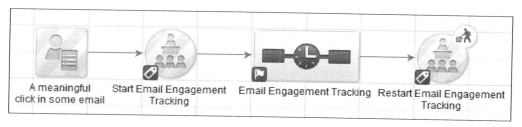

6. Double-click into the sequence and add two **Tag** steps, as follows:

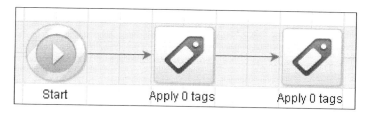

7. Double-click into the first **Tag** step and configure it to apply the **Hot** engagement tag; click on **Save**:

8. Double-click into the second **Tag** step and configure it to remove all the other engagement tags and the functional tag; click on **Save**:

9. Drag out a **Delay Timer** and two new **Tag** steps:

10. Double-click on the timer, configure it to wait 30 days, and then run on any day at 12 AM; click on **Save**:

11. Double-click into the next **Tag** step and configure it to remove the **Hot** tag; click on **Save**:

12. Double-click into the last **Tag** step in the chain and configure it to apply the **Warm** tag; click on **Save**:

13. At this point, we may want to leave canvas notes to track the different segments, as follows:

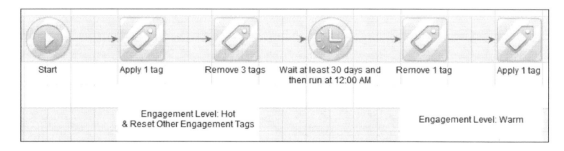

14. Repeat this **Delay** - **Tag** switching structure for the remaining **Cold** tag, as shown in the following image:

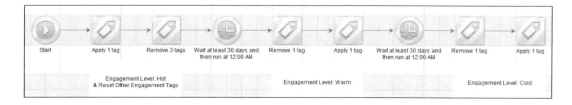

15. On the upper-right side of the page, click on **Draft** to mark the sequence as **Ready**.

16. On the upper-left side of the page, click on **Back to Campaign** and publish the campaign.

17. In our other e-mails throughout Infusionsoft, anytime there is a meaningful link that, when clicked, means the person is engaged, apply the functional tag:

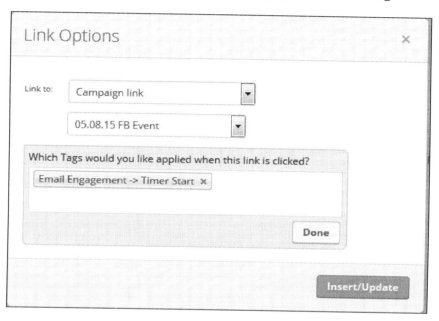

How it works...

The first time someone clicks on a link that auto-tags them with the functional tag, they are tagged as **Hot** and then the tags switch as time passes. If they click on another link that applies the functional tag in the future, the second tag goal will pull them out of the sequence and then the first tag goal will add them back into the sequence. When this happens, any previously applied tags will be removed and the **Hot** tag is reapplied. To ensure that this always happens, we set the second tag goal as an entry point.

There's more...

In this recipe, we are switching tags every 30 days. However, depending on the business, we may want to extend or shorten the tag-switching cycle.

These tags can be used in conjunction with lead scoring to help sales representatives find out who is the most active and thus should be contacted first:

We may also want to add a **Super Hot** tag that is only present for a short period of time. Again, this can help sales representatives find out who is in front of their e-mails right now and therefore might be a great person to call right now since we know they are active:

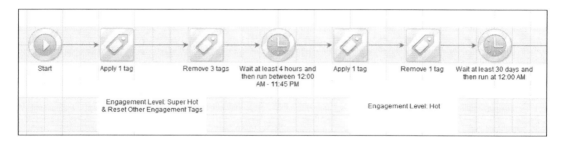

Tracking engagement levels is a pretty good stat for the dashboard. All we have to do is create a saved contact search for each tag and then put them into a **Custom Statistics** widget on the dashboard:

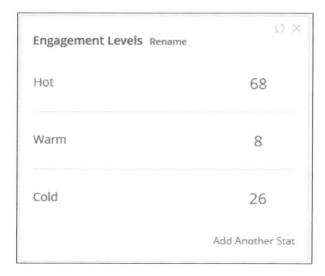

See also

▸ For a campaign template similar to this recipe, download the **Track Email Engagement** campaign from the Infusionsoft Marketplace

▸ For a similar resettable timer model that tracks the time from the last purchase, see the *Segmenting by last purchase date* recipe in *Chapter 6, Wowing New Customers with Great Experiences*

▸ To learn more about lead scoring, see the *Setting up lead scoring* recipe in *Chapter 5, Selling with a Sales Team*

▸ To learn how to make saved searches for these engagement tags, see the *Creating a saved search or report* recipe in *Chapter 9, Your Dashboard and Reporting - Make Better Decisions*

Filtering out new hire applicants

Our small business doesn't need any employees that cannot follow basic instructions. Those are the kinds of employees that can cause all sorts of problems in many different areas of the business.

In fact, even considering them for an interview is a big waste of time.

Fortunately, with Infusionsoft, we can create a simple *hoop* for a new applicant to jump through to make sure that they can follow basic instructions. The idea behind this recipe is to position the initial application submission as a two-step process, where the applicant has to confirm their e-mail address in order to reach step two.

Getting ready

We need to be logged in to Infusionsoft, inside a specific account, and in a new campaign.

How to do it...

1. Drag out a web form, a landing page goal, an e-mail confirmation and two sequences; connect and rename accordingly:

2. Double-click on the **Task to Contact** sequence at the end of the chain.

3. Add a **Task** step as follows:

Start   Task to Contact
               New Applicant

4. Double-click on the **Task** step and configure it for the user to contact the new applicant:

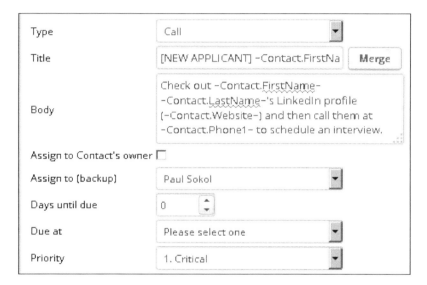

5. In the upper-right corner of the page, click on **Draft** to mark the task as **Ready**; in the upper-left corner of the page, click on **Back to Sequence**.

6. In the upper-right corner of the page, click on **Draft** to mark the sequence as **Ready**.

7. In the upper-left corner of the page, click on **Back to Campaign**.

8. Double-click on the part 2 landing page to configure it.

9. Add a **Logo** snippet at the top of the page.

10. Using the **Field Snippets** tab, drag out a **Hidden** snippet.

11. Using the **Which Field** dropdown, select **Email**, leave the **Field Value** empty, and click on **Save**:

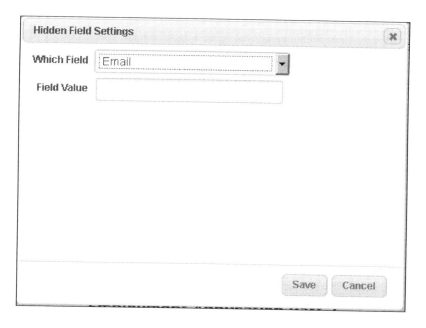

12. Add a **Divider** and **Title** snippet beneath the hidden field; change the text to indicate that this is the second part of the employment application:

13. Drag out an **Other** snippet.

14. Using the **Which Field** snippet, choose **Append to Person Notes** at the bottom of the list.

15. Change the label to ask about their previous experience, mark the field as **Required** and click on **Save**:

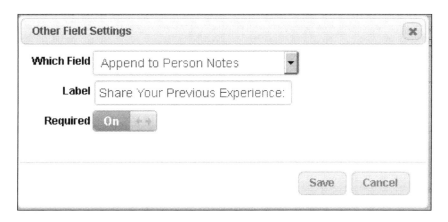

16. Repeat steps 13 to 15 for any remaining questions we want to collect; it is recommended to only have three to five questions:

17. Click on the **Submit** button to change the call to action.

18. Change the button label to `Submit Employment Application` and click on **Save**:

19. Click on the **Thank-you Page** tab at the top of the page.

20. Add a **Logo** and **Title** snippet, then adjust the message to notify the applicant that we have received their information. See the following example:

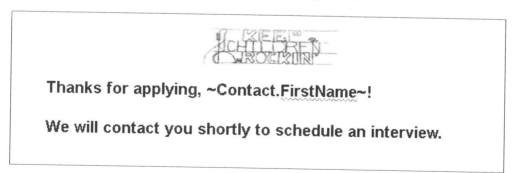

21. In the upper-right corner of the page, click on **Draft** to mark the landing page as **Ready**.

22. In the upper-left corner of the page, click on **Back to Campaign** and publish the campaign.

23. After publishing, click on the **Edit** tab in the upper-left corner of the page:

24. Double-click into the **Complete Application** sequence.

25. Add an **Email** step:

26. Double-click on the **Email** step and write a message thanking the potential applicant for confirming their e-mail and driving them to complete their application, as follows:

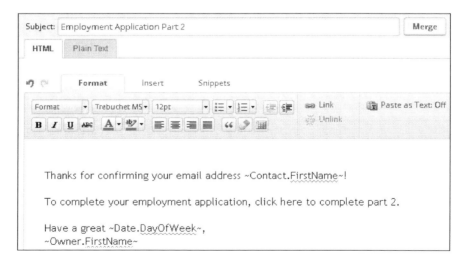

27. Highlight the call to action text and click on **Link** in the toolbar:

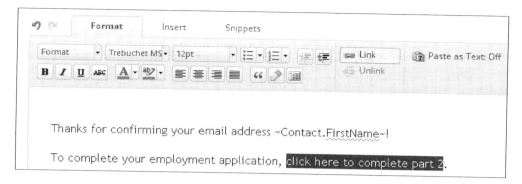

28. Using the **Link To:** dropdown, select **Hosted landing page**:

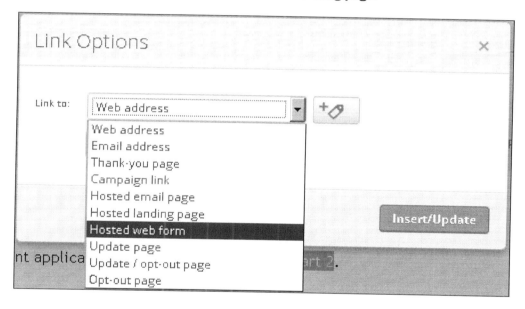

29. Begin typing the name of the landing page:

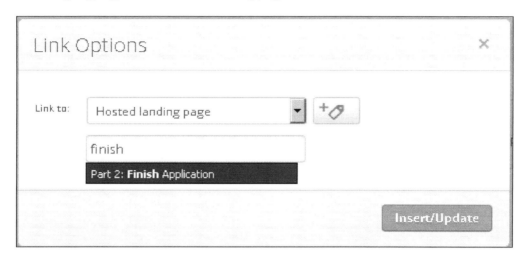

30. Click on the name of the landing page and then click on **Insert/Update**.
31. In the upper-right corner of the page, click on **Draft** to mark the e-mail as **Ready**; in the upper-left corner of the page, click on **Back to Sequence**.
32. In the upper-right corner of the page, click on **Draft** to mark the sequence as **Ready**.
33. In the upper-left corner of the page, click **Back to Campaign**.
34. Double-click on the **Email Confirmation Request** sequence:

35. Double-click on **Confirmation Email**.

36. Adjust the message to notify the potential applicant that, after confirming, they can complete their application, as follows:

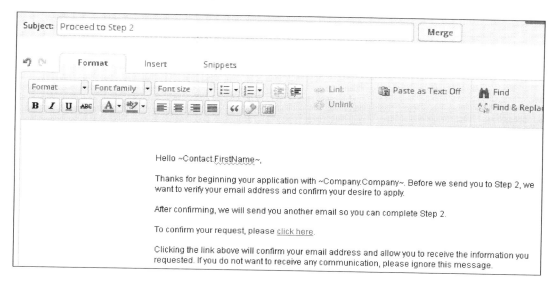

37. In the upper-right corner of the page, click on **Draft** to mark the confirmation e-mail as **Ready**; in the upper-left corner of the page, click on **Back to Sequence**.

38. In the upper-right corner of the page, click on **Draft** to mark the sequence as **Ready**.

39. In the upper-left corner of the page, click on **Back to Campaign**.

40. Double-click on the **Part 1** web form.

41. Add a **Logo** and **Title** snippet; adjust the text to frame the application process:

42. Add the following fields as required:

- **First Name**
- **Last Name**
- **Phone Number**
- **Email**

43. Add an **Other** snippet.

44. Using the **Which Field** dropdown, select **Website** and change the label to **LinkedIn URL**; click on **Save**:

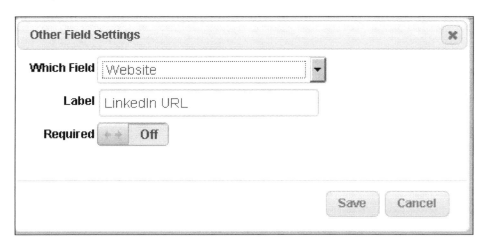

45. Click on the **Submit** button and change the button label to Proceed to Step 2:

46. Click on the **Thank-you Page** tab at the top of the page.

47. Add a **Logo** and **Title** snippet, then adjust the message to notify the applicant that they need to confirm their e-mail address before moving on to step two:

Thanks for beginning your application, ~Contact.FirstName~!

Before completing step 2, you'll need to confirm your email address. Check your inbox right now for the link!

48. In the upper-right corner of the page, click on **Draft** to mark the web form as **Ready**.

49. In the upper-left corner of the page, click on **Back to Campaign** and publish the campaign.

How it works...

When someone applies, they will submit the first web form, which sends them an e-mail confirmation. Upon confirming their e-mail address, they will receive an e-mail immediately linking them to the part 2 landing page. We will only receive a task to contact the applicant if they complete part two, thus saving us time interviewing people who cannot follow basic instructions.

There's more...

We can extend this recipe to fully systematize the hiring process with some additional internal forms after the part 2 landing page.

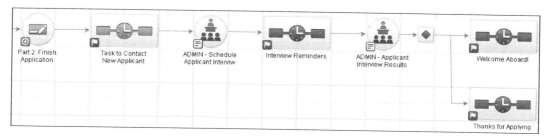

If we are hiring for different positions, we can clone this recipe and create a hiring funnel for each position being offered.

The **Filebox** on a contact record is accessible via the API. This can be used to add an **Upload Your Resume** function.

See also

For a campaign template similar to this recipe, download the **Easy Hiring** campaign from the Infusionsoft Marketplace.

Creating a true e-mail preferences center

The e-mail subscription management options available out of the box with Infusionsoft are limited because they do not show current subscription status.

Traditionally, Infusionsoft users use tags to track someone's e-mail subscription. However, if we use a custom field to track subscription status, we can build a web form that operates like a true e-mail preference center.

Getting ready

We need to be logged in to Infusionsoft, inside a specific account, and in a new campaign. In addition to this, we also want to have a dropdown-type custom field created to track an e-mail subscription status with two values: **Yes** and **No**.

How to do it...

1. Drag out a web form and rename it accordingly:

Any newsletter email   Newsletter Subscription
Centre

2. Double-click on the web form to edit it.
3. Remove all fields from the form.

4. Add a **Logo** and **Title** snippet; update the text to indicate that this is an e-mail preference center:

5. Using the **Field Snippets** tab, drag out a **Hidden** field.

6. Using the **Which Field** dropdown, select **Email**; leave the field value empty and click on **Save**:

7. Using the **Field Snippets** tag, drag out an **Other** field.

8. Using the **Which Field** dropdown, select the custom field we are using to track this particular e-mail subscription; mark the field as **Required** and click on **Save**:

9. Click on the **Submit** button to change the call to action.

10. Change the button label to `Update My Preferences`, center align the button, and click on **Save**:

11. Our web form should now look like a basic subscription management page as follows:

12. At the top of the page, click on the **Thank-you Page** tab.

13. Modify the thank you page content to indicate that the contact has just updated their preferences:

14. At the top of the page, click on **Settings**.

15. Verify that **Auto-populate** has its option selected:

16. On the upper-right side of the page, click on **Draft** to mark the form as **Ready**; on the upper-left side of the page, click on **Back to Campaign**.

17. Publish the campaign.

18. The next time we send a newsletter, include a link to this **Hosted web form** in the footer:

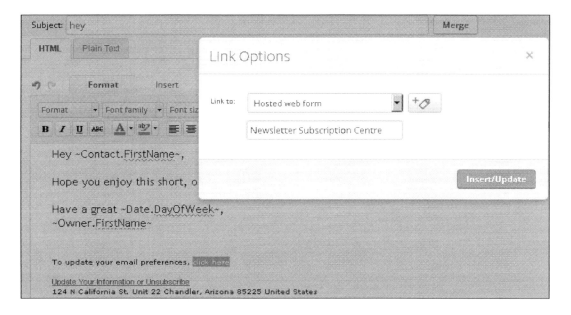

How it works...

When someone clicks on the link to manage their e-mail preferences, the form will prepopulate the contact's e-mail in the hidden field as well as the current value for the subscription custom field. If they make any changes and submit the form, their record will reflect their preferences.

There's more...

If we have more than one subscription, we can include them all on the preference form. However, we may want to strategically create one preference form per subscription, depending on the business:

We can add extra options to the dropdown values to give further communication control or allow people to select their preferred frequency:

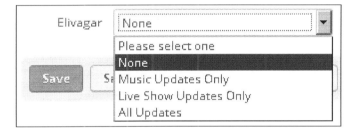

See also

To learn how to create a custom field to track e-mail subscriptions, see the *Creating custom fields* recipe in *Chapter 2, Critical Tools for Mastery*.

Using lead sources to track ROI

There is a fairly popular John Wanamaker quote floating around the Internet that reads as follows:

> *"Half the money I spend on advertising is wasted; the trouble is I don't know which half."*

What he is referring to is his inability at the time to track which marketing assets were providing a return on the investment.

Fortunately, thanks to Infusionsoft, we can track the cost for different lead sources, which can be used for native **Return On Investment** (**ROI**) reporting right in the software.

Getting ready

We need to be logged in to Infusionsoft and inside a specific account.

How to do it...

1. Hover over the main navigation, and in the **Marketing** column, click on **Lead Generation**:

My Nav	CRM	Marketing	E-Commerce	Admin
Contacts	Contacts	Campaign Builder	E-Commerce Setup	Branding Center
Campaign Builder	Companies	Email & Broadcasts	Orders	Infusionsoft Account
Email & Broadcasts	Opportunities	Lead Generation	Products	Users
Legacy	Referral Partners	Templates	Actions	Import Data
Templates	Visitors	Legacy	Promotions	Data Cleanup
Opportunities			Legacy	
Edit	Reports Settings	Reports Settings	Reports Settings	Reports Settings

2. In the **Lead Sources** section, click on **Create Lead Source**:

3. Give the new lead source a name and a description and then click on the green **Save** button at the bottom of the page:

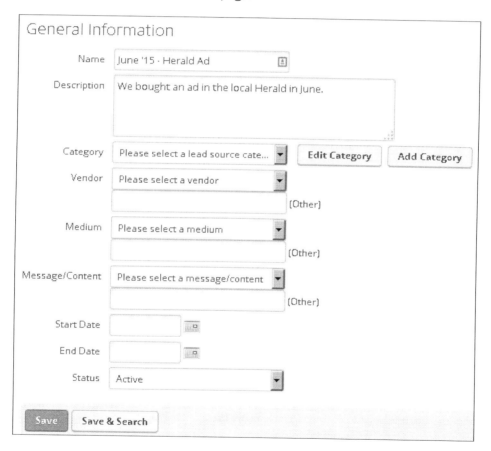

4. After the page reloads, click on the **Expenses** tab at the top:

5. Click on the **Add Expense** button:

6. Log the cost for this particular lead source and click on **Save**:

Add Expense ✕

Occurrence

Type   One Time Expense ▾ ⑦
Date Incurred   06-17-2015

Details

Title   Herald Ad
Amount 250
Notes   Found in the Business section

Cancel   Save

7. We will now see this cost in the **Recent Expenses** section at the bottom of the page:

How it works...

When someone has this lead source on their contact record as well as an order recorded, that will populate in the ROI reports:

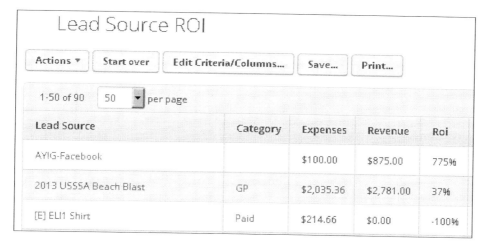

There's more...

The ROI reports can be found in the **Marketing** reports:

Sequence Step Recipients	This shows Contacts that have received an item within a Sequence
Lead Source ROI	This shows ROI by leadsource.
Lead Source ROI By Category	This shows ROI by leadsource category.
Web Analytics	This shows the pages that have been tracked by your tracking code.

When contacts have this lead source, the **Expenses** tab will give an overview of the number of contacts and cost per contact in the upper-right corner of the page:

It is recommended to take full advantage of the **Category**, **Vendor**, **Medium**, and **Message/Content** fields in the lead source. This empowers better reporting and deeper insights. This is particularly helpful when we have different variations of marketing messages as it allows us to quickly see which ones are performing best:

When a lead source is no longer relevant, we can set it as **Inactive**. This prevents future contacts from being added to the lead source accidentally by an end user; inactive lead sources are not visible when manually selecting a lead source for a contact. This can keep our list of lead sources clean while retaining all historical data for reporting:

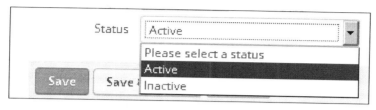

If a certain lead source has a fixed monthly expense, we can create a recurring expense that will add to the cost progressively each month until the end date. This allows us to create a rolling ROI since the expense is dynamic over time:

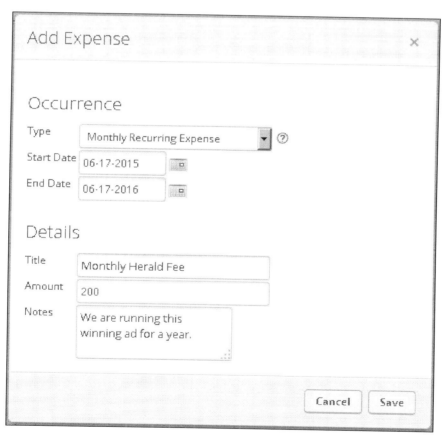

We can add a hidden **Lead Source** field to any web form or landing page to ensure that new contacts will be properly sourced:

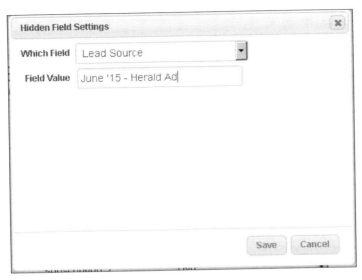

We can also drive different traffic sources to the same web form/landing page and dynamically pass different lead sources through the URL. This way, it is easy to test different variations of a particular marketing message without having to create a unique web form/landing page for each variation.

To do this, we need to have a hidden **Lead Source** field with an empty value. Then, when linking to the web form/landing page, we can append `?inf_field_LeadSourceId=xx` to the URL where `xx` is the lead source ID.

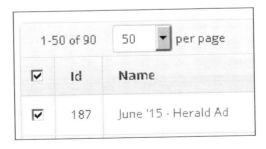

 This only works when driving traffic to the JavaScript version of a web form or a hosted landing page because those have a built-in function to prepopulate form fields from URL parameters.

See also

To learn how to create a custom field to track e-mail subscriptions, see the *Creating custom fields* recipe in *Chapter 2, Critical Tools for Mastery.*

Managing campaign model variations with versioning

An esoteric function of the campaign builder is the ability to save different campaign model configurations. This can be helpful when reusing common elements of a campaign but other elements change. For example, seasonal promotions or a product launch.

It is also helpful when innovating and improving an existing model. It allows us to safely make changes to the model that can be rolled back if necessary.

Getting ready

We need to be logged in to Infusionsoft, inside a specific account, and in a particular campaign.

For this example, we are going to show how a product that is only sold twice a year, during the winter and during the summer, can be easily updated for the season.

The campaign model we are going to start with looks like this, and we will be updating it for the winter season:

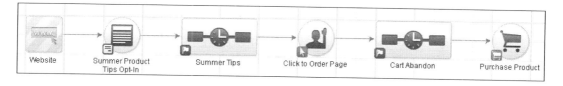

How to do it...

1. Using the **Campaign** dropdown in the upper-left corner of the page, click on **Save Version**:

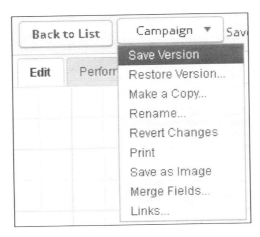

2. Click on **OK** on the confirmation message dialog box:

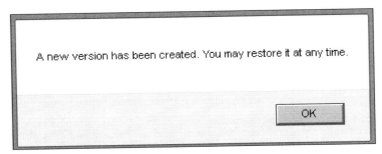

3. Update the campaign model with the changes we need; be sure to retain any sequence content that we will want to reuse in the future.

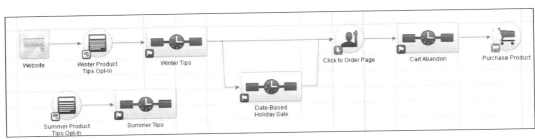

4. Using the **Campaign** dropdown in the upper-left corner of the page, click on **Save Version**.

5. Finish the campaign. Publish and use it.

6. When it is time for the summer season, using the **Campaign** dropdown in the upper-left corner of the page, click on **Restore Version**:

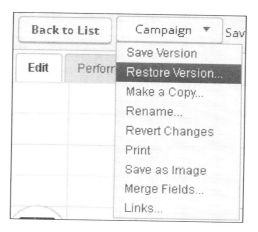

7. Click on the version we want to restore; this will restore the campaign model for the summer version:

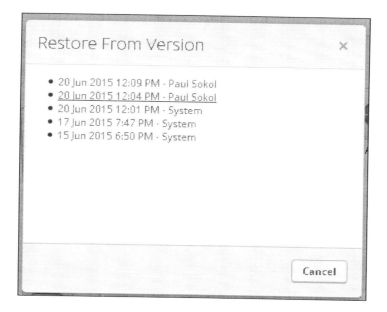

How it works...

Saving a campaign version takes a *snapshot* of the campaign model structure, including all the structures within a sequence. When we restore a campaign, it loads this structure as it was when the version was saved.

There's more...

Campaign versioning does *NOT* include the sequence step content; it only includes the sequence layout. For example, if we make changes to an e-mail's content and then restore to an older version, it will restore the sequence layout but still retain the current e-mail (assuming that the same e-mail object is in the older version). This is why it is recommended to disconnect but not delete any sequence content that we plan to reuse. **Cloning** sequences can be very handy in these situations.

A campaign version is generated automatically whenever a campaign is published. We can tell which versions were automatically created because they will be accredited to *the system* instead of a specific user.

There is a similar restoration function available within an **Email** step:

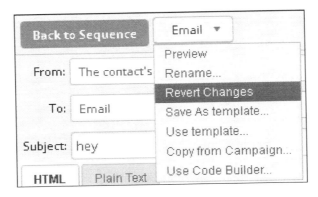

When using the **Revert Changes** function, it will restore the e-mail content to whatever was present upon first opening the e-mail; this was the last saved state for the content. Please be aware that previewing an e-mail does save the e-mail content on the backend so it can be displayed. Hence, if you have previewed an e-mail since opening it, the **Revert Changes** function will restore the content to the last time it was previewed.

Adding groups of contacts to a campaign sequence

Most campaigns start when someone performs a particular action such as filling out a web form. However, there are certain situations where we need to manually add a group of contacts to a particular campaign sequence, such as a product launch to the existing list of customers.

Getting ready

We need to have a campaign already published and a list of contacts we want to add into it.

How to do it...

1. Perform a contact search for the group of people we want to add into the campaign.
2. Using the **Actions** dropdown, select **Start/Stop a Campaign Sequence**:

3. Using the dropdown menus, select the **Campaign** and the specific sequence within the campaign we want to add this list of contacts to:

4. Click on the **Process Action** button.

How it works...

This function adds the list of contacts to the campaign sequence specified, thus launching the campaign.

There's more...

This function can also be used to stop a specific campaign entirely, we just have to select **Stop** in the first dropdown:

Checking for duplicate contact records

Ideally, every human will only have one contact record in the database. In the real world, this doesn't always happen. This can lead to strange experiences such as an existing customer receiving a promotion for a product they have already purchased. Needless to say, this doesn't enhance customer experience.

Fortunately, Infusionsoft has a built-in function to check for duplicate contact records.

Getting ready

We need to be logged in to Infusionsoft and inside a specific account.

How to do it...

1. Hover over the main navigation and in the **Admin** column, select **Data Cleanup**:

My Nav	CRM	Marketing	E-Commerce	Admin
Contacts	Contacts	Campaign Builder	E-Commerce Setup	Branding Center
Campaign Builder	Companies	Email & Broadcasts	Orders	Infusionsoft Account
Email & Broadcasts	Opportunities	Lead Generation	Products	Users
Legacy	Referral Partners	Templates	Actions	Import Data
Templates	Visitors	Legacy	Promotions	Data Cleanup
Opportunities			Legacy	

Edit	Reports	Settings	Reports	Settings	Reports	Settings	Reports	Settings

2. Click on **Check for Duplicate Contact Records**:

⚙ Clean Up Your Data

Modify Existing Records
This allows you to update existing records in Infusionsoft by importing a csv file that contains the corresponding Infusionsoft Ids.

Check for Duplicate Contact Records
This allows you to find duplicate contact records in your database.

3. On the screen that explains how duplicate checking works, click on the green **Next** button at the bottom of the screen; it is recommended to stop and read how duplicate checking works.

4. Using the radio options, select **Check all records. (May take a long time).** and click on the green **Next** button:

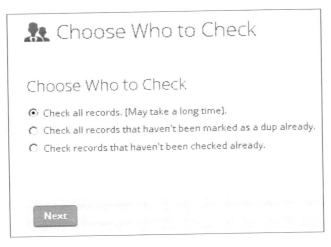

5. On the next page, scroll down and ensure that all **Stages** are checked and click on **Next**.

6. On the alert that displays, click on **OK** to begin the **deduping** process:

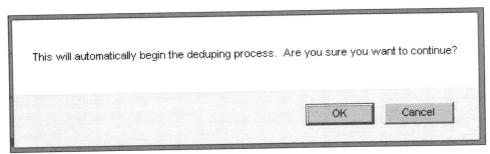

7. As the deduping occurs, we will see a status bar; this may take a while depending on the amount of contacts being checked:

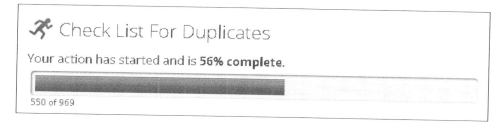

8. When the deduping is done, we will get a confirmation message:

How it works...

This function uses the built-in deduping logic inside Infusionsoft to generate a list of contact records it believes may be duplicates.

There's more...

It is highly recommended to perform a duplicate check (and reconcile any duplicates found) after importing a list of contacts to minimize spam complaints from accidentally sending the same e-mail multiple times to a single person.

It is recommended to check for duplicates periodically, say every quarter. To save system resources, we can only check records that haven't been checked already:

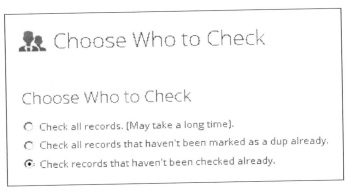

We can further speed up the duplicate checking process by searching across fewer fields. In particular, unless the business makes heavy use of phone numbers or addresses, we can perform a satisfactory duplicate check just against an e-mail alone:

Stages

☐ STAGE 1: **First Name + Last Name + One Other Field**
    ☐ CHECK: FirstName + LastName + Company

    ☐ CHECK: FirstName + Email

    ☐ CHECK: LastName + Email

    ☐ CHECK: FirstName + LastName + StreetAddress1

    ☐ CHECK: FirstName + LastName + Fax1

    ☐ CHECK: FirstName + LastName + Phone1

☐ STAGE 2: **Email + One Other Field**
    ☐ CHECK: Email + Fax1

    ☐ CHECK: Email + StreetAddress1

    ☐ CHECK: Email + Phone1

☑ STAGE 3: **One Field Check**
    ☑ CHECK: Email

See also

To learn how to merge duplicate contact records discovered by this function, see the next recipe, *Cleaning up duplicate contact records*.

Cleaning up duplicate contact records

The previous recipe will only return a list of contacts the system thinks may be duplicates. It is still necessary to merge any duplicate records found.

Getting ready

We need to be logged in to Infusionsoft , inside a specific account, and have already performed a duplicate check.

How to do it...

1. Hover over the main navigation and in the **Admin** column, select **Data Cleanup**:

My Nav	CRM	Marketing	E-Commerce	Admin
Contacts	Contacts	Campaign Builder	E-Commerce Setup	Branding Center
Campaign Builder	Companies	Email & Broadcasts	Orders	Infusionsoft Account
Email & Broadcasts	Opportunities	Lead Generation	Products	Users
Legacy	Referral Partners	Templates	Actions	Import Data
Templates	Visitors	Legacy	Promotions	Data Cleanup
Opportunities			Legacy	
Edit	Reports Settings	Reports Settings	Reports Settings	Reports Settings

2. Click on **View Duplicate Contact Records**:

3. On the duplicate results screen, in the left column, click on **Manual Merge**.

4. This will display three columns. The left and right columns will show the available data in the duplicate records.

5. The center column consists of the data that will be merged into the resulting contact record. We can click on the arrows either side of this column to move data:

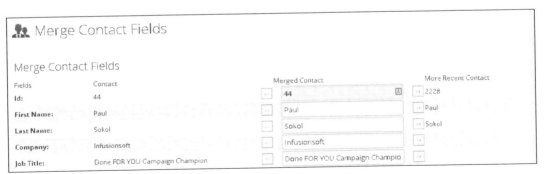

6. When we have selected the data to be merged into the resulting contact record, at the bottom of the page, click **Merge & Return to Search**:

7. On the alert that displays, click on **OK** to merge the records and return to the list of potential duplicate contacts:

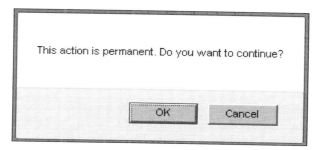

How it works...

This function takes the two contact records and merges them into one with the data that was selected. It will merge all associated data, including tags, notes, orders, and so on.

There's more...

Occasionally, we will have good information for the same field such as two working phone numbers. To avoid losing data, it is recommended that we copy the good data into our clipboard and then after the merge, place the data in another field (for example, **Phone 2**). The **Merge & View Contact** button at the bottom of the page makes this very easy.

There are certain instances where a contact record is actually not a duplicate. For example, it is very possible to have two different John Smiths in the database. In this case, we can click on **Mark as Not Duplicates** to keep the two records separate and prevent them from being flagged as duplicates in the future.

If a lot of duplicates are found, there are ways to automatically merge contact records in bulk:

 Clean Up Your Data

Modify Existing Records
This allows you to update existing records in Infusionsoft by importing a csv file that contains the corresponding Infusionsoft Ids.

Check for Duplicate Contact Records
This allows you to find duplicate contact records in your database.

View Duplicate Contact Records
View a list of contact records that are considered duplicates.

Merge Duplicate Contact Records By Overwriting Old Data With New Data
This will overwrite all older data with the newest data for all duplicate contact records.

Merge Duplicate Contact Records By Only Adding New Data, Not Overwriting Old Data
This will only add data that doesn't already exist for all duplicate contact records. This is typically used to ensure that valid email addresses for people are not overwritten.

The **Merge Duplicate Contact Records By Overwriting Old Data With New Data** option will overwrite any fields on the older record (based on when it was created) with the fields from the newer record. The **Merge Duplicate Contact Records By Only Adding New Data, Not Overwriting Old Data** option will only fill in fields that aren't present in the older record. For example, if both records have an e-mail address but the old record doesn't have a phone number and the new one does, the phone number will be in the merged record while retaining the older e-mail address. While these functions are convenient, for the most reliable data integrity, it is preferred to perform the manual merge as outlined in this recipe.

See also

To learn how to get a list of duplicate contact records, see the previous recipe, *Checking for duplicate contact records*.

Collecting W-9 forms from referral partners automatically

To close this chapter, we're going to explore how to automatically collect necessary tax documents from our referral partners. Since the author is American, this recipe is going to be for a U.S. tax form, but the recipe will work for any tax document in any country.

Specifically, we are going to be collecting a **W-9 form**.

Getting ready

We need to be logged in to Infusionsoft , inside a specific account, and inside a new campaign.

We also need to have a functional tag created to trigger this particular campaign.

How to do it...

1. Drag out a new tag goal, note goal, and sequence. Connect and rename them accordingly:

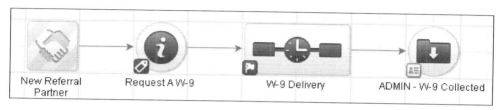

2. Double-click on the tag goal and configure it for the functional tag; click on **Save**:

3. Double-click on the note goal and configure it for tracking when a W-9 has been collected; click on **Save**:

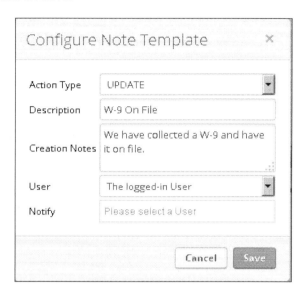

4. Double-click into the **W-9 Delivery** sequence.

5. Drag out two **Email** steps and two **Delay Timers**. Connect and rename them accordingly:

6. Double-click into the first e-mail step and write a message requesting a W-9 from the referral partner, including a call to action to download the form and reply with it attached:

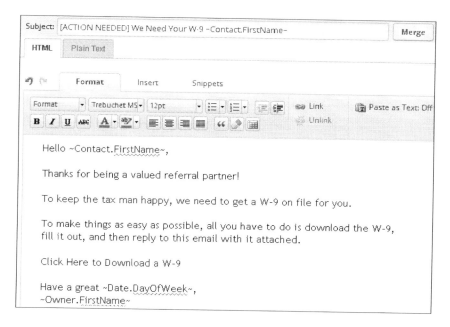

7. Highlight the download call-to-action and click on the **Link** button in the toolbar:

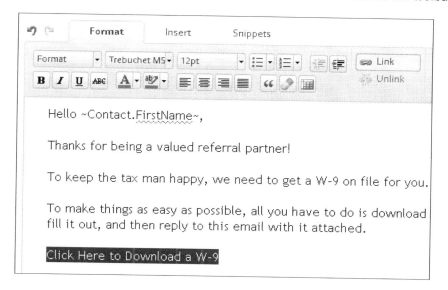

8. Configure the link for a direct download to the W-9 form and click on **Insert/Update**; this can easily be found by searching online:

9. In the upper-right corner of the page, click on **Draft** to mark the e-mail as **Ready** and click on **Back to Sequence**.

10. Double-click the first **Delay Timer**, configure it to wait 1 week, and then run on any weekday at 8 AM; click on **Save**:

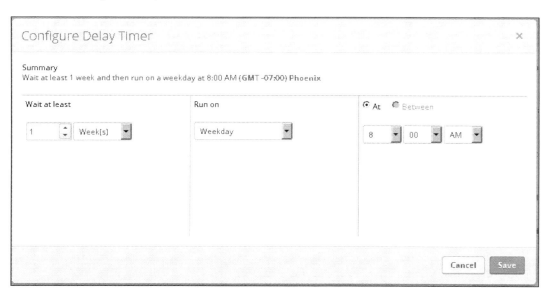

11. Double-click on the second e-mail step and write a reminder message about the W-9 form and include another call to action to download the form and send it back:

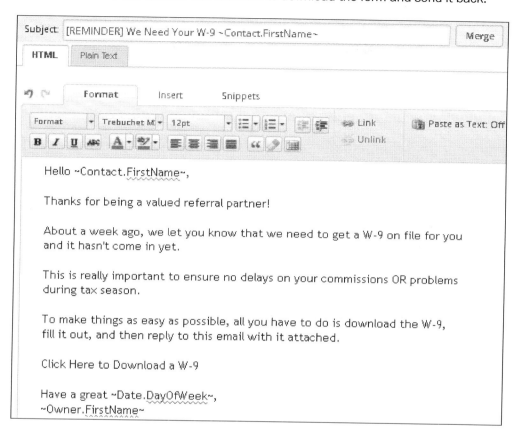

12. Configure the download link with the W-9 form URL, as we did in step 8.

13. In the upper-right corner of the page, click on **Draft** to mark the e-mail as **Ready** and click on **Back to Sequence**.

14. Double-click the second **Delay Timer**, configure it to wait 1 week, and then run on any weekday at 8 AM; click on **Save**:

15. In the upper-right corner of the page, click on **Draft** to mark the sequence as **Ready** and then click on **Back to Campaign**.

16. Publish the campaign.

How it works...

When the functional tag is applied to a referral partner's contact record, they will automatically receive an e-mail asking for the tax form. If a user does not apply the Admin note indicating that the form has been returned, the referral partner will receive a reminder e-mail after one week.

There's more...

To fully automate this process, it is recommended to apply the functional tag after someone signs up to be a referral partner.

At its core, this recipe is a document collection strategy, which means that it can be used to collect any type of document, not just tax forms.

9

Your Dashboard and Reporting - Make Better Decisions

In this chapter, we will cover the following topics:

- ► Creating a saved search or report
- ► Adding custom statistics to your dashboard
- ► Configuring your dashboard
- ► Setting a user's default start page
- ► Automating saved search or report delivery
- ► Building the perfect sales rep dashboard
- ► Reporting on who is in a campaign
- ► Reporting on who is in (or was in) a specific campaign sequence
- ► Reporting on who is queued to receive a specific campaign step
- ► Reporting on who received a specific campaign step
- ► Reporting on who completed a specific campaign goal

Introduction

In the book *A Scandal in Bohemia*, Sherlock Holmes states that:

> *"It is a capital mistake to theorize before one has data. Insensibly one begins to twist facts to suit theories, instead of theories to suit facts."*

At its core, Infusionsoft is a database, which means our business is swimming in an ocean of valuable data. The purpose of this chapter is to empower us to fish for meaningful insights that we can use to drive business decisions. This way, we can make informed and educated decisions as opposed to just guessing.

Creating a saved search or report

One of the most valuable skills we can develop as an Infusionsoft user is knowing how to properly search for and display meaningful data. There are two ways we can search through the database. We can do a direct query on the different tables (contacts, opportunities, orders, and so on) or we can use the built-in reports that come out of the box.

The good news is that no matter which method we use, the process to search, display, and save such data is the same. Hence, while this recipe will demonstrate a specific search example, we can extend these ideas to any data inquiry.

Specifically, this recipe will search for a group of contacts with a specific tag and then save it for quick access in the future.

Getting ready

We need to be logged in to Infusionsoft and inside a specific account.

How to do it...

1. Hover over the main navigation menu and in the **CRM** column, click on **Contacts**. If a previous search is displaying when the page loads, click on the **Start Over** button at the top of the list, as follows:

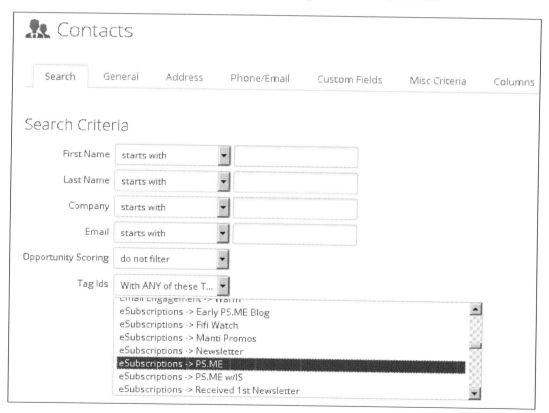

2. In the **Tag Ids** list box, find and select the tag we want to search for:

3. In the tabs at the top of the search options, click on **Columns**:

4. The **Custom Columns:** box on the left-hand side is the data that will be displayed upon performing the search. To show more data, select the data field we want to see in the box on the right-hand side and click on the **<<** symbol between the boxes:

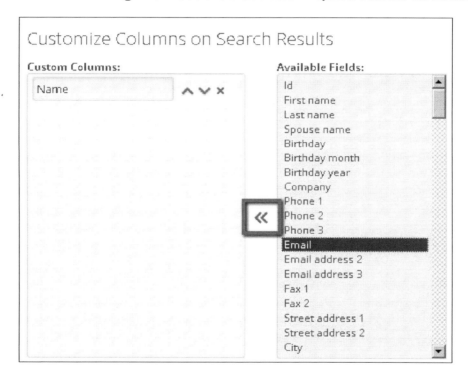

5. This will move the data field from the box on the right-hand side to box on the left-hand side:

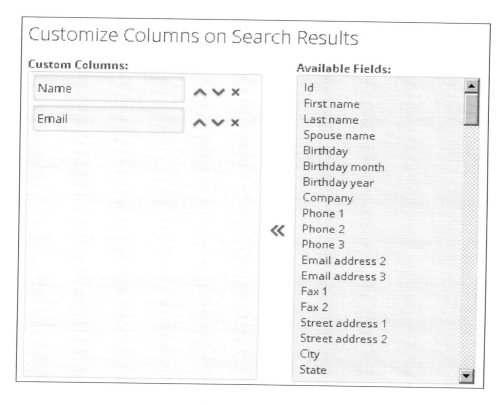

6. Once we have selected the data fields we want to display, scroll down the page and click on the green **Search** button:

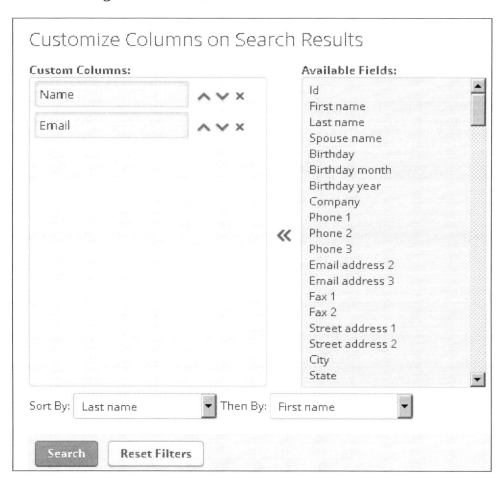

7. This will display the results for the search criteria we selected:

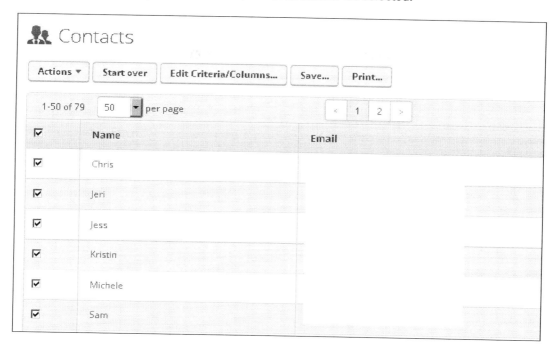

8. In the buttons above the search results, click on the **Save...** button; this will open a pop-up window:

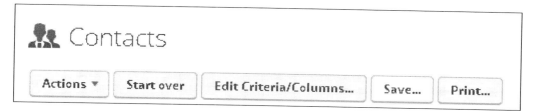

9. Give this search a name and click on the green **Save** button:

10. The next time we want to access this saved search, we can use the dropdown in the upper-right corner of the page:

How it works...

The search filter criteria and data fields selected make up a saved search or report. From here, we can use this saved search to customize our dashboard, send automated e-mails to a user with the search results, or run mass actions.

There's more...

The word *report* is sometimes a misnomer when searching for data inside Infusionsoft. The list of contacts we generated in this recipe could colloquially be referred to as a *newsletter subscribers report*, but in actuality, it is just a straight database query. Reports, formally, are ways to manipulate data (such as an opportunity stage move conversion percentages) or access data that isn't a standard record type (such as a campaign's performance). It is an important skill for an Infusionsoft user to know when to do a search and when to use a formal report. For example, if we wanted to find a *report* of all the sales opportunities that are overdue, we would simply do an opportunity search with the **Next Action Date** criteria for dates in the past.

We can raise a direct query on the following record types:

- ▶ **Contacts**
- ▶ **Companies**
- ▶ **Opportunities**
- ▶ **Referral Partners**
- ▶ **Orders**

We can also perform a search on e-mail broadcasts by clicking on any option in the **Marketing** menu and then hovering over **Email & Broadcasts**:

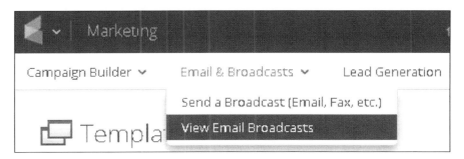

We can also perform a search on subscriptions by clicking on any option in the **E-Commerce** menu and then hovering over **Orders**:

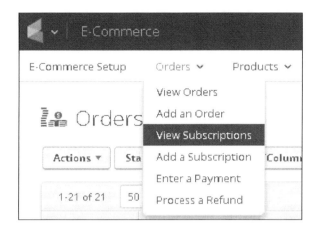

The different reports for the various sections of Infusionsoft can be accessed by hovering over the main navigation menu and clicking on the **Reports** link in the footer of each section. Searching and saving these reports functions in the exact same way as doing a direct database query. It is highly recommended to spend some time becoming familiar with the different reports available for the different sections.

When selecting the data fields to display, we can control the order they display by using the arrows to the right of the field:

We can also select how the data should be sorted upon search by using the dropdowns at the bottom of the **Custom Columns** tab:

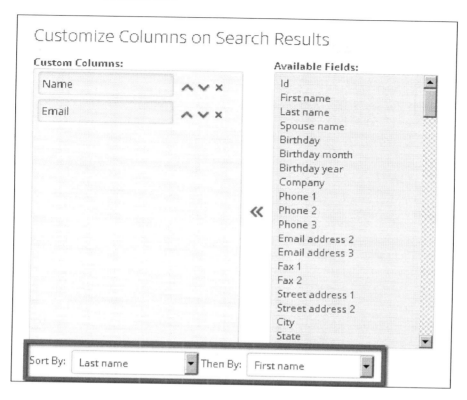

After the search has been performed, we can typically click on the data header to sort by that column; certain data types don't have this sorting functionality:

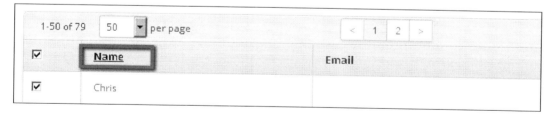

If we have a search that we plan to access often, after saving it, we can use the **Options** dropdown to add it to our favorites:

Clicking the **Add to Favorites...** option will open a pop-up window where we can configure how it will be displayed in the **Your Favorites** menu:

Upon clicking **Save**, we will be able to quickly access it from the **Your Favorites** menu in the navigation:

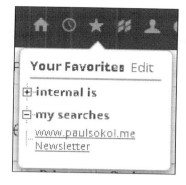

By default, any saved searches or reports can only be seen by the user that created them. However, there is a **Share/Unshare...** option that allows us to share what we create with other users:

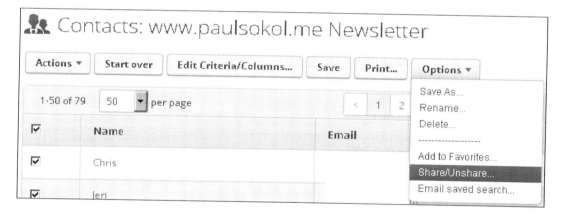

After performing a search or a report, depending on the record type being queried, we will have a list of actions that can be performed on a group for records. It is highly recommended that you become familiar with the different actions available for the different record types.

For example, these are the available actions when searching contact records:

Note how some of the options change if we do an opportunity search that consists of specific actions related to certain sales pipeline functions:

See also

▸ To learn how to add saved searches and reports to a user's dashboard, see the next recipe *Adding custom statistics to your dashboard* or the following one, *Configuring your dashboard*

▸ To learn how to send saved searches or reports to the e-mail on file for a user, see the *Automating saved search or report delivery* recipe later in this chapter

Adding custom statistics to your dashboard

Now that we know how to create saved searches and reports, we can add those directly to our dashboard. However, there are certain situations where seeing the full details is unnecessary.

This recipe is going to cover how we can take a saved search or report and display it as a statistic on the dashboard for faster consumption.

As with the previous recipe, while we are going to cover a specific example, the process to create a custom statistic is the same regardless of the search or report being used.

Getting ready

We need to be logged in to Infusionsoft, inside a specific account, and have a saved search available.

How to do it...

1. In the upper-right corner of the navigation, hover over the *house* symbol and click on **Dashboard**:

2. In the upper-right corner of the dashboard, click on **Add Widgets**:

3. To the right of the **Custom Statistics** option, click on **Add to Dashboard**, as shown in the following screenshot:

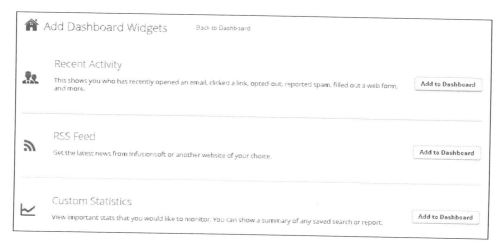

4. Using the second dropdown, select the record type containing the saved search, as shown in the following screenshot:

5. Using the third dropdown, select the saved search we want to display, as follows:

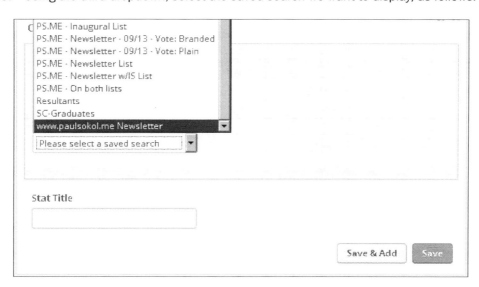

6. Give the stat a meaningful title and click on **Save**:

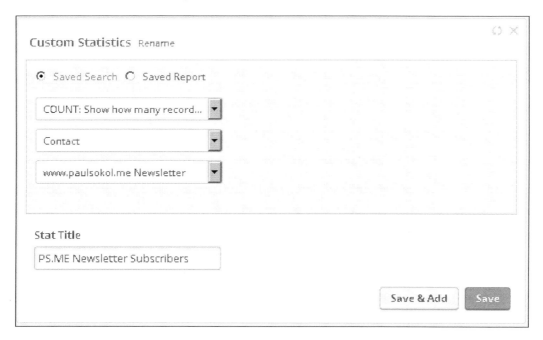

7. This will display the custom statistic based on the saved search:

How it works...

The **Custom Statistics** widget loads the saved search in the background and then displays a count of the number of records found. This will work for any saved search or report.

There's more...

By default, the **Custom Statistics** widget performs a count of the records. However, there are four other types of statistics that can be leveraged:

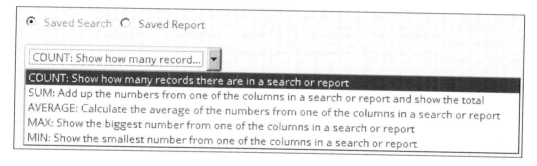

If we choose one of the other options, we will also have to select which data field we want to perform the calculation on:

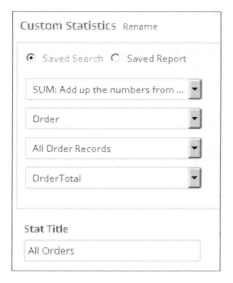

This is one way to easily keep track of vital e-commerce data:

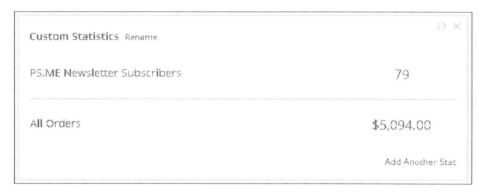

We can have as many **Custom Statistics** widgets on our dashboard as we want. To keep them organized, we can rename the different widgets using the **Rename** function at the top of each one:

If we are running calculations on a saved report, we will have to select the **Saved Report** radio button when configuring the statistic in order for the relevant reports to be selectable:

A **Custom Statistics** widget can have up to 10 stats per widget:

We can use the same search or report for more than one statistic:

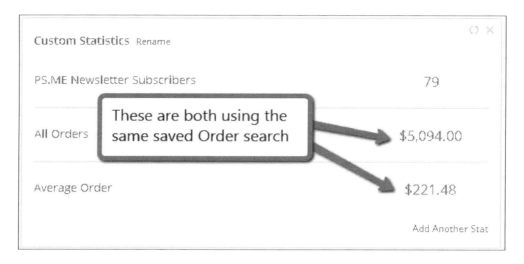

See also

▶ To learn how to create saved searches or reports, see the previous recipe *Creating a saved search or report*

▶ To further learn about all the different dashboard customizations available, see the following recipe *Configuring your dashboard*

Configuring your dashboard

Now that we know how to create saved searches/reports and how to create custom statistics from those, we can now learn how to configure our dashboard.

Infusionsoft's dashboard can be extremely powerful when we configure it for critical business information. It should be thought of as *ground control* for our business, displaying important metrics and vital signs.

Since every business is different, this recipe is going to cover the different functionality available to set up and organize our dashboard.

Getting ready

We need to be logged in to Infusionsoft and inside a specific account.

How to do it...

1. In the upper-right corner of the navigation, hover over the *house* symbol and click on **Dashboard**.

2. In the upper-right corner of the dashboard, click on **Change Layout**.

3. Select the dashboard layout we want to use by clicking on **Use This**. It is recommended to use the biggest layout, so we have the most room to display critical information:

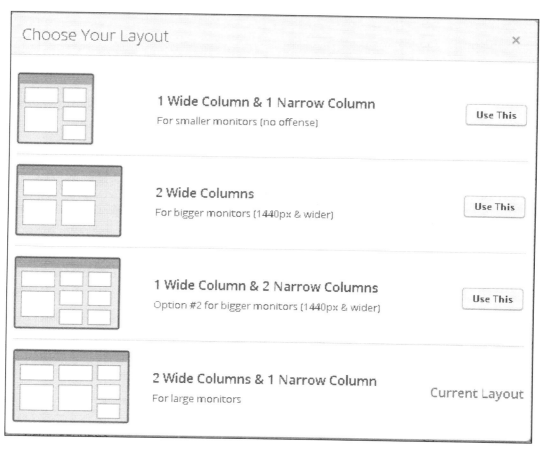

4. To organize the different widgets, we can drag and drop the widget's title for better placement:

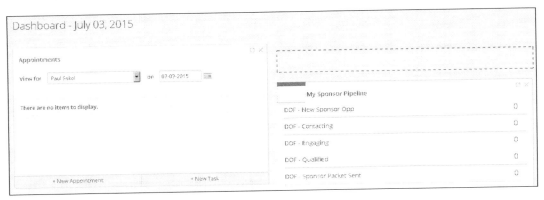

5. To add more widgets, we can click on **Add Widgets** in the upper-right corner of the page and then click on **Add to Dashboard**:

How it works...

The dashboard can contain a variety of widgets to provide valuable insights into our business.

There's more...

Each dashboard is configured at the user level. When adding a new user, it is recommended to log in with them and help them configure their dashboard for their roles and responsibilities. To save time, as the admin, we can build any relevant saved searches or reports and share them with different users before doing this. See the *There's more...* section of the first recipe in this chapter to learn how to do this.

If we want to display the details of a particular saved search or report, we can use the **Saved Search or Saved Report** widget:

We can also add a saved search or report directly to our dashboard when we save it:

If we are using fulfillment lists that are going to a user, we need to use the **Fulfillment Jobs** widget for those jobs to display and be properly worked:

It is recommended to add every widget to your dashboard, so we can become familiar with how each one operates. While we won't necessarily use every widget, and we can delete them afterwards, it is a wonderful learning exercise to become fully versed in the dashboard's capabilities.

See also

 ▸ To learn how to create saved searches or reports, see the first recipe in this chapter, *Creating a saved search or report*

 ▸ To learn how to use the **Custom Statistics** widget, see the previous recipe *Adding custom statistics to your dashboard*

Setting a user's default start page

There are many different options that can be configured for each user. One of the lesser known abilities is the option to set which page displays upon logging in. This can be a massive time saver, especially for those users who log in multiple times a day.

Getting ready

We need to be logged in to Infusionsoft and inside a specific account.

How to do it...

1. In the upper-right corner of the navigation, hover over the *person* symbol and click on **Edit My Profile**, as follows:

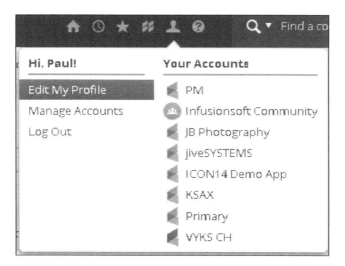

2. In the tabs at the top of the page, click on **Preferences**:

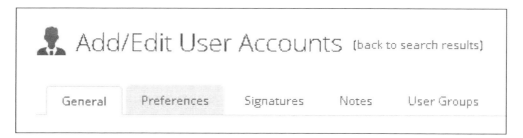

3. In the **Misc** section, next to the **Default Start Page** setting, select the radio button for what we want to display upon login; click on **Save** at the bottom of the page:

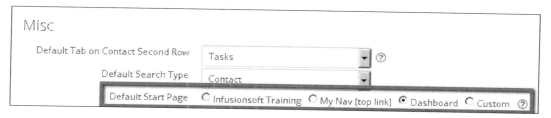

How it works...

This setting controls what a user will see upon logging in.

There's more...

We can make any main navigation item display upon loading by selecting the **My Nav** (top link) option. This will load whichever menu option is configured at the top of the **My Nav** section of the navigation:

If we want a page to load that is not available in the main navigation, we can select the custom option and configure it for the URL of the page we want. To do this, go to the page we wish to load upon login and then set the **Custom** option as everything after the `.com` in the URL.

For example, if we wanted the subscription search to load upon login, we would set the custom value as `/app/nav/link?navSystem=nav.accounting&navModule=order&navLink=search-subscription`:

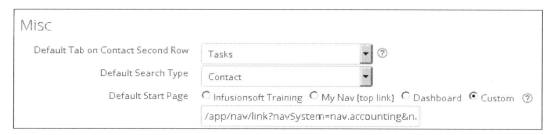

Automating saved search or report delivery

There are certain scenarios where receiving a saved search or report automatically via e-mail can be beneficial. For example, a saved search for all opportunities with a **Next Action Date** of today.

One of the most esoteric functions of a saved search/report is the ability to automate the sending of it to a user on a particular schedule.

Getting ready

We need to be logged in to Infusionsoft, inside a specific account, and looking at an existing saved search or report.

How to do it...

1. Using the buttons at the top of the search/report, click on **Options** and then **Email saved search....** This will open a pop-up window:

2. In the list box of days, select the day(s) we wish to receive the automated e-mail. Hold the *Ctrl* key and click to select multiple days:

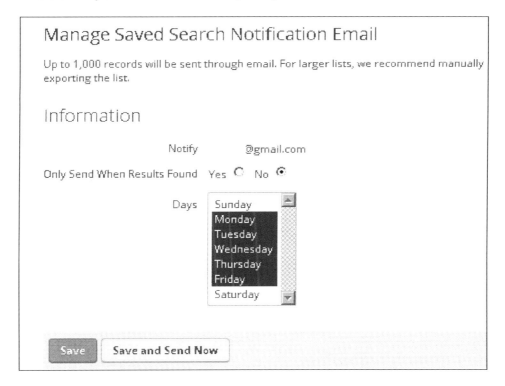

3. Click on the green **Save** button.

How it works...

On the morning of the days that have been selected, the user will receive an e-mail with the saved search/report results.

There's more...

To prevent inbox bloat, we can select **Yes** on the **Only Send When Results Found** option. This will ensure that an automated e-mail is only sent if the particular search/report returns results for that day. For example, if we want a saved search of opportunities with **Next Action Date** in the past, but there are none, this would prevent a useless e-mail from being delivered.

This function is performed per user, so if we want more than one person to receive it, each user must have access to the saved search/report and perform this recipe.

See also

To learn how to create saved searches or reports, see the first recipe *Creating a saved search or report* in this chapter.

Building the perfect sales rep dashboard

Opportunities inside Infusionsoft are, in the author's opinion, one of the most powerful tools available to not only drive sales, but provide valuable insights into what it is working and what isn't in the sales process.

In order to ensure that nobody slips through the cracks, there is a particular configuration of the dashboard for a sales rep that ensures that they can start their day off with focus and work the leads that need attention today.

While nothing can ever be perfect, this configuration ensures that a sales rep's dashboard can act as a very reliable *ground control* for them to see exactly how their pipeline is operating.

For this recipe, we will be creating two saved opportunity searches and then configuring the dashboard.

Getting ready

We need to be logged in to Infusionsoft, inside a specific account, and should already have our opportunity stages configured.

How to do it...

1. Hover over the main navigation and, in the **CRM** section, click on **Opportunities**:

2. Search with the following criteria:

    ❑ **Search | Stage**: All stages selected *except* win/loss

    ❑ **Search | Owner**: Current user

    The **Search Criteria** window will look like this:

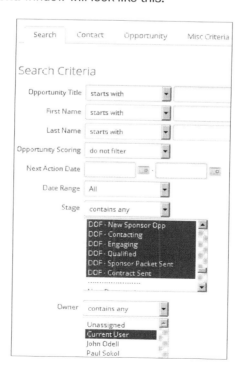

3. Now, in **Custom Columns**, under the **Columns** tab, select the following fields:

    ❑ **Opportunity**

    ❑ **Contact name**

    ❑ **Stage**

    ❑ **Next action date**

    ❑ **Next action notes**

4. Scroll down and set the **Sort By:** dropdown to **Next action date**:

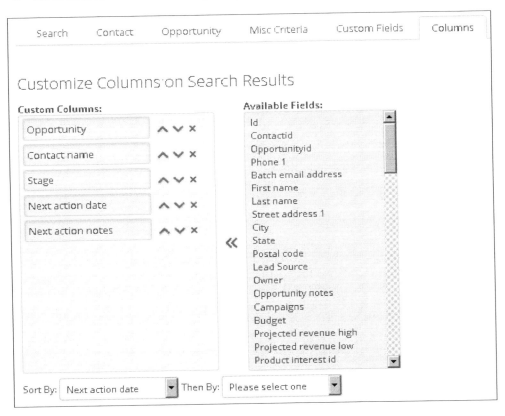

5. Click on the green **Search** button.

6. When the search loads (and it may be empty), click on the **Save...** button above the results; this will open a pop-up window, as follows:

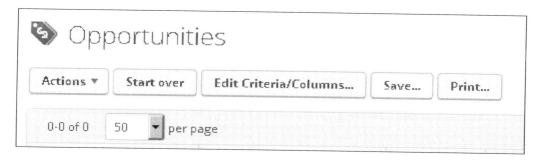

7. Name the search My Opportunities, select all the users who will be working on opportunities, and click on **Save**:

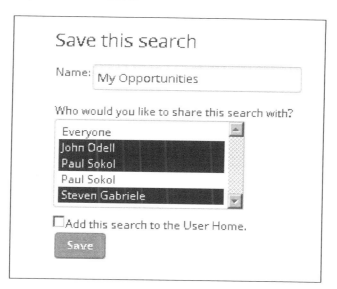

8. After the search saves, click on the **Edit Criteria/Columns...** button; this will open a pop-up window, as follows:

9. In the **Misc Criteria** tab, modify this search by setting the **Next Action Date Custom Interval** as 365 days ago and/or -1 days after today and then scroll down and click on the green **OK** button:

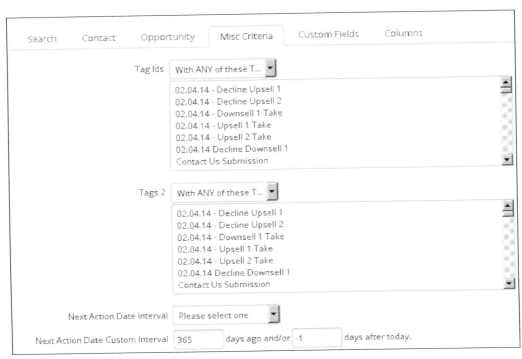

10. When the search loads (and it may be empty), click on the **Options** dropdown above the results and also click on **Save As...**; this will open a pop-up window:

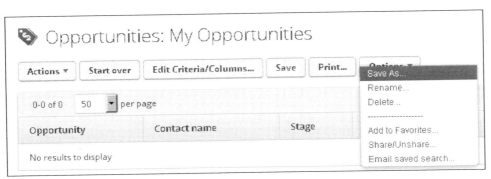

11. Name the search `Overdue Opportunities`, select all the users who will be working on opportunities, and click on **Save**:

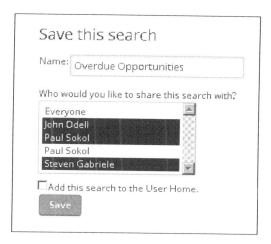

12. After the search saves, hover over the *house* symbol in the upper-right corner of the navigation and click on **Dashboard**:

13. Using the **Add Widgets** button in the upper-right corner of the dashboard, add the following widgets:

   ❑ **Calendar Items**

   ❑ **Pipeline Stages**

   ❑ **Tasks**

14. At the bottom of the **Pipeline Stages** widget, click on **Settings** and configure it to show only our user's stats, the relevant sales stages, rename it as My Pipeline, and then click on **Save**:

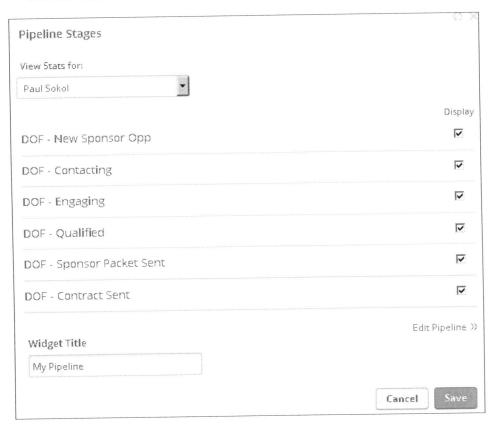

15. Using the **Add Widgets** button in the upper-right corner of the dashboard, add two **Saved Search or Saved Report** widgets.

16. Configure both widgets for the two saved searches we created earlier in the recipe:

17. Click and drag the widgets to organize the dashboard, as shown in the following screenshot:

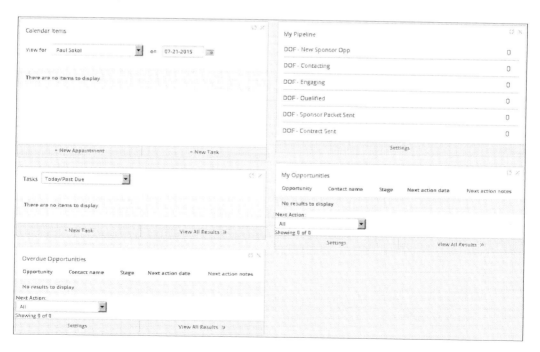

How it works...

Every morning, the sales rep can log in, and the **Calendar Items** widget will show any opportunities with a next action date of today. This should be their focus. Upon completing those, they can work on any tasks that may be assigned to them and catch up on any overdue opportunities. By following this workflow impeccably, it ensures that no leads will ever slip through the cracks.

The right column acts like a 10,000-foot view into the state of their current pipeline.

There's more...

Each sales rep will need to configure their own dashboard. This is why we created the searches and shared them with other users, it saves them from setting up the searches on their own. A sales rep can follow this recipe starting at step 12 once the searches have been saved.

The **Overdue Opportunities** saved search is looking for next action dates that are -1 day after today, in other words, anything due yesterday or before. Using negative numbers as criteria in searches/reports (assuming that the search field is looking for a whole number) is a very handy tool to have in our back pocket.

Tasks and opportunities will both show up on a user's calendar. Even though we are showing tasks, it is recommended to only use these for secondary or auxiliary action items; the opportunity's next action date should always contain the next primary thing that needs to occur. For example, if an appointment is scheduled, we can set the next action date as the actual appointment and then create a one-off task to send the meeting invitation.

See also

- For a more in-depth look at creating saved searches or reports, see the first recipe *Creating a saved search or report* in the chapter
- For more information on how we can configure the dashboard, see the *Configuring your dashboard* recipe earlier in this chapter
- For help setting up opportunity stages, see the *Setting up a sales pipeline* recipe in *Chapter 5, Selling with a Sales Team*
- To learn how to properly work with an opportunity, see the *Working sales opportunities* recipe in *Chapter 5, Selling with a Sales Team*

Reporting on who is in a campaign

To close this chapter, we are going to go in depth into campaign reporting and all the different angles we can hit the database.

This recipe will cover how to see who, in general, is active in a particular campaign.

Getting ready

We need to be logged in to Infusionsoft, inside a specific account, and need to have a campaign published with contacts flowing through it.

How to do it...

1. Hover over the main navigation, and in the **Marketing** section, click on **Campaign Builder**:

2. Find the campaign we want to report on and in the **Active Contacts** column, click on the number:

3. This will display the list of contacts active in the campaign.

How it works...

This report displays all the contacts who are active within a sequence, any sequence, within the campaign.

There's more...

This report operates like any normal search or report, so we can customize the data to display by clicking on the **Edit Criteria/Columns...** button.

This report can also be accessed through the marketing reports:

Click Through Percentage Search By Contact	Click Through Percentage By Contact
Click Through Percentage Search By Email	Click Through Percentage Search By Email
Unique Campaign Contacts	This shows unique Contacts who are in a specific Campaign
Campaign Contacts	This shows Contacts who are being marketed to by Campaign Sequences.
Campaign Contacts Waiting	This shows Contacts who are waiting for a step within a Campaign Sequence.

See also

For a more in-depth look at modifying searches or reports, see the first recipe *Creating a saved search or report* in this chapter.

Reporting on who is in (or was in) a specific campaign sequence

This recipe will cover how to see who is active in a particular sequence within a campaign.

Getting ready

We need to be logged in to Infusionsoft, inside a specific account, and need to have a campaign published with contacts flowing through it.

How to do it...

1. Hover over the main navigation and in the **Marketing** section, click on **Campaign Builder**.

2. Find the campaign we want to report on and open it.

3. Click on the **Performance** tab in the upper-left corner of the page:

4. Hover over the sequence we want to report on and click on the blue *person* icon in the upper-right corner, as shown in the following image:

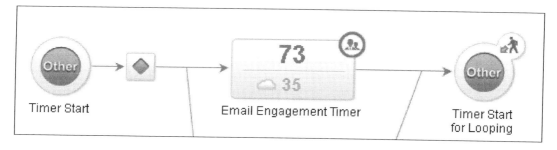

5. This will display the list of contacts active in that specific sequence within the campaign.

How it works...

This report displays all the contacts who are active within the chosen sequence of the campaign.

There's more...

By default, this report is showing contacts who are active in the sequence, but there are actually three other states a contact can be in with respect to a specific sequence:

- **Active**: This means the contact is in the sequence and is waiting to receive all the steps within it, including a timer at the end of a flow.

- **Queued**: This means the contact received all the steps within a campaign and did not move ahead in the campaign. They did not achieve a goal further down the line, and they didn't automatically flow into another sequence. This is the orange number seen in the **Performance** view.

- **Done**: This means that the sequence has *done* its job and pushed a contact ahead to a goal or they automatically flowed into another sequence.

If we click on **Edit Criteria/Columns...** from this report, we can select the sequence state we wish to report on:

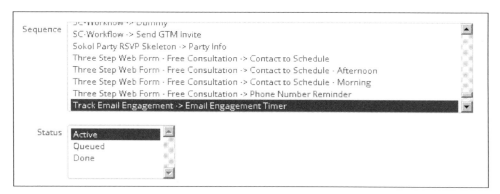

For the **Done** status, we can also filter by when a contact stopped the sequence as well:

This report can also be accessed through the marketing reports:

Click Through Percentage Search By Email	Click Through Percentage Search By Email
Unique Campaign Contacts	This shows unique Contacts who are in a specific Campaign
Campaign Contacts	This shows Contacts who are being marketed to by Campaign Sequences.
Campaign Contacts Waiting	This shows Contacts who are waiting for a step within a Campaign Sequence.
Campaign Goal Completion	This shows Contacts who have completed Campaign Goals

See also

For a more in-depth look at modifying searches or reports, see the first recipe *Creating a saved search or report* in the chapter.

Reporting on who is queued to receive a specific campaign step

This recipe will cover how to see who is waiting to receive a particular step within a sequence.

Getting ready

We need to be logged in to Infusionsoft, inside a specific account, and should have a campaign published with contacts flowing through it.

How to do it...

1. Hover over the main navigation, and in the **Marketing** section, click on **Campaign Builder**.
2. Find the campaign we want to report on and open it.
3. Click on the **Performance** tab in the upper-left corner of the page.
4. Hover over the sequence we want to report on and double-click on the sequence itself.

5. Hover over the timer before the step we want to report on and click on the blue *person* icon in the upper-right corner:

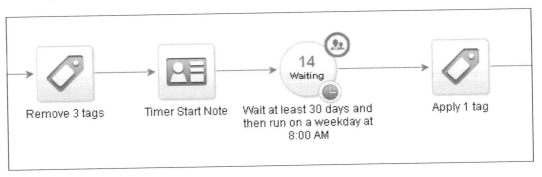

6. This will display the list of contacts in that specific sequence who are waiting for the next step.

How it works...

This report displays all the contacts who are queued to receive the next step in the sequence.

There's more...

If we click on **Edit Criteria/Columns...** from this report, we can also filter by when a contact is scheduled to receive the step:

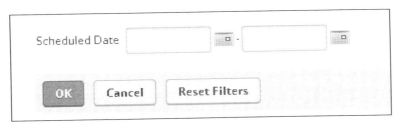

This report can also be accessed through the marketing reports:

Unique Campaign Contacts	This shows unique Contacts who are in a specific Campaign
Campaign Contacts	This shows Contacts who are being marketed to by Campaign Sequences.
Campaign Contacts Waiting	This shows Contacts who are waiting for a step within a Campaign Sequence.
Campaign Goal Completion	This shows Contacts who have completed Campaign Goals
Sequence Step Recipients	This shows Contacts that have received an item within a Sequence

See also

For a more in-depth look at modifying searches or reports, see the first recipe *Creating a saved search or report* in this chapter.

Reporting on who received a specific campaign step

This recipe will cover how to see who has already received a particular step within a sequence.

Getting ready

We need to be logged in to Infusionsoft, inside a specific account, and need to have a campaign published with contacts flowing through it.

How to do it...

1. Hover over the main navigation, and in the **Marketing** section, click on **Campaign Builder**.
2. Find the campaign we want to report on and open it.
3. Click on the **Performance** tab in the upper-left corner of the page.

4. Change the dropdown in the upper-left corner of the page to **Historical**:

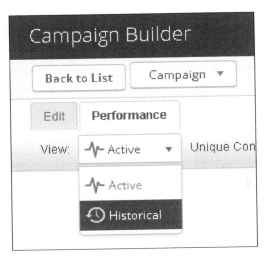

5. Hover over the sequence we want to report on and double-click on the sequence itself.

6. Hover over the step we want to report on and click on the *blue* person icon in the upper-right corner, as follows:

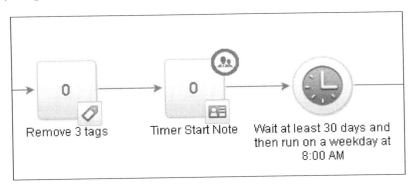

7. This will display the list of contacts in that specific sequence who have received that campaign step in the past 24 hours.

How it works...

This report displays all the contacts who received this step in the sequence within 24 hours.

There's more...

Once we have switched to **Performance** mode, we can change the date range to the last 30 days, using the dropdown in the upper-right corner of the page:

If we click on **Edit Criteria/Columns...** from this report, we can customize the date range for the report:

This report can also be accessed through the marketing reports:

Campaign Contacts Waiting	This shows Contacts who are waiting for a step within a Campaign Sequence.
Campaign Goal Completion	This shows Contacts who have completed Campaign Goals
Sequence Step Recipients	This shows Contacts that have received an item within a Sequence
Lead Source ROI	This shows ROI by leadsource.
Lead Source ROI By Category	This shows ROI by leadsource category.

See also

For a more in-depth look at modifying searches or reports, see the first recipe *Creating a saved search or report* in this chapter.

Reporting on who completed a specific campaign goal

This recipe will cover how to see who has achieved a particular goal within a sequence.

Getting ready

We need to be logged in to Infusionsoft, inside a specific account, and need to have a campaign published with contacts flowing through it.

How to do it...

1. Hover over the main navigation, and in the **Marketing** section, click on **Campaign Builder**.

2. Find the campaign we want to report on and open it.

3. Click on the **Performance** tab in the upper-left corner of the page.

4. Change the dropdown in the upper-left corner of the page to **Historical**.

5. Hover over the goal we want to report on and click on the *blue* person icon in the upper-right corner:

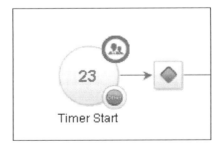

6. This will display the list of contacts that have achieved the campaign goal.

How it works...

This report displays all the contacts who have achieved a particular campaign goal in the past 24 hours.

There's more...

Once we have switched to **Performance** mode, we can change the date range to the last 30 days, using the dropdown in the upper-right corner of the page.

If we click on **Edit Criteria/Columns...** from this report, we can customize the date range for the report:

This report can also be accessed through the marketing reports:

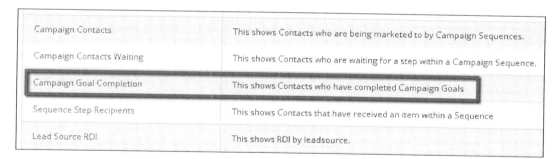

Campaign Contacts	This shows Contacts who are being marketed to by Campaign Sequences.
Campaign Contacts Waiting	This shows Contacts who are waiting for a step within a Campaign Sequence.
Campaign Goal Completion	This shows Contacts who have completed Campaign Goals
Sequence Step Recipients	This shows Contacts that have received an item within a Sequence
Lead Source ROI	This shows ROI by leadsource.

See also

For a more in-depth look at modifying searches or reports, see the first recipe *Creating a saved search or report* in this chapter.

10
Pushing the System with Hacks

In this chapter, we will cover the following topics:

- ▸ Creating a custom confirmation link inside campaign builder
- ▸ Creating a custom unsubscribe link inside campaign builder
- ▸ Triggering automation from an e-mail open
- ▸ Sending form submissions to different thank you pages based on custom fields
- ▸ Adding a calendar dropdown to date type fields on forms
- ▸ Hiding order forms until a link is clicked
- ▸ Using images as form submit buttons
- ▸ Making any text a social sharing link
- ▸ Making any link an unsubscribe link
- ▸ Creating an evergreen sales funnel with an expiring offer

Introduction

Everything in this chapter is officially unsupported and should any of the recipes in this chapter break, Infusionsoft support cannot help you!

Sorry for yelling, just wanted to make it clear that the recipes in this chapter are definitely *use at your own risk*. Now, while these hacks have been working for a while, there is no guarantee that they will continue to work. For all of these, we'll absolutely want to test thoroughly after configuring to ensure that it still works on our implementation.

When these masterful tricks are wielded properly, they can create world-class automated experiences, the kinds of thing that will cause our peers to inquire "How did you do that?".

Creating a custom confirmation link inside campaign builder

When confirmation links (formerly known as *double opt-in links*) were introduced to the campaign builder, the functionality was heavily restricted to prevent abuse of the new confirmation system. Primarily, the ability to control what the link text actually says, and what contacts see upon confirming, were both uneditable.

This hack uses a legacy merge field to insert custom confirmation links into a campaign builder e-mail.

Getting ready

We need to be logged in to Infusionsoft and inside a specific account.

How to do it...

1. Hover over the main navigation and in the **Marketing** column click on **Settings**:

My Nav	CRM	Marketing	E-Commerce	Admin
Contacts	Contacts	Campaign Builder	E-Commerce Setup	Branding Center
Campaign Builder	Companies	Email & Broadcasts	Orders	Infusionsoft Account
Email & Broadcasts	Opportunities	Lead Generation	Products	Users
Legacy	Referral Partners	Templates	Actions	Import Data
Templates	Visitors	Legacy	Promotions	Data Cleanup
Opportunities			Legacy	
Edit	Reports Settings	Reports Settings	Reports Settings	Reports Settings

2. In the **Marketing Settings** menu on the left-hand side of the page, click on **Automation Links**:

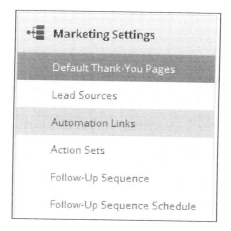

3. In the **Confirmation Links** section, click on the **Create Confirmation Link** button. This will open a pop-up window:

4. Give the new confirmation link a meaningful name:

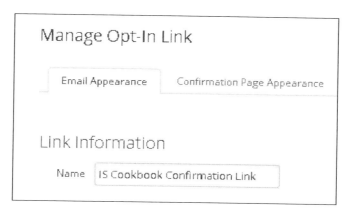

5. Scroll down the page and in the **Link Text** field, type the text you wish to be hyperlinked when the recipient receives the confirmation e-mail. Then click on the green **Save** button:

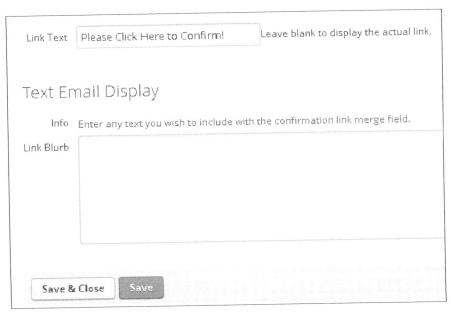

6. When the page reloads, make note of the confirmation link ID in the window's URL. Once we have the confirmation link ID, we can close the window:

7. Go into an e-mail step within campaign builder.

8. At the appropriate point in the e-mail, manually type in the merge field ~OptIn_xx~ where xx is the confirmation link's ID:

9. Finish the e-mail and mark it as **Ready**, mark the sequence as **Ready**, and publish the campaign.

How it works...

When a contact receives this e-mail, they will see a working confirmation link in place of the merge field, containing the text we set in step 5 hyperlinked.

There's more...

To quickly check whether we have entered the merge field properly, we can preview the e-mail using the **Email** dropdown in the upper-left corner of the e-mail builder. If the confirmation link text displays properly, the link has been properly configured:

If we wish to automate based on a contact clicking on this confirmation link, we are unable to use a link click goal: it will not track legacy links. However, when configuring the confirmation link after we have the link ID, we can configure an action to apply a functional tag:

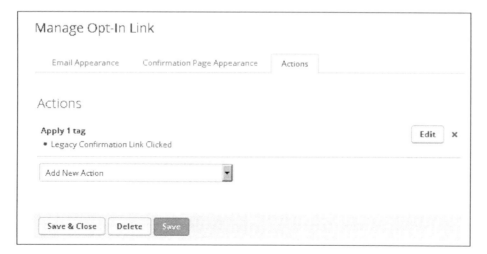

From there, we will want to add a tag goal to remove the contact from the custom confirmation sequence:

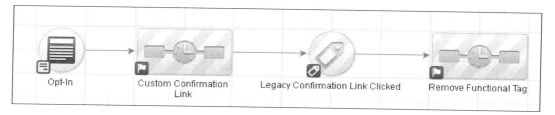

Using the tactic mentioned earlier, we can create an automated confirmation follow-up in case the contact doesn't confirm their e-mail address right away:

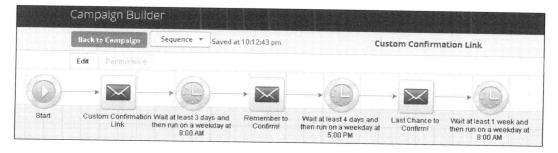

We also have some control over what a contact sees upon confirming their e-mail address. After we have the link ID, we can click on the **Confirmation Page Appearance** tab at the top and customize the experience:

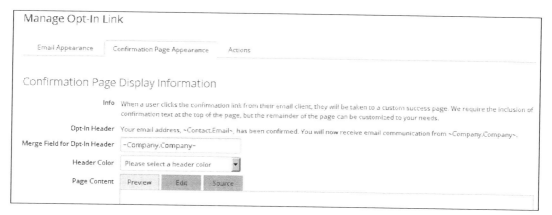

While this confirmation page does support HTML, it is a direct violation of Infusionsoft's acceptable use policy to automatically redirect from this page using a code snippet. This kind of behavior will get an Infusionsoft app shut down quickly, so its not worth the risk!

The **Header Color** option changes how the required confirmation text displays to the contact:

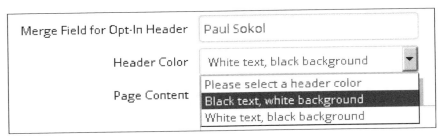

This is what the **Black text, white background** option looks like:

This is what the **White text, black background** option looks like:

See also

To learn how to add custom unsubscribe links to an e-mail, see the next recipe *Creating a custom unsubscribe link inside campaign builder*.

Creating a custom unsubscribe link inside campaign builder

Out of the box, an e-mail inside campaign builder has limited unsubscribe control.

Similar to the previous recipe, we can use a legacy merge field for an **Unsubscribe** link with more customization.

Getting ready

We need to be logged in to Infusionsoft and inside a specific account.

How to do it...

1. Hover over the main navigation, and in the **Marketing** column, click on **Settings**.
2. In the **Marketing Settings** menu to the left of the page, click on **Automation Links**.
3. In the **Update / Opt-out Links** section, click on the **Create Update / Opt-Out** button. This will open a pop-up window:

4. Give the new opt-out link a meaningful name:

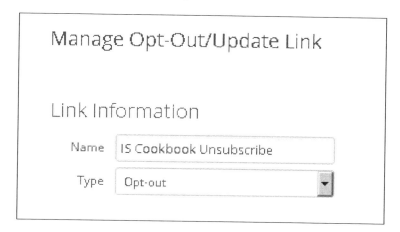

5. Scroll down the page, and in the **Link Text** field, type the text you want the unsubscribe link to be hyperlinked with in an e-mail, and click on the green **Save** button:

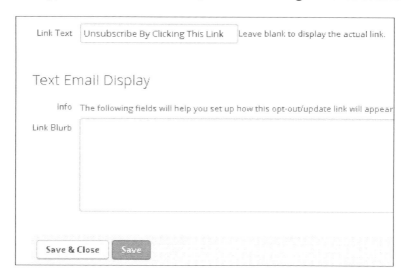

6. When the page reloads, make note of the opt-out link ID in the window's URL. Once we have the opt-out link ID, we can close the window:

7. Go into an e-mail step within campaign builder.

8. At the appropriate point in the e-mail, manually type in the merge field ~OptOut_xx~ where xx is the opt-out link's ID:

9. Finish the e-mail and mark it as **Ready**, mark the sequence as **Ready**, and publish the campaign.

How it works...

When a contact receives this e-mail, they will see a working unsubscribe link in place of the opt-out merge field, containing with the text we set in step 5 hyperlinked.

There's more...

To quickly check if we have entered the merge field properly, we can preview the e-mail using the **Email** dropdown in the upper-left corner of the e-mail builder. If the opt-out link text displays properly, the link has been properly configured:

If we wish to automate based on a contact opting out, then when we're configuring the opt-out link, after we have the link ID, we could configure an action to apply a functional tag:

See also

To learn how to add custom confirmation links to an e-mail, see the previous recipe *Creating a custom confirmation link inside campaign builder*.

Triggering automation from an e-mail open

Tracking e-mail opens is directly impacted by the recipient's e-mail software, because tracking an open can only occur when an e-mail's HTML is loaded.

Not all e-mail software loads the full HTML automatically, so automating based on an e-mail open is not super reliable.

Despite this instability in the automation confidence, automating based on e-mail opens can still be leveraged by another legacy merge field hack.

Getting ready

We need to be logged in to Infusionsoft and inside a specific account. We also want to have a functional tag created for the e-mail open.

How to do it...

1. Hover over the main navigation and in the **Marketing** column click on **Settings**.

2. In the **Marketing Settings** menu to the left of the page, click on **Automation Links**.

3. In the **Automation Link** section, click on the **Create Link** button. This will open a pop-up window:

			Create Link
Automation Link			
Edit	Name		Delete

4. Give the new link a meaningful name:

Manage Automation Link

Link Information

Link Name (so you can find it easily in Infusionsoft)

IS Cookbook Email Open Automatic

5. Scroll down the page and click on the green **Save** button:

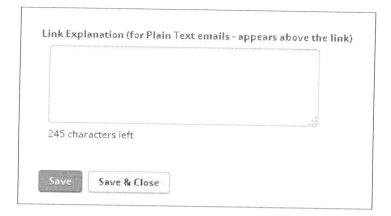

6. When the page reloads, click on the **Actions** tab at the top of the page.
7. Using the dropdown, click on **Add New Action** and select **Apply/Remove tag**:

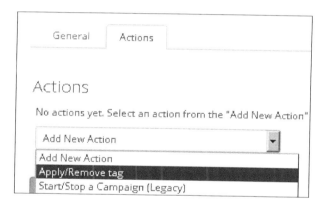

8. Select the functional tag from the list box:

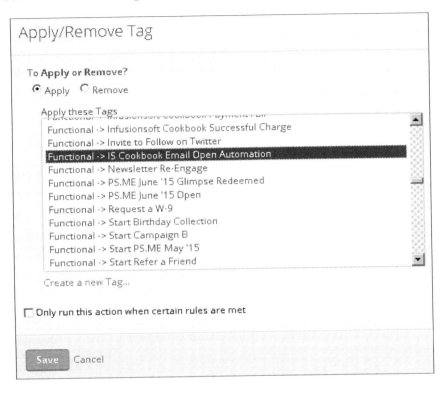

9. Click on the green **Save** button:

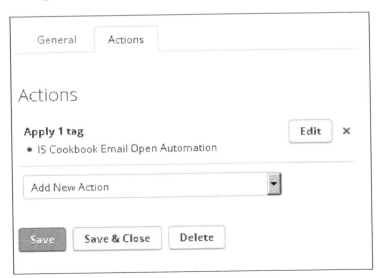

10. Take note of the automation link ID in the window's URL; once we have the link ID, we can close the window:

11. Go into an e-mail step within campaign builder.

12. Using the **Snippets** tab at the top of the e-mail editor, add an **HTML** snippet:

13. In the **HTML Code** snippet box, type in `<img src="~Link-xxxx~" width="1" height="1" />` where `xxxx` is the link's ID. Click on **Save**:

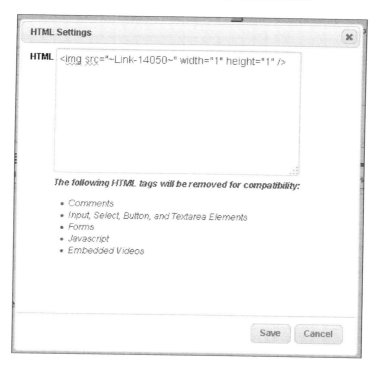

14. Finish the e-mail and mark as **Ready**, mark the sequence as **Ready**, and return to the campaign canvas.

15. Drag out a new tag goal, rename it and connect it to the sequence containing the e-mail we just wrote:

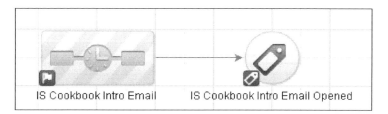

IS Cookbook Intro Email   IS Cookbook Intro Email Opened

16. Double-click on the tag goal and configure it for the functional tag, then click on **Save**:

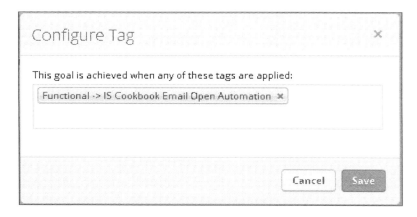

17. Publish the campaign.

How it works...

When a contact receives this e-mail and their e-mail client loads the full HTML, the functional tag will be applied, automating based on the open. This hack places an automation link as the *source* for a 1x1 image in the e-mail. When the image is *loaded*, it simulates a click, which is how we connect the open to a tag application.

There's more...

To the best of the author's knowledge, this hack was originally discovered and shared with the community by Tyler Garns.

Automating based on an e-mail open can be used to strategically ensure important messages get read:

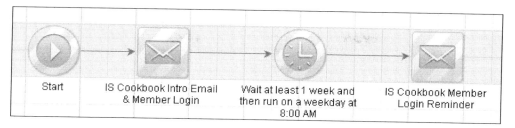

In these cases, since it is possible that someone has opened the e-mail previously, we have to carefully craft our copy for both people who had opened it, and people who hadn't.

Here is an example of how the login reminder e-mail can read:

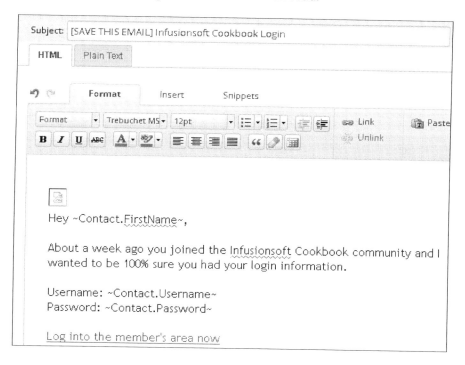

When written this way, even if someone already has the recipient's information, it just seems like a nice gesture.

Automation based on e-mail opens should be used carefully because of this lack of confidence. If we must have confidence in the automation, a link click goal is more reliable.

If we wish to have a *series* of e-mails that have automation based on opens, we will want to set up each series e-mail with its own open automation structure to ensure clean reporting and easy maintenance/improvements:

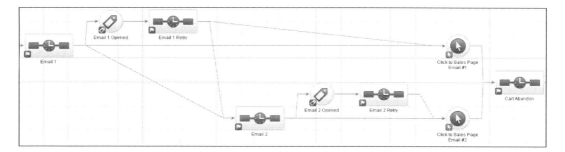

Sending form submissions to different thank you pages based on custom fields

When campaign builder was introduced, it provided the ability to use merge fields on the form's thank you page.

This hack uses a simple piece of JavaScript to pull information from a customer merge field and redirect based on the fixed possible values.

Getting ready

We need to be logged in to Infusionsoft, inside a specific account and a campaign with a web form or landing page. We also want to have:

- A custom field created that has fixed values (dropdown, radio button, Yes/No, and so on) to control the redirect. In this example, we have a custom dropdown type called `Subscription2` with two possible values: **No** and **Yes**.

- A URL for each different thank you page.

How to do it...

1. Open the web form or landing page and go to the **Thank-you Page** tab.

2. Add an **HTML** snippet.

3. In the **HTML** snippet, write the following and make sure to use the proper merge field value and page URLs. Click on **Save**:

HTML Settings

```
HTML   <script type="text/javascript">
       var x='~Contact._Subscription2~'
       if (x == 'No')
       {var url = 'URL_FOR_NO_IN_SUBSCRIPTION2';}

       else if (x=='Yes')
       {var url =
       'URL_FOR_YES_IN_SUBSCRIPTION2';}

       else
       {var url = 'DEFAULT_URL';}

       var delay = 0;

       setTimeout(function(){window.location.href = url;},
       delay);
       </script>|
```

The following HTML tags will be removed for compatibility:

* *Comments*
* *Input, Select, Button, and Textarea Elements*
* *Forms*

How it works...

This code is a simple switching mechanism. It pulls the value of a custom field with fixed values and then checks it against the possible values. When it finds a match, it stores the proper URL and then redirects the page to said URL. If no match is found, there is a default fallback URL to ensure nobody gets lost.

There's more...

To the best of the author's knowledge, this hack was originally discovered and shared with the community by Todd Meyer.

Depending on the person's Internet speed, they may see the form's thank you page briefly.

Any merge field can be used to control the switch, not just custom fields. However, when using field types that don't have a fixed number of values, there is a risk someone doesn't redirect to the right place.

If we wish to redirect to another page that has the contact's e-mail prepopulated in the background of another web form / landing page, we can add an e-mail merge field to the redirect URL:

```
if (x == 'No')
{var url = 'https://www.mywebsite.com/form-
thank-
you-no?inf_field_Email=~Contact.Email~';}
```

Adding a calendar dropdown to date type fields on forms

When a user is filling out an internal form inside Infusionsoft, and they are populating a date field, the system shows a calendar picker.

However, if we place a **Date** type field on a web form, the contact must enter the date in a specific format, otherwise it doesn't properly capture the information.

This hack uses a simple piece of JavaScript to add a calendar picker to **Date** type fields on a web form or landing page.

Getting ready

We need to be logged in to Infusionsoft, inside a specific account and inside a campaign with a web form or landing page. We also want to have a **Date** type field we wish to use (either a default one or custom field).

In this example, we have a custom **Date** field type named `Appointment Date`.

How to do it...

1. Open the web form or landing page with the date.
2. If the **Date** field isn't already on the form, add it.
3. Add an **HTML** snippet.
4. In the **HTML** snippet, write the following and make sure to use the proper merge field value. Click on **Save**:

```
<link rel="stylesheet" type="text/css"
href="https://ajax.googleapis.com/ajax/libs
/jqueryui/1.8.11/themes/base/jquery-ui.css" />
<style>
#ui-date-picker-div {
    font-size: 12px;
}
</style>
<script src="https://ajax.googleapis.com
/ajax/libs/jqueryui/1.8.11/jquery-ui.min.js"
type="text/javascript">
</script>
<script>
    jQuery(document).ready(function(){

jQuery('#nf_custom_AppointmentDate').css('widt
h', '100px');
jQuery('#nf_custom_AppointmentDate').datepick
er();
    });
</script>
```

How it works...

This code uses a built-in calendar picker from an online Google library and associates it with the **Date** type field.

There's more...

To the best of the author's knowledge, while this hack has evolved over time, it was originally discovered and shared with the community by Brent Crandall.

To check whether we entered the code properly, we can use the test function in the upper-right corner of the page:

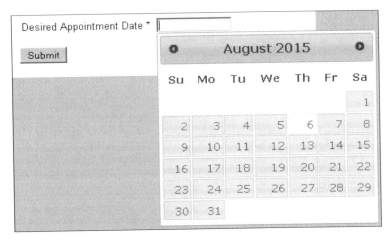

Hiding order forms until a link is clicked

A typical online form goes from a sales page to an order form. This means that someone on the sales page has to click a link and then wait for the order page to load. In a world where attention is becoming a super rare commodity, page load speed can impact sales.

This hack takes page load speed out of the equation by having the sales page and order form all in one. However, when the page loads for the first time, only the sales page portion displays. Once someone clicks on the call to action link, the order form reveals itself.

Getting ready

We need to be logged in to Infusionsoft and inside a specific account. In addition to this, we need to have:

- ▸ A working order form
- ▸ The sales page copy

How to do it...

1. Open the order form, and in the tabs at the top, click on **HTML Areas**:

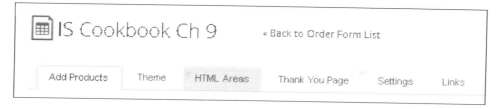

2. In the **Custom Header** area, write the following, then click on **Save**:

```
<script type="text/javascript"
src="https://ajax.googleapis.com/ajax/libs/jquery/1.8.1/jquery.js">
</script>
<script type="text/javascript">
$(document).ready(function(){
$("#content").hide();
$("#IMAGE").hide();
});

</script>
<script type="text/javascript">
$(document).ready(function(){
$("#show").click(function(){
    $("#content").show(500);
    $("#IMAGE").show(500);
  });
});
</script>
<p align="center">Your Sales Page</p>
<br>
<a align="center" href="#content" id="show">Cart Button</a>
```

3. Beneath the custom code box, click on **Preview** and verify that the order form is hidden until the link is clicked, as follows:

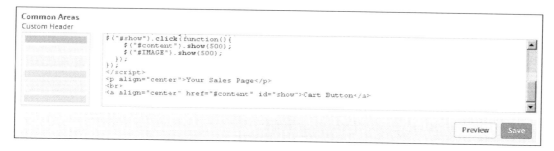

4. Replace the placeholder **Your Sales Page** HTML with your actual sales page HTML and finish configuring the order form.

How it works...

This code takes the content and IMAGE sections of the page (order form and logo respectively) and hides them upon page load using jQuery. There is also a small function that says whenever the element with the name #show is clicked, it should display those hidden sections. Finally, the Cart Button link is given the ID #show and points to the anchor in the page where the order form starts.

There's more...

This is how the experience works. First, the page loads and we just see the sales page:

Your Sales Page

Cart Button

After clicking, the theme's logo and order form display:

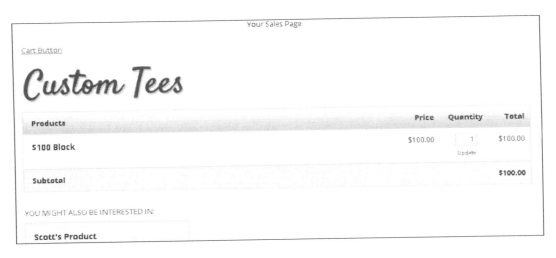

There are a lot of different parameters for the .show() function in jQuery. This can be used to adjust the time to display and other neat things.

Using images as form submit buttons

If we want to spice things up a bit with a really fancy call-to-action button, we can use an image as the submit button on a web form or landing page.

This hack uses a simple piece of JavaScript to adjust the CSS of the submit button on a web form or landing page.

Getting ready

We need to be logged in to Infusionsoft, inside a specific account and inside a campaign with a web form or landing page. We also want to have a hosted URL for the image.

How to do it...

1. Open the web form or landing page.

2. Add an **HTML** snippet.

3. In the **HTML** snippet, write the following and make sure that the width and padding-left are set to the image's actual width and that the height is the image's actual height. Click on **Save**:

```
HTML  <style>
        div.infusion-submit{ width: 110px; overflow:
      hidden; }

      div.infusion-submit button {
      background-image: url(URL_FOR_IMAGE);
      background-color: transparent;
      background-repeat: no-repeat;
      background-position: 0px 0px;
      border: none;
      cursor: pointer;
      height: 50px;
      padding-left: 110px;
      vertical-align: middle; }
      </style>
```

How it works...

This code adjusts the CSS properties of the submit button by using the image as the background image.

There's more...

For extra impact, use an animated `.gif` as the call-to-action button.

Making any text a social sharing link

The social sharing snippets in the e-mail builder are powerful ways to give recipients an easy way to share an e-mail to their networks. However, we have no control over how these share buttons display visually.

This hack uses a hidden system merge field to construct the same link built by those snippets.

In this recipe, we are going to create a link that acts as a Twitter share.

Getting ready

We need to be logged in to Infusionsoft, inside a specific account and inside a campaign with an e-mail that we wish to insert a social share link into.

How to do it...

1. Open the e-mail.
2. Highlight the text we wish to make a social sharing link and click on **Link** in the toolbar.
3. Set the URL as `https://appname.infusionsoft.com/app/socialShare/~EmailSent.Id~/~EmailSent.PartialHash~/T` and click **Insert/Update**.

How it works...

The link we manually build the same link that the system generates on the backend from a Twitter social share snippet.

There's more...

To create a social share link for Facebook or Google+, change the end of the link to `F` or `G` respectively.

This can also be used to link an image as a social share button, which means we can use custom graphics for social share calls to action.

See also

To learn about how to get the most out of social shares, see the recipe *Maximizing social sharing of your e-mails* in *Chapter 3, Attracting Leads and Building Your List*.

Making any link an unsubscribe link

Even with the ability to customize an unsubscribe link, sometimes there are situations where the way they display doesn't work, or we wish to use an image as the unsubscribe link.

This hack leverages the same system merge fields as the previous recipe to build an unsubscribe link.

Getting ready

We need to be logged in to Infusionsoft, inside a specific account and inside a campaign with an e-mail into which we wish to insert the unsubscribe link. In addition to this, we need to have a custom unsubscribe link created, and know the link's ID.

How to do it...

1. Open the e-mail.

2. Insert the unsubscribe link's merge field (more information about this merge in the *See also* section of this recipe).

3. Send the e-mail to yourself as a test.

4. When it comes in, hover over the link.

5. Note the first set of numbers after the link's ID in the URL; this is what we need:

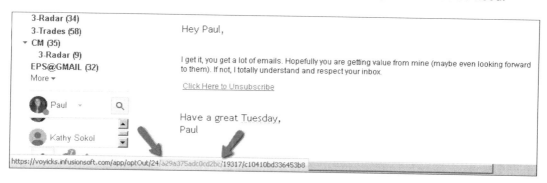

6. Right-click on the link and copy the link's URL.

7. Open a text editor and paste the link's URL in it. Keep this open.

8. Go back to the e-mail into which we wish to insert the unsubscribe link.

9. Highlight the text we wish to make an unsubscribe link and click on **Link** in the toolbar.

10. Set the URL as `https://appname.infusionsoft.com/app/optOut/xx/yyyyyyyyyyyyyyyy/~EmailSent.Id~/~EmailSent.PartialHash~` where xx is the unsubscribe link's ID and yy is the hash string we identified in step 5 (use the text editor to easily copy/paste this value). Then click on **Insert/Update**.

How it works...

The link we manually built is the same link that the system generates on the backend from an unsubscribe link.

There's more...

This can also be used to link an image as an unsubscribe button, which means we can use custom graphics for unsubscribe calls to action.

This hack can also be used for *update only* type unsubscribe links.

In step 6, we reference copying the link's URL after right-clicking. The specific name of this function upon right-clicking is different depending on which browser you use.

In Internet Explorer, the specific function name is:

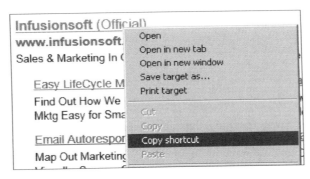

In Firefox, the specific function name is:

In Chrome, the specific function name is:

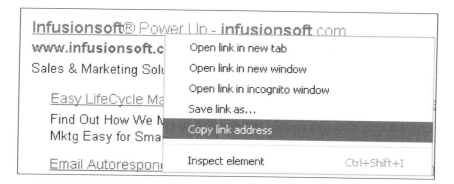

Once we have built this link, we can save time in the future by storing it somewhere easy to retrieve, such as Evernote. Then, the next time we need it, we can jump immediately to step 10 and copy/paste it in.

See also

To discover the unsubscribe merge field, learn how to find the link ID and how to customize unsubscribe links, see the recipe earlier in this chapter, *Creating a custom unsubscribe link inside campaign builder*.

Creating an evergreen sales funnel with an expiring offer

When it comes to automated experience design, few things compare to the amazing power of an evergreen sales funnel with an expiring offer. We *open the cart* when someone reaches a certain point within a campaign and then *close the cart* after a fixed period of time. This tactic for driving urgency is extremely powerful.

The idea behind an evergreen sales funnel is that the cart opens and closes with respect to each individual, as opposed to a classic *launch* where it opens and closes for everyone at the same time.

This hack leverages a merge field behind a link where the field value is dynamic.

For this example, we are going to assume that after someone opts in, the cart is open for 7 days and then closes:

Getting ready

We need to be logged in to Infusionsoft, inside a specific account and inside a campaign. In addition to this, we need the following:

► A live sales page/order form

► A *cart closed* page

► A custom Text field to hold the cart URL

► All sales e-mails written

How to do it...

1. Open the sequence, in this example we have three sales e-mails before the cart closes:

2. Open the first sales e-mail.

3. Somewhere in a text object, insert the merge field for the custom field holding the URL.

4. Highlight the cart URL merge field and copy/cut it:

5. Highlight the call-to-action in the e-mail and set the web address as the custom field value. Click on **Insert/Update**:

6. For all call-to-action links in this e-mail and the others in the sequence, set the destination as this merge field.

7. Back to the sequence, add a **Set Field Value** step and rename appropriately:

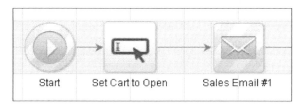

Start   Set Cart to Open   Sales Email #1

8. Double-click on the **Set Field Value** step to configure.

9. Using the **Field Value** dropdown, select the custom field for the cart URL:

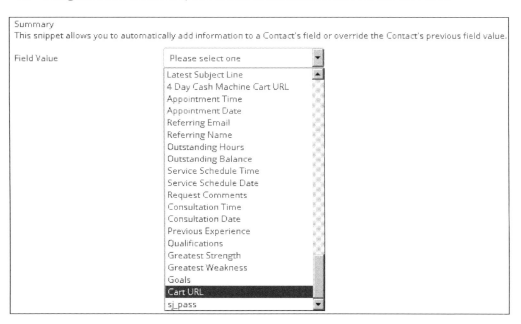

Summary
This snippet allows you to automatically add information to a Contact's field or override the Contact's previous field value.

Field Value   Please select one

Latest Subject Line
4 Day Cash Machine Cart URL
Appointment Time
Appointment Date
Referring Email
Referring Name
Outstanding Hours
Outstanding Balance
Service Schedule Time
Service Schedule Date
Request Comments
Consultation Time
Consultation Date
Previous Experience
Qualifications
Greatest Strength
Greatest Weakness
Goals
Cart URL
sj_pass

10. Set **Field Value** as the **Cart URL** for the active sales page/order form, as follows:

Summary
This snippet allows you to automatically add information to a Contact's field or override the Contact's previous field value.

Field Value   Cart URL

Cart URL   http://www.website.com/sales-page

11. In the upper-right corner of the page, click on **Draft** to mark the step as **Ready** and then go **Back To Sequence**.

12. At the end of the e-mail flow, add a **Delay Timer** and another **Set Field Value** step. Rename it appropriately:

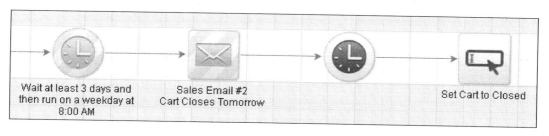

Wait at least 3 days and then run on a weekday at 8:00 AM — Sales Email #2 Cart Closes Tomorrow — Set Cart to Closed

13. Double-click the timer and configure it so that the cart will *close* at the appropriate time:

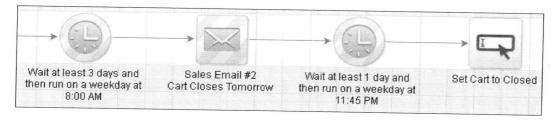

Wait at least 3 days and then run on a weekday at 8:00 AM — Sales Email #2 Cart Closes Tomorrow — Wait at least 1 day and then run on a weekday at 11:45 PM — Set Cart to Closed

14. Double-click on the **Set Field Value** step to configure.

15. Using the **Field Value** dropdown, select the custom field for the cart URL.

16. Set the field value as the URL for the *cart closed* page:

Summary
This snippet allows you to automatically add information to a Contact's field or override the Contact's previous field value.

Field Value | Cart URL
Cart URL | http://www.website.com/cart-close

17. In the upper-right corner of the page, click on **Draft** to mark the step as **Ready**.

18. Finish the campaign and publish.

How it works...

When someone enters the sequence, the cart URL custom field is populated with the value of the active sales page. This way, when someone clicks on the e-mail, they will be able to make a purchase. After the 7 days, the cart URL field is populated with the value of the *cart closed* page. Now if someone clicks, they will find that the offer has *expired*.

There's more...

Since the links in every e-mail are pointing to the custom field value, whenever someone clicks, they will go to whichever URL is set at that moment in time. Hence, when the *cart is open*, they can purchase because the field value is pointing to the active sales page. When the *cart is closed*, they will see the closed page because the field value is pointing there. Even if they go back to old e-mails when the *cart was open*, because the field value is still pointing to the closed page, they still cannot redeem the offer.

We may wish to change the cart URL back to the *cart closed* URL in the sequence after the purchase goal.

This hack only changes the URL inside the Infusionsoft database; there is nothing to stop someone from looking back in their browser history and finding the active sales page even after the cart has *closed*.

See also

To learn more about products and order forms, see the relevant recipes in *Chapter 4, Selling Products Online and Getting Paid*.

Index

A

Acceptable Usage Policy (AUP) 73
automated appointment reminders
  sending 179-184
automated cart abandon follow-up
  implementing 127-130
automated Happy Birthday messages
  building 258-266
automated Twitter offer
  building 73-82
automation
  on lead score achievement 198-202
  triggering, from e-mail open 428-433

B

Billing Automation trigger 191
birthday collection mechanism
  setting up 247-258
Bit.ly 66
bounced e-mail addresses
  reconciling 308-315
builders 14

C

calendar
  configuring 4
calendar dropdown
  adding, to date type fields on forms 436, 437
campaign builder
  custom confirmation link, creating 418-424
  custom unsubscribe link, creating 425-428
campaign links
  about 20
  using 20-22

campaign merge fields
  about 18, 54
  using 18-20
campaign model variations
  managing, with versioning 347-350
campaign reporting
  defining 405, 406
campaigns
  chaining 35-38
campaign sequence
  Active 408
  Done 408
  Queued 408
  reporting 406-409
campaign templates
  installing, from Marketplace 32
CAN-SPAM address block
  configuring 8-10
company's logo
  configuring 6, 7
components, referral partner program
  commission program 290
  defining 290
  referral tracking links 290
contacts
  queued, for receiving next step in
    sequence 409-411
Contact Us form
  creating 46-50
custom confirmation link
  creating, inside campaign builder 418-424
Customer Relationship Management
    (CRM) 14
customer satisfaction survey
  creating 228-238

customer welcome campaign
building 222-227
custom fields
creating 14-16
custom statistics
adding, to dashboard 382-387

D

dashboard
configuring 388-391
custom statistics, adding to 382-387
database segmentation
tags, creating for 23, 24
decaying lead score 197
deduping process 354
default start page, user
setting 392-394
downsell chain
building 146-153
duplicate contact records
checking 353-357
cleaning up 357-360
dynamic lead scoring 197

E

e-mail engagement levels
tracking 315-323
e-mail preferences center
creating 334-339
e-mails
custom opportunity fields, merging
into 184-192
social sharing, maximizing on 55-60
end users 14
Escape Hatch tag 38
evergreen sales funnel
creating 445-450

F

Facebook account
connecting 5
failed automated billing attempts
collecting 130-136

FAQ workflows
time, saving with 174-178
Filebox 334
form submissions
sending, to different thank you pages based
on custom fields 434, 435
form submit buttons
images, using as 440, 441
Frequently Asked Questions (FAQs) 174

G

great user experiences
creating, with tasks 28-30
groups of contacts
adding, to campaign sequence 351, 352

I

images
used, as form submit buttons 440, 441
inactive e-mails
re-engaging, in database 275-284
inbound phone call lead capture
building 88-93
Infusionsoft
about 1
users, creating 10, 11
Infusionsoft Certified Partner 11
in-person events
about 60
leads, collecting from 60-63
internal forms
about 25
using, for workflow 25, 26

L

landing page 73
last purchase date
segmenting by 216-222
lead generation
offline media, leveraging for 64-67
Lead Generation Card 73
lead magnet
about 50
forms 50

lead magnet delivery
building 50-55
leads
collecting, from in-person events 60-63
lead scoring
setting up 193-198
lead sources
used, for tracking ROI 340-347
Lifecycle Marketing
about 45
Attract 45
Sell 45
Wow 45
link
creating, as Twitter share 442
login, Infusionsoft customers
URL 304
logo snippet 8
long-term prospect nurture
building 202-214

M

Marketplace
campaign templates, installing from 31, 32
merchant account
about 105
setting up 105-110
merge fields
using 16, 17
My Day
working 39-44

N

new hire applicants
filtering 323-334
note template
using 87
using, for workflow 26, 27

O

OAuth
using 5
offline media
leveraging, for lead generation 64-67

one-click upsell
building 146-153
creating 136-146
order forms
about 35, 118
building 118-127
hiding 438-440
order form theme
creating 119-121
OR logic
using 196

P

payment gateway 111
Pay Per Click (PPC) 93
pipeline 156
Pipeline Automation trigger 190
PPC lead generation funnel
creating 93-102
product options
fixed 116
typed 116
products and subscriptions
creating 111, 112
purchase version, recurring 113-118
single purchase version 112

Q

QR code
creating 67

R

recurring event 19
referral partner program
setting up 290-299
referral partners
W-9 forms, collecting from 360-366
referral partner sign-up form
building 299-304
referral request
creating 68-73
report
creating 368-382

report delivery
  automating 394-396
ROI (Return On Investment)
  about 63, 213
  tracking, lead sources used 340-347
round robins
  using, for sales team 168-174

S

sales opportunities
  working 162-168
sales pipeline
  Contacting 156
  Deposit Secured (Win) 156
  Engaging 156
  Lost 156
  New Opportunity 156
  Qualified 156
  Quote Accepted 156
  Quote Finalizing 156
  Quote Sent 156
  setting up 156-161
sales rep dashboard
  building 396-404
sales team
  round robins, using for 168-174
saved search
  automating 394-396
  creating 368-382
sequence 46
social media following
  increasing 84-87
soon-to-be-expired credit card
  updating automatically 268-274
specific campaign goal completion
  reporting 414, 415
specific campaign step, receiving
  reporting 411-414

T

tags
  creating, for database segmentation 23, 24
tasks
  great user experiences, creating with 28-30
testimonial request
  performing 238-246
traffic source 46
Twitter account
  connecting 6
Twitter offer goal 74

U

unsubscribe link
  building 443-445
user group 172
user signature
  setting up 2-4

V

Vaynerchuk opt-out
  building 284-290
versioning
  campaign model variations, managing
    with 347-350

W

W-9 forms
  about 360
  collecting, from referral partners 360-366
web analytics
  setting up 102, 103
web form goal 46
web forms
  connecting 32-35
workflow
  internal forms, using for 25, 26
  note templates, using for 26, 27

About Packt Publishing

Packt, pronounced 'packed', published its first book, *Mastering phpMyAdmin for Effective MySQL Management*, in April 2004, and subsequently continued to specialize in publishing highly focused books on specific technologies and solutions.

Our books and publications share the experiences of your fellow IT professionals in adapting and customizing today's systems, applications, and frameworks. Our solution-based books give you the knowledge and power to customize the software and technologies you're using to get the job done. Packt books are more specific and less general than the IT books you have seen in the past. Our unique business model allows us to bring you more focused information, giving you more of what you need to know, and less of what you don't.

Packt is a modern yet unique publishing company that focuses on producing quality, cutting-edge books for communities of developers, administrators, and newbies alike. For more information, please visit our website at www.packtpub.com.

Writing for Packt

We welcome all inquiries from people who are interested in authoring. Book proposals should be sent to author@packtpub.com. If your book idea is still at an early stage and you would like to discuss it first before writing a formal book proposal, then please contact us; one of our commissioning editors will get in touch with you.

We're not just looking for published authors; if you have strong technical skills but no writing experience, our experienced editors can help you develop a writing career, or simply get some additional reward for your expertise.

Microsoft Dynamics CRM 2013 Marketing Automation
Implement effective marketing strategies using Microsoft Dynamics CRM 2013

Alok Singh   Sandeep Chanda   [PACKT] enterprise

Microsoft Dynamics CRM 2013 Marketing Automation

ISBN: 978-1-78217-722-7   Paperback: 128 pages

Implement effective marketing strategies using Microsoft Dynamics CRM 2013

1. Hands-on and illustration focused guide for beginners and expert marketers.

2. Detailed features of marketplace solutions explained to help marketers understand advanced e-mail marketing concepts and capture profile and product usage data through web and social channels.

3. Step by step information on creating marketing lists, campaigns, campaign responses, dashboards and reports with lots of screen shots for easy illustration.

Final Cut Pro X Cookbook
Edit with style and ease using the latest editing technologies in Final Cut Pro X

Jason Cox

Final Cut Pro X Cookbook

ISBN: 978-1-84969-296-0   Paperback: 452 pages

Edit with style and ease using the latest editing technologies in Final Cut Pro X!

1. Edit slick, professional videos of all kinds – music videos, promos, documentaries, even feature films.

2. Add hundreds of built-in animated titles, transitions, and effects without complicated keyframing.

3. Learn tons of time-saving workflows to tricky, yet common editing scenarios.

Please check **www.PacktPub.com** for information on our titles